THE GOLDEN AGE OF ISLAM

North-Holland Medieval Translations

Volume 2

General Editor
RICHARD VAUGHAN
University of Hull

NORTH-HOLLAND PUBLISHING COMPANY – AMSTERDAM • OXFORD
AMERICAN ELSEVIER PUBLISHING COMPANY, INC. – NEW YORK

THE
GOLDEN AGE
OF ISLAM

By
MAURICE LOMBARD

Translated by
JOAN SPENCER

1975

NORTH-HOLLAND PUBLISHING COMPANY – AMSTERDAM • OXFORD
AMERICAN ELSEVIER PUBLISHING COMPANY, INC. – NEW YORK

Library of Congress Catalog Card Number: 74 83268
North-Holland ISBN for the series: 0 7204 9000 6
North-Holland ISBN for the hardbound: 0 7204 9001 4
North-Holland ISBN for the paperback: 0 7204 9003 0
American Elsevier ISBN for the hardbound: 0 444 10788 6
American Elsevier ISBN for the paperback: 0 444 10824 6

Publishers:

NORTH-HOLLAND PUBLISHING COMPANY – AMSTERDAM
NORTH-HOLLAND PUBLISHING COMPANY, LTD. – OXFORD

Sole distributors for the U.S.A. and Canada:
AMERICAN ELSEVIER PUBLISHING COMPANY, INC.
52 VANDERBILT AVENUE
NEW YORK, N.Y. 10017

This book was originally published in French under the title
"L'Islam dans sa première grandeur".
Published by:
Flammarion et Cie — Paris

PRINTED IN THE NETHERLANDS

General Editor's preface

This translation of Maurice Lombard's *L'Islam dans sa première grandeur*, published in 1971, will provide the English-speaking student and general reader with new historical perspectives and with an elegantly organized corpus of new or hitherto little-known data about the Muslim World between its first formation as a result of the Arab expansion of the seventh century and its disintegration in the eleventh century. That is, about a great part of the civilized world in the Age of the Umayyad caliphs of Damascus and their Abbasid successors in Baghdad. This was a time when the West was primitive, poverty-stricken, backward; overrun by barbarians, confused, illiterate, depopulated, and primarily rural. But in the East the integrated economy and the world civilization of Islam, which extended from Cordoba to Samarkand, maintained and developed the tradition of wealth, cultural and artistic achievement, and thriving urban life which it had absorbed from its predecessors, the civilizations of Greece, Egypt, Persia, and the ancient cities of the Middle East. It is this Islamic economy and civilization which Maurice Lombard here portrays at its height and brilliantly sets into its context of satellite, in part semi-civilized, peripheral worlds — black North Africa, the barbarian West, the region of Russian rivers, and the Byzantine Empire. Above all he brings the economic historian's expertise to bear on the Muslim World, showing how the entire edifice was sustained by the circulation of products of all kinds, but especially of slaves — both black and white — and of gold. All this constitutes a highly original account of Islamic history in which events take second place to long-term economic structures, and these in their turn give way to the eternal unchanging truths of geography. What we have, indeed, is a masterpiece of the *Annales* school of French historians.

In view of this it is not surprising that, after 1948, Maurice Lombard was a colleague of Fernand Braudel in the Sixième Section of the Ecole pratique des hautes études at Paris; the famous Sixième Section which deals with Sciences économiques et sociales. Lombard was born in Algeria in 1904. He studied in the Universities of Algiers and Paris and conducted prolonged researches in Italy, Spain, and Egypt before being appointed a lecturer in the University of Rennes in 1942.

The book translated here was derived from lecture notes and other material left by the author at the time of his death in 1965, and was put together by his colleagues in the Sixième Section. The translator, Mrs J. Spencer, wishes to place on record her gratitude to Dr Robin Ostle, who read through and emended her text, which has been extensively revised by myself. The list of sources, bibliography, and chronology of the Muslim World promised in the preface to the French edition have not materialized and are not supplied here. Indeed it has been thought best to omit the few scattered footnotes of that version, but its maps and diagrams have been retained.

May 1974   Richard Vaughan
                                                       General Editor

Contents

List of figures

Introduction

The Early Middle Ages — from the founding of Constantinople in the fourth century to the great Crusading movement beginning in the eleventh century — was in every sphere and in every respect an Oriental period of history. This is especially true of the three centuries running from the middle of the eighth century to the middle of the eleventh, and coinciding with the zenith of the Muslim era. It was the Muslim East which provided the driving force behind economic and cultural life; the West was a void — an area in which all commercial and intellectual activity had ceased after the decline and fall of Rome and the subsequent barbarian invasions. But to understand the economic supremacy of the Muslim World one must look back to the period of conquests from the mid seventh to the mid eighth century. This was the time when the Muslim World assumed its main features.

The conquests were carried out initially by the Arabs in Arabia, Bedouin camel-drivers who formed the first military force in Islam under the leadership of the Quraysh chiefs of Mecca, who were themselves city-dwellers and traders, and owned the great caravans. Apart from the desert and the grazing areas of the Arabian Peninsula, the Arabs set their sights on the countries of the Fertile Crescent, namely Mesopotamia, Syria, and Egypt. But, in addition to this Arab element, the armies of Islam were to absorb into their ranks contingents raised from subject peoples, and these contingents in their turn continued the initial impetus. Thus, the Iranians penetrated central Asia, the Syro-Egyptians entered North Africa, and the Berbers of North Africa advanced into Spain and Sicily.

These invaders, whether Arabs or non-Arabs, were never to form more than a minority in the countries they occupied. Their role in history was to create a vast religious and political domain, to unite in one great Empire disparate territories and diverse peoples, then to be absorbed into the ancient populations they had conquered. Under the cloak of the Caliphate and Islam the former societies of Eastern antiquity continued their activity unbroken. When the Arabs left their desert they settled in densely populated areas: Mesopotamia, Iran, Egypt — countries with oases or cities, with populations long settled there, and ancient historical traditions. A long history of urban settlement is deeply rooted in these Eastern countries which possessed some of the most ancient civilizations in the world.

Here, the Arab element was confined to one single wave of invaders who came from a desert and not from one of those hinterlands of forest with clearings under cultivation as in central Europe, or steppes with grazing land as in Asia, which have constantly produced barbarian invaders in successive waves to settle in the rural, wooded, and thinly populated West. Here in the East, a handful of conquerors was rapidly absorbed, merging with the urban masses who enjoyed a superior civilization. The Arabs settled in the cities or in camps set up opposite them, which were in turn the nucleus of future cities: Kufa, Fustat, and Kairouan. The explanation of this phenomenon lies in the need to remain in a group, and in the preference felt by the Arab merchant and Arab Bedouin for the city, to which was added a marked distaste for the plough and for settling on the land. All these people wished to enjoy for themselves the pleasures offered by the city. The hard core who did not were swiftly relegated to the desert or isolated in certain regions of the steppes. The best example of this is the case of the Hilalian Bedouins, who moved from the Arabian Desert to Sinai, then from Sinai to Cyrenaica and the Maghreb.

The peoples originally existing in the East in Classical times —

Arameans, Persians, Egyptians — maintained their identity throughout the Arab invasion. This makes it important to discover the part played by the conquerors *vis-à-vis* these peoples.

In political terms the conquest was expressed by the construction of a vast empire, the Islamic State, symbolized by the Caliphate; in the religious sphere it established Islam, the religion resulting from the Koranic revelation vouchsafed to Muhammad; in the linguistic field it meant the spread of the Arab language; in the economic field the main result of this historical phenomenon was the uniting of very different territories into one vast whole. But once the conquest was completed, the Arabs disappeared from the scene to merge with the older populations already inhabiting the area, whether Iranian, Semitic, Egyptian, Berber, or Iberian. This was still to hold good during the second phase of conquest, indeed the small size of the Syrian contingents and of the Berber population in tenth-century Muslim Spain was marked.

How is one to explain the ease and rapidity of a conquest achieved by so small a number of warriors? There was, in fact, every reason why the Arabs should be hailed as deliverers by the older populations of the Semitic World of Syria and Mesopotamia and by the Egyptians. Apart from the ethnic and linguistic relationship linking some of these peoples to the Arabs, they had long been in subjection to Rome, then to Byzantium in the west, and to the Persian Sassanid Empire in the east. They were in a state of permanent revolt against the administrations of Constantinople and Ctesiphon, and this revolt, as always in the East, had a religious tinge and a social basis. The Byzantine Empire was racked by heresies; Nestorianism and Monophysitism were the main rivals to the established orthodoxy. In Sassanid territory there grew up Manichaeism, Judaism, and Christianity, all of which conflicted with the official religion, Mazdaism.

The democratic, egalitarian, and cosmopolitan tendencies of the Islamic message found an echo in these movements of social and religious revolt. This explains in part why the conquest was so easy. Another reason was the need for stability and peace which prompted the urban populations to support the conquering power, from whom they hoped for protection against anarchy and nomad depredations. In the end the only stubborn resistance came from the Berbers. Just as they had in former times rebelled against Carthage and Rome, and were later to rebel against the Turks, so now they were in a constant state of open or veiled rebellion against Muslim domination.

Relations with subject peoples were in every instance made easier by the toleration shown by the invaders, who in religious matters were indifferent, not to say sceptical. Hence there were no persecutions or forced conversions. The conquerors imposed only one firm condition, and it was of a fiscal nature. A treaty of capitulation, correctly drawn up and entered into with the religious authorities guaranteed, in exchange for the raising of taxes by the notables of the various communities, freedom of worship and freedom to engage in economic activity.

The conquest was so swift that it did not produce any hiatus or break with the past, but allowed things to go on as they had before, in every sphere: institutions, administrative machinery and personnel, legal processes, offices, taxes, and even currency. The two main currencies, the dirhem of Sassanid silver and the denarius of Byzantine gold, continued in circulation until the eighth century. In the economic sphere the cities and commercial networks — structures of vital importance — were left unchanged. The Egyptian *annona*, a levy on grain, originally sent to Rome, then to Constantinople when the imperial power was transferred there, was not abolished by the Muslim authorities, but simply redirected to the holy cities of Arabia via the Red Sea, then to Damascus, the capital of the Umayyad Caliphate. The tax itself was thus retained, but to the advantage of the Muslim community. One of the economic features of the conquest was the taxation of non-Muslims only, until the Caliphate, faced with the possibility of losing by conversions to Islam a taxable commodity of ever-increasing importance, instituted a basic tax applicable to Muslims and non-Muslims alike.

Nor did the conquest leave a trail of destruction. No cities were burned down or sacked, with the single exception of the pillaging of Sassanid palaces filled with gold. There was in consequence no disorganization; the subject peoples provided as a matter of course the administrative framework, the mental equipment of civilized peoples. The recent Christian, Jewish, or Persian converts, known as *mawali* (clients), were to play a decisive role in the elaboration of this syncretic civilization we style 'Muslim'. Even the codification of Arabic grammar, even the establishment of the definitive text of the Koran, was to involve the participation of non-Arabs, those heirs of a long Oriental tradition of skill in intellectual techniques.

And so the Muslim East, comprising the former Sassanid (Mesopotamia and Iran) and Byzantine territories (Syria and Egypt), functioned as the crucible of a synthetic civilization which later spread throughout the whole of Islam; eastwards into central Asia, westwards into Ifriqiya (Tunisia and eastern Algeria), to the Maghreb al-Aqsa, the Far West (Barbary, Spain, and Sicily). Hence the eastern part of this area, the former Byzantine and Sassanid territories, enjoyed continuous development but with greatly increased impetus, while the western part enjoyed a genuine revival. My own view runs directly counter to H. Pirenne's famous thesis. I believe that it was because of the Muslim conquest that the West regained contact with Oriental civilizations and, through them, with the major world movements in trade and culture. Whereas the great barbarian invasions of the fourth and fifth centuries had caused an economic regression in the West under the Merovingian and Carolingian dynasties, the creation of the new Islamic Empire brought with it an astonishing development in this same area. The Germanic invasions provoked a decline in the West, but the Muslim invasions caused a revival of its civilization. The question whether the advent of the barbarians in the West interfered with economic continuity or led to regression is thus soon answered: if the same question is asked of the Arab conquest, and its effect on the entire Muslim Empire, it must be answered quite differently. Not only was there no break in continuity, but there was an extraordinarily rich development.

Three distinct problems must here be stated and considered separately: Islamization, Arabization, and Semitization.

Islamization is the conversion of ancient populations to the new religion, Islam, a conversion enjoying the fiscal advantages bestowed on the new converts when they embraced the Faith, namely the abolition of the *jizya* (poll-tax).

The term 'Arabization' is to be understood in the purely linguistic sense. No important infusion of 'Arab' blood took place, and very few specifically 'Arab' traditions were introduced into the newly conquered territories. The process often mistakenly termed 'Arabization' is really Semitization, Orientalization, i.e. the adoption of a set of moral concepts, taboos, cosmogonies, mental and practical systems belonging to the Semitic (or, more accurately, Semitized) populations of Syria-Mesopotamia, and especially the section of these populations which represents the directive and motive force. These are the urban populations bearing the accumulated weight of all the older civilizations from the very earliest times, civilizations from which they derived delicacy and refinement, intellectual and commercial skills, the need for firmly established order, together with a deficiency in the warlike virtues – a trait common to many populations of later antiquity – which made it necessary to have recourse to mercenaries. The Muslim conquests were primarily battles won by the Bedouin of Arabia who emerged from their deserts along routes already clearly marked, and descended upon the tightly packed towns on the fringe of their domain, mere groups of town-dwellers, whose needs were supplied by the surrounding *fellahin*. Later on these conquests were made by the Berbers, Sanhaja nomads or sturdy Kutama mountain-dwellers, and still later, by Turks, Kurds, and Daylamites. From these sources of mercenary warriors Islam drew her military strength.

Semitization was quite a different matter; it was the urban civilization of the ancient syncretic East – the Persian Empire and the Hellenistic kingdoms – carried beyond the confines of Semitic territory along several channels and by several different means. Foremost among these was the Arab tongue: the religious language of the Koran, the language of government, the official and administrative language, the language of large-scale commerce and foreign trade, and the language of literary and scientific civilization. Greek, Iranian, Indian, and Chinese ideas have come down to us for the most part in Arabic translations, i.e. by means of a Semitic transmission. Semitization also took place along the routes of the Levantine commercial diaspora from the Isthmus region, mainly through the dispersion and migration of small numbers at a time and because of the establishment of religious communities at strategic points along the major trade routes. Fresh arrivals gradually swelled the ranks of these tiny groups of pioneers. At the same time they multiplied, advanced, prospected, set up fresh centres while still retaining reliable positions to fall back on, with which they maintained more or less loose contact, sometimes broken by schisms, sometimes strengthened by regroupings or by a common dependence on the same centre. This was the origin of the Jewish communities with Hebrew or Aramaic as their written language, and Arabic as their spoken language, and the Nestorian communities with Syriac as the written language and Arabic as the spoken language.

Finally, it should be noted that the three processes I have briefly analysed, namely Islamization (religion), Arabization (language), and Semitization or Orientalization (civilization), appeared and developed initially in cities. The urban setting proved congenial to their development because of a certain pre-established harmony, and the influence of the cities spread out over the surrounding countryside. The Muslim World, from the eighth to the eleventh centuries, was the centre of a prodigious urban activity. Those regions in which urban life was most intense were the first to undergo these influences and were the most deeply affected. The rest remained on the fringe or right outside the movement; some areas were left completely untouched by it. In North Africa, for example, there was a distinction between Arabic-speaking cities which had undergone Oriental influence, and the Berber-speaking mountain regions which Islamization had barely touched.

The area of conquest extended from central Asia to Spain, bringing under Muslim rule — either within her borders or within her sphere of influence — the territories situated at the heart of the Ancient World. At that period these were the most important territories, in economic terms, because of their agricultural, industrial, or mining output, and also because of their commercial organization, e.g. transport and caravan networks, and lastly because of their active populations. These resources were, from then on, placed at the disposal of wider commercial circuits and more extensive economic activities.

These territories included countries with the most fertile soils, such as Mesopotamia and Egypt with their oases and long tradition of irrigation, also the vast North African plains which produced corn and oil, and lastly Andalusia. There were mining countries, the Caucasian-Armenian group, North Africa, and Spain. As well as this direct production, the Muslim World exercised control over the routes leading to the world's most important gold-mines — south-east Africa, the Sudan, and central Asia. There were also centres of highly developed craft industries in Iran, Mesopotamia, Syria, and the Egyptian Delta.

Great ports provided the Muslim World with ships, dockyards, and seafaring populations. There were three enormous complexes: first, shipping in the Persian Gulf and the Red Sea, which Arab and Persian sailors opened up towards the Indian Ocean and which was complemented by the river-boats of the Euphrates and Tigris; next the ports of Syria and Egypt, foremost of which was Alexandria, backed by the river-boats of the Nile; finally the ports on the Sicilian Strait and the Strait of Gibraltar, supported by the river-boats on the Guadalquivir. Caravan towns also possessed transport systems which dominated the Mesopotamian routes (running westwards towards Syria and eastwards towards Iran and central Asia), the Arabian routes, and the Berber trading routes crossing the Sahara. The system presupposed a caravan network complete with beasts of burden (camels, dromedaries, horses, mules, asses) and a specialized body of escorts, guides, merchants, and caravan-owners. These were the trading peoples of the East, traditionally the leaders in world commerce, and they were known by the term 'Syri' (Levantines). They were the true successors of the Phoenicians.

Finally there were stocks of gold which came from Sassanid palaces and Byzantine churches and which further strengthened the economic power of the Muslim World. This was in any case ensured by its monopoly of the traffic between the Far East, the Indian Ocean and the West on the one hand, and between Central

Africa and the Mediterranean on the other. Thus Islam occupied a key position, at the point of intersection of the major trade routes of that period. Only one route lay beyond her control, and that was the road across the steppes, from the Far East to Mongolia, to central Asia, and from there to the Hungarian plains. It was a nomad route, a highway running north of the old Asiatic and Mediterranean civilizations. Similarly, one major trading centre remained outside Muslim territory, namely Byzantium.

It is clear, then, how admirably placed the Muslim World was, at the heart of the Ancient World. Islam was not a civilization which suddenly landed from another planet, but something closely linked with the history of all those areas which surrounded its cradle, and to which it subsequently spread. For the black populations, the advent of Islam, from the Sudan to the West African coast, was to prove one of the major influences on the history of modern Africa. From the Indian Ocean, Islamization was to spread as far as Indonesia. In central Asia the Turks and the Chinese felt the same impact. The earliest Muslim advance resulted in the Islamization of the Turks, who themselves were the cause of a Chinese Islam today numbering perhaps more than 30,000,000. Lastly, in the area of Byzantium and the Christian West, Islam travelled along the routes leading from the Mediterranean to central Europe, as far as the Baltic countries. This provoked further encounters and intrusions, when one considers Scandinavian expansion, aimed at the countries round the Black Sea and the Caspian Sea.

For Islam, all these countries were so many economic horizons to be prospected. It left its mark on every one, either in the religious sphere by conversions, or in the commercial sphere, as discoveries of Islamic currency have attested. From all these places Islam imported the most varied merchandise, which led to a very lively flow of trade.

The centre of the Muslim World was situated in the Isthmus region, bounded by the Persian Gulf, the Red Sea, the Mediterranean, the Black Sea, and the Caspian Sea. It was, therefore, set at the intersection of two major economic units: the Indian Ocean area and the Mediterranean area. These two territories, united in

Hellenistic times but later split into two rival worlds, the Roman-Byzantine and the Parthico-Sassanian, were now reunited by the Muslim conquest, so as to form a new, vast territory which was economically one.

This unity rested on large-scale trading relations along caravan and maritime routes, on one main currency, the Muslim dinar, and one international commercial language, Arabic. It was also made easier by the emergence of a new world open to fresh techniques, and favouring the combination of Byzantine and Oriental methods and their spread throughout the Muslim World.

Finally, the unity mentioned above was helped by the reintroduction into world trade of the great consumer markets of the western Mediterranean in the guise of new towns: Kairouan, Tunis, and Fez; or old towns with a new lease of life: Seville, Cordoba, and Palermo. These great new urban centres of the Muslim West found themselves closely linked with their opposite numbers in the East, old Hellenistic cities like Alexandria or Antioch, or newly founded cities like Cairo or Baghdad.

This last circumstance is of vital importance: indeed, the establishment or the revival of an urban network was to give the new world of Islam its economic, social, and cultural framework. A complete system of relations was built up from one city to the next, and these cities were, once again, the strong points, the motive force of economic life. The pre-eminence of the city in the Muslim World from the eighth to the eleventh centuries is a major feature of the period under consideration. From Samarkand to Cordoba, Muslim civilization was a remarkably unified urban civilization, with considerable movement of men, merchandise, and ideas within it, a syncretic civilization superimposed upon the original regional system, whether rural or nomadic.

And so the Muslim World may be seen as a series of urban islands linked by trade routes. But this superb urban organization received a mortal blow in the form of the crises, the disturbances, the invasions of the second half of the eleventh century. They impeded the powerful flow of trade, thereby provoking the decline of the cities. Henceforward the Muslim World was not a united whole, but divided. There was a Turkish Islam, a Persian

Islam, a Syrian Islam, an Egyptian Islam, and a Maghreb Islam. Gone was the single Muslim civilization and in its place was a resurgence of regional particularisms, embodied in a number of different Muslim civilizations.

I propose, therefore, to deal with the Muslim World country by country. I shall examine each one from the geographical standpoint, with reference to natural conditions, and physical and human setting. Then I shall discuss the economic and social aspects, for example the heritages of former civilizations still continuing on the soil from which they sprang, in and through the same populations, the same techniques, the same mental attitudes, often the same beliefs, which were to some extent modified by new factors. After the period of the Ecumenical Caliphate, the Umayyad Caliphate, which ended in the middle of the eighth century, these particularisms reappear and assume concrete form as States, as dynasties which could be styled more or less 'national' provided the term were not taken in the very modern sense. These were the Umayyads of Spain, the Tulunids and Fatimids of Egypt, the Tahirids and Samanids of eastern Iran.

This move towards differentiation has been called, mistakenly in my view, 'the dismemberment of the Abbasid Caliphate'; it would be far better to call it the development of the Muslim World, the transition from the Caliphate *Khilafa* to the Bilad al-Islam.

PART I

THE TERRITORIES OF ISLAM:
REGIONS AND NETWORKS

CHAPTER 1

The Isthmus region

The first country to be considered is Arabia, from whose deserts Islam sprang, followed by those regions acquired in the initial conquest, namely Egypt, Syria, and Mesopotamia.

Arabia

To appreciate the dual role — positive and negative — which Arabia played in the Muslim World, we must look back to pre-Islamic peoples and visualize them in their geographical setting of oases and deserts, with the latter functioning more or less as grazing land. In the north-west oasis, in places such as Yathrib (Medina), dwelt settled farmers from whom Muhammad recruited his earliest followers, those who were to form his very first troops, the *Ansar* or 'companions'. Next came the citizens of Mecca, Ta'if, and Judda, the Qurayshites, who were bankers and masters of the caravan trade, and the maritime traders of the southern ports of the Yemen and Oman. Lastly came the Bedouin living in the habitable areas of the central desert as stock-rearers and carriers, who manned the caravans and were all imbued with warlike virtues.

It was not long before the *Ansar* were ousted by the rich bourgeois of Mecca who had realized how useful the new religion could

be to their trade and so joined the ranks of Islam. The most
powerful clan, that of Umayya, old-established Qurayshites,
achieved their conquests by relying on the warlike strength of the
Bedouin — they first supplied them with arms and then allowed
them to keep their booty. As a result the Umayyads extended the
range of their political power as far as Damascus, a point from
which they commanded the termini of the trade routes. In this
way central Arabia — Hijaz and Nejd — lost its inhabitants and
with them its economic power. The Bedouin gradually merged
with the older urban civilizations of the East, where the political
masters were the indigenous scribes of the *diwan* who continued
to write in Pahlavi and Greek.

Under Umayyad rule there was still some social mobility between the newly conquered countries and Arabia. The Bedouin
who could not be absorbed were driven back into the desert. At
the beginning of the eighth century the Banu Hilal and the Banu
Sulaym were deported by 'Abd al-Malik to the Suez Isthmus,
where they were used as caravan escorts and led a nomadic life of
plunder. By the middle of the eleventh century their descendants
were to be launched into Ifriqiya by the Fatimids. However, the
Umayyad caliphs retained emotional links with the Arabian Desert
through their entourage and also because of the charm still exercised by pre-Islamic Arabic poetry, which depicts life in the desert.
These caliphs, though possessing a palace built of stone, also had
another made of canvas in which they made frequent visits to the
Syrian Desert or Badiya. These links were broken with the advent
of the Abbasids and their new associates the Khorasanians, who
came from eastern Iran.

From the eighth century onwards Arabia was politically dead, a
province forgotten by the new dynasty. The same was true in the
sphere of commerce: Mecca and Medina ceased to be the centres
of large-scale caravan trade. The area lost its role of middleman, its
position at the centre of things, because of the conquests and the
capture of the caravan termini used by the Byzantines and Sassanids in Syria and Mesopotamia. From this period the caliphs,
now in possession of the Red Sea route and the Persian Gulf route,
neglected the one in between which crossed Arabia. Under Umay-

yad rule, Egyptian corn was still unloaded in the port of Judda, but the Arabian Peninsula gradually became a dead weight, and by the Abbasid era it was completely isolated. Now, Egyptian corn no longer reached the holy cities of the Hijaz, but was redirected to Mesopotamia and Baghdad, and was carried by the roundabout sea route of the Red Sea and the Persian Gulf to the port of Basra. But despite all these adverse factors, a certain amount of peripheral activity connected with the major trade routes still went on in Arabia.

There was one particular sphere in which Arabia continued to play a positive role. It remained the religious centre of Islam, with its holy cities, Mecca and the Ka'ba Sanctuary, Medina and the Tomb of the Prophet. Along the roads converging on Mecca from Egypt, Syria, Mesopotamia, the Indian Ocean, and Ethiopia, travelled widely differing modes of thought: Mazdaism, Judaism, Eastern Christianity, Buddhism, and Negro fetishism, all of which influenced the Koran. These same routes which once had carried conquering armies now brought pilgrims to the holy cities of Islam. To make the Pilgrimage (*Hajj*), the peoples of the Maghreb travelled via Cairo and the Suez Isthmus, those from Iran via Baghdad and Kufa, and those of the Yemen and Oman came direct. This vast movement of pilgrims was to create a fresh road network and a set of economic conditions specific to the pilgrimages. For example, the Faithful needed food and transport; they required the *ihram*, the large piece of seamless cloth which they used as a ritual garment; they wished to buy more or less valuable souvenirs of their pilgrimage, such as pieces of turquoise cut to order. But there was also the trade carried on by the pilgrims themselves, who took advantage of the *Hajj* to do business at the great fair near Mecca in the month of Muharram. A governor was in residence there to represent the caliph and levy taxes. It was the government's way of exploiting pilgrimages at the fiscal level, while the Bedouin turned them to their economic advantage. That was the positive side of Arabia's role, and she was never exploited politically. Spiritual authority was elsewhere, for the caliph, as religious head, resided in Baghdad or Cairo. The cities of the Hijaz were no more than holy places.

A further positive feature was the vital role played by Arabia in the slave-trade. The habit of importing into Arabia slaves from Ethiopia — Somalis and Bantus (Zanj) — which had begun before the advent of Islam, went on. The early ninth century saw the creation in the Yemen of the town of Zabid, an important black-slave market, during the Ziyadid dynasty (819–tenth century). Medina became a centre where very valuable slaves were educated to become singers, musicians, dancers, and so on. Some of these slaves became very famous, for example Ishraq as-Suwaida', the learned female slave. Even Slav and Indian slaves were sent to this school at Medina to learn the 'Medina chant', very much in favour at the Abbasid Court. This was a chant which took its rhythm from the *qadib* or wooden stick, a kind of percussion music which spread throughout the Muslim World and later, by way of the Andalusian chant, developed into the *cantus mensurabilis* of the West.

Finally, the earliest developments in Arab horse-breeding, by crossing the Berber and Iran strains, took place on the high pla-teaux of the Najd, in an eminently suitable climate.

Arabia's role during the Muslim era can, therefore, be summed up as follows: she was no longer an important transit route and participated in world trade only along her periphery; she had her own trade circuit along the roads taken by pilgrims to the holy cities; she was a centre for the redistribution and training of slaves; finally she was a centre for rearing Arab thoroughbreds with a pedigree going back five generations.

Egypt

Egypt has been called the 'gift of the Nile'; she should also be called the 'achievement of the *fellah*'. Her geographical setting is especially important. The Nile Valley was the scene of ceaseless toil by farmers who built and maintained a vast irrigation system requiring very exact regulations, statute-labour, and a continuous mobilization of the labour force. This requisition system, the *litur-gies* system of the Byzantine era, was to persist after the Muslim conquest. The Aphrodito papyri have preserved very many requisi-

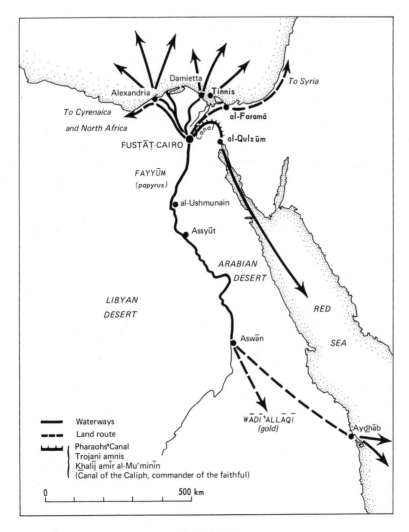

Fig. 1. Egypt.

tion letters calling upon a mobile peasant work force — a mass of labourers always obliged to serve and always available.

The country's two major products were corn and flax. Egypt,

one of the granaries of the Ancient World, now sent its corn to the Muslim holy cities and to Baghdad. The flax, which Pliny had praised for its high quality, kept its good reputation. It should be noted that cotton, which grew in Syria, did not appear in Egypt until the ninth century, that is long after the sugar-cane had been introduced into the Nile Valley.

The density of the population along the river, which was indeed extraordinary, struck all the travellers in the Early Middle Ages. One of them called it a 'city street' — a sort of ribbon development along the banks of the Nile. The older urban centres expanded, while new cities constantly sprang up. On the site of Cairo alone there grew up Fustat (seventh century), al-'Askar (eighth century), al-Qata'i' (ninth century), and al-Qahira (tenth century). The city reached the peak of its development at the end of the tenth century with about 500,000 inhabitants. But there were other densely populated urban areas along the river-bank, for example Qus, Qift, and Aswan (about 100,000 inhabitants) at the First Cataract.

The Nile formed the main trunk route and has a raised earth embankment running parallel with it from the Delta to Aswan, known as the 'Wall of the Old One' — the name in Arabic is 'sadd al-Ajuza'. It was a caravan route along· which travelled, as if on a causeway, convoys mounted on asses or camels. Of course the main route was still the Nile itself with its busy, swarming river-craft, as many boats, according to contemporaries, as there were at Baghdad and Basra put together. There were old-fashioned, square-sailed boats and modern ones with a triangular, 'lateen' sail which appeared in the ninth century and made it possible to sail very close to the wind, a point of some importance for river navigation.

The maintenance and replacement of craft on the Nile, together with those of the Mediterranean and Eritrean ports, required enormous amounts of timber. Byzantine Egypt had two arsenals, one at Alexandria for the Mediterranean fleet and the other at Clysma for the Red Sea fleet. The Muslims possessed eight: the two just mentioned, three at Fustat (Roda-Island, Fustat, and al-Maks in the north), one at Damietta, one at Rosetta, and one at as-Salihiyya on the eastern arm of the Nile. As well as being urgently needed for the naval dockyards, timber was in demand for building in towns, and as fuel in industries dependent on fire, such as glass-making and ceramics. Wood was also needed to make cauldrons for holding the liquid from the sugar-cane; for sugar-refining was practised in Egypt, which was an old centre of Hellenistic alchemy. This constantly growing need for wood could not be met by Egypt alone. Every tree in the country, including palm trees, was entered on a land survey chart. The fleet enjoyed a monopoly of all wood capable of being used in shipbuilding. Even so, Egypt was obliged to resort to trading far afield; she brought teak from India via the Red Sea, and timber from the backwoods of the Adriatic, thanks to Venetian contraband trading.

Not only was Egyptian civilization short of timber; it also lacked iron, so that it was obliged to buy swords abroad from India and from 'Firanja', i.e. 'the Franks'. Because of its close dependence on communications with other territories, it was a contingent civilization; but for its gold resources it would not have survived at all, because timber and iron were at that time essential to any urban civilization.

The population of Egypt was mainly composed of Copts, *qubti*, from the Greek word *Aigyptios.* The old Egyptian word is *Misr,* in Hebrew *Misraim.* In the Middle Ages the term 'Bilad Misr' was used to designate Egypt and 'Misr' for the capital. The physical types in Egypt are remarkably stable, as may be seen by comparing Egyptians of today with those depicted in the underground chambers of the Pharaohs. The language was Ancient Egyptian: hieroglyphic, hieratic, demotic, and finally Coptic. The Egyptians used a distorted Greek alphabet eked out with one or two signs. The Egyptian population formed a homogeneous bloc, the Greek element being concentrated mainly in Alexandria, an alien town which seemed a mere appendage to Egypt. When it was captured by Arab troops in 643, the garrison and the most important Greek families of Alexandria fled the country, which meant that the alien element in the Egyptian population disappeared. On the other hand, considerable Jewish colonies, which were not assimilated and did not mingle with the Coptic population, continued to

live in Alexandria, at Bilbays on the eastern arm of the Delta, the
arrival-point of the Syrian route, as Aswan, in Elephant Island
from which caravan routes left for Nubia, Ethiopia, and the Red
Sea, at the points at which the Nile ceased to be navigable, and
also at Fustat.

Similarly, the activity of the Egyptian population, on the economic and even on the religious level, continued without a break.
The numerous conversions to Islam were often a pretext for evad-
ing the taxes which bore hard on non-Muslims, for example the
poll-tax (*jizya*). In the second half of the seventh century, under
Muawiya, this tax yielded no less than 5,000,000 dinars, then
under Harun ar-Rashid, at the beginning of the ninth century,
4,000,000, and shortly afterwards only 3,000,000. In the same
way Egypt made the transition from Sunnite Islam to the 'Alid
(Shi'ite) Islam of the Fatimids.

The basic Coptic element was not materially altered by the
arrival of the Arabs, a mere handful of invaders who were in any
case welcomed as liberators by the whole Levantine World, which
felt a sense of relief and renewal. The peoples under Byzantine
rule were in revolt against the administration, and this revolt had,
in Egypt and Syria, assumed a religious guise, as a conflict between
the Monophysite heresy and Byzantine orthodoxy. Their national
awareness was rather negative. 'We felt it no slight advantage',
wrote Michael of Syria later, 'to be delivered from the cruelty of
the Romans, from their wickedness, their anger, their cruel zeal
towards us, and instead to be left in peace.' There was in fact no
national resistance to the Caliphate in Egypt. The revolt of the
Delta Copts against al-Ma'mun (829–830) was provoked by fiscal
matters and must be regarded as one of the major social movements resulting from the new economic conditions prevalent in
the Muslim World.

And so Egypt, with her ancient civilization and almost un-
varying ethnic types, came under Muslim rule. She was short of
timber and iron, but her agricultural products, corn, flax, and
papyrus, were of world-wide importance. Finally, and most important of all, she provided gold, concealed in large quantities in the
ancient tombs of the Pharaohs. This gold was recovered, melted

down, and launched into monetary circulation. Later it was used to mint the beautiful Egyptian dinars, three of which, according to Nasir-i-Khusraw, were in the early eleventh century equivalent to three and a half Nishapur dinars.

Mesopotamia and Syria

The region stretching in an arc to the north of the Arabian Desert and roughly corresponding to Syria and Mesopotamia is often referred to as the 'Fertile Crescent'. It is not a homogeneous zone but is in fact a series of oases separated by rock-strewn plateaux or arid steppes often deteriorating into desert, and lying between the edge of the Anatolian Plateau (Taurus and Anti-Taurus), the edge of the Iranian Plateau (Zagros and Luristan), and the sea (Syria and Palestine). These oases are of varying extent and need irrigation and unbroken toil if they are to flourish. Without constant attention the soil quickly reverts to marsh or desert-like steppe; this happened during periods of insecurity, and then nomads returned and took over the ruins.

During the period which concerns us, Lower Mesopotamia was fully productive after a long series of irrigation operations carried out up to the Sassanid era. The crop-bearing area was extended because of the zones recently irrigated and drained, particularly on the edge of the great marshes (al-Bata'ih) into which the Euphrates runs, south of Kufa, and which even today are still nothing but an expanse of reeds. This is the marshy zone into which the Zotts were deported with their buffaloes from the banks of the Indus; they spent some time there before staging an uprising and being transferred to Syria and the Anatolian marshes (eighth century). It was there, too, that the black slaves (Zanj) fled in revolt in the ninth century, and held out against attack in flat-bottomed boats and camouflaged huts in the middle of the reeds. The Government pursued a policy of internal colonization recommended by jurists of the Abbasid era such as Abu Yusuf Ya'qub (died 798). He accorded the right to own property and an exemption from taxes to any pioneer who reclaimed 'dead land' (*ard mawat*). The result

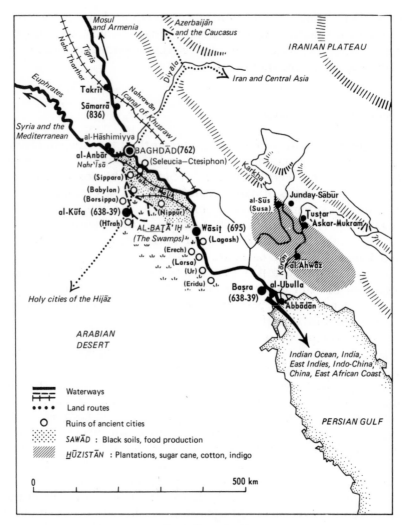

Fig. 2. Mesopotamia.

was to increase the amount of irrigated land and to bring conquered territory under cultivation, particularly that of the Sawad,
made up of alluvial deposits brought by the river, fertile black

earth which bore food crops needed to supply the populations concentrated in the cities.

Lower Mesopotamia, the centre of the Abbasid Caliphate, witnessed extraordinary urban development at this period. Some of its capitals, Baghdad, Basra, Kufa, Wasit, and Samarra, had hundreds of thousands of inhabitants. The Sawad territory, because of its fertility but also, as in Egypt, because of the unremitting labour of the *fellahin* both in cultivation and irrigation, partly supplied the needs of these vast urban areas. The land grew palm trees, corn, barley, and also rice, which had been known since the Sassanid era and was introduced into the Mediterranean Basin in Muslim times. Even so, the country had to import certain foodstuffs, such as corn from Egypt and meal from Syria.

However, as was stated above, the Mesopotamian oasis was not continuous, but broken up into several regions with different characteristics. Foremost among them was Khuzistan, formerly Susiana, the south-eastern part of Lower Mesopotamia, including the basins of the Karun and the Karkha, where the Sassanians had already carried out massive improvements, including retaining-dikes and navigable irrigation canals. From the end of the Sassanid era it was the most important area for growing sugar-cane, a plant which came from India and then spread a considerable way westwards during the Muslim era. Throughout the Muslim West the largest supplies of sugar came from Khuzistan. This was brown sugar, the kind we call 'soft brown sugar' or, after certain technical advances had taken place in Egypt, it was transparent sugar, *qand* (from which we derive the word 'candy'). The labourers on the plantations were mainly Bantu (Zanj) slaves from the east coast of Africa, who made their way to Khuzistan via southern Arabia, Oman, and the Iranian coast between Mekran and Kirman.

Next comes the Sawad, between the marshes (al Bata'ih) and a line running from Takrit to Hit, covered with cornfields, barley-fields, rice-fields, and date-palms. Finally, Upper Mesopotamia (Jazira) included a string of oases along the Tigris (Mosul, Amid-Diyar Bakr) and the Khabur region up to the bend in the Euphrates. Nowadays the area is a wild and empty steppe, where only nomadic shepherds live, but in those days there were vast colonies

of settlers. For Arab geographers the great speciality of al-Jazira
was the cotton from Khabur, which was exported to Mosul (cotton 'muslin'), to Baghdad (coloured silk embroidered on cotton,
or *baghdadi* material), or to Akhlat and the other Armenian textile
centres. These cotton crops were irrigated by underground channels (*qanat*) the idea for which came from central Asia. With the
removal of the frontier between the Byzantine and Sassanid empires, as a result of the establishment of the larger unified territory
of the Muslim World, cotton became acclimatized in northern and
then southern Syria. The latter region became, in the Middle Ages,
the main cotton-supplier for the whole of the Mediterranean
World.

From the bend made by the Euphrates as it flows from Syria to
Mesopotamia, the land slopes gradually up to the Syrian foothills
in the form of a great inclined plane covered with steppes containing grazing land. The southern aspect is more barren (Badiyat
ash-Sham), but even here it is possible to breed animals because
they can change pasture between the borders of the Badiyat in
summer and the central area in winter; here camels and horses
were bred for transport. This region functioned rather like a turn-
table, where every kind of contact was made and from which a
complete road system fanned out. It was the intersection-point of
the sea and river route reaching northern Syria from the Indian
Ocean via the Tigris and the Euphrates, and the continental route
also linking Iran and Baghdad with Syria by the bend in the
Euphrates.

Syria, like Mesopotamia, is made up of a series of rich, fertile
oases, formed from alluvium loosened from the rocky surface of
the uplands by the erosion caused by torrential rain which scored
gullies and uprooted trees as it rushed down the slopes. In Cilicia,
irrigation made it possible to grow tropical crops such as sugar-
cane and cotton. In the Biqa (the Crusaders knew it as 'Bouquee')
corn was grown. In Ghawr ('the hollow'), a rift-valley containing
lakes, the Jordan, and the Dead Sea, tropical crops were also
grown: sugar-cane, cotton, later on rice, which was introduced
during the Muslim era. The Damascus oasis, watered by streams
flowing down from the Anti-Lebanon and Mount Hermon, was

one enormous garden, the Ghuta, a kind of orchard planted with walnut trees, olive trees, fig trees, and other fruit trees. In the Middle Ages preserves from Damascus were famous the world over; they were made from Damascus fruits and Syrian sugar. Similarly, along the coast, there was a series of garden oases which were of necessity very tiny, because here the faulted boulders drop sheer down to the sea. It is a long strip of littoral plains, often broken by a spur of mountain. This coastline offered shelter for ports — the so-called 'ladders of the Levant' — which were successively used by Phoenician, Hellenistic, Roman, and Byzantine navies, and finally by the Muslim navies, whose arsenals used the timber grown in northern Syria and the Lebanon. This is the Mediterranean aspect of the countries along the Persian Gulf.

From the demographic point of view the populations of Syria and Mesopotamia were almost an extension of the Semites of Arabia — a Semitized rather than a Semitic society — as regards customs, language, and mental attitudes. They constituted the outer fringe of the Arab World, the melting-pot in which were mingled several successive waves of Semites from Arabia, the last of which coincided with the seventh-century conquest. The older non-Aryan populations existed side by side with the Aryans who had recently come down from the semicircle of mountains to the north (Asia Minor, Armenia, Iran); indeed every race from Asia and Africa was present, for this is accessible terrain, a transition zone exercising a strong attraction because of its large towns, the site of a very ancient urban civilization both exogamous and polygamous, and including slaves and mercenaries of every colour and tongue: Negroes, Turks, Slavs. The main body of the population was Semite but it had absorbed and assimilated constant and numerous additions, and the mixing of races became more marked under Muslim rule.

The great unifying factor was language, and it must be stated at once how easy it was to move from one Semitic language to another, because of the principle of the triliteral root which is often retained, even when the vocalization is different.

The 'Syri' of the Early Middle Ages who had seen the Eastern horizon closed to them by the Sassanid 'wall' and had turned to the barbarian West until its reserves of gold were exhausted, now saw opening up in the East a vast economic field under a single rule — the Muslim World. And so the diaspora was renewed, this time towards Mesopotamia. Here, as in the Indian Ocean, there was rivalry between Jacobites and Nestorians. The Aramean World had closed its ranks from the Persian Gulf to the Mediterranean and sent out far to the east and west powerful networks of inter-penetrating communities, points of stimulus both in the economic and in the cultural field. This *rapprochement* was not achieved smoothly or without struggle and rivalry between the Syrian and Mesopotamian elements.

The capital of the Umayyad Caliphate was Damascus, on the edge of the Badiyat ash-Sham. Although Mesopotamia was torn by constant revolts in Kufa and Basra, the last Ummayad ruler, Marwan II (744—750), intended to move the capital from Damascus to Harran in Upper Mesopotamia, so as to straddle Syrian Aramea and Babylonian Aramea. After the Abbasid conquest Damascus was ruled out as a capital because it was the home of the last remaining Umayyad supporters. Iranian influences — Khorasanian troops, counsellors from eastern Iran, the Barmekids — swayed the decision in favour of Mesopotamia, on the Iranian side. This was Aramean territory, but had already, in Sassanid times, absorbed certain Iranian traditions. After several attempts to found a capi-tal, all in Mesopotamia, in particular an attempt by the first Abba-sid caliph, Abu'l-'Abbas as-Saffah to found it near Anbar, at the point where the Nahr 'Isa or 'Jesus Canal' flows into the Euphra-tes, the second Abbasid caliph, al-Mansur, founded Baghdad at the other end of the Nahr 'Isa, where it flows into the Tigris. At the time the site was occupied by a few villages and a Nestorian mon-astery. The population of this city was imported from the four corners of the Muslim Empire, but the core was Aramean. The Nahr 'Isa and the Euphrates, and the route leading from Balis, the 'Syrians' port' to Antioch, Damascus, and Jerusalem, now effec-tively linked the two centres of the Muslim World, Mesopotamia and Syria.

CHAPTER 2

The Iranian World

Despite its close proximity to the Semitic World where both Arabic and Aramaic were spoken, with Arabic rapidly predominating, and despite its proximity to the Isthmus region with its perennial rivalry between the Persian Gulf routes and the Red Sea routes (a struggle which flared up in the twentieth century between Egypt and Syria, and Iraq and Jordan), the Iranian Plateau seems like another world, inhabited by different people speaking a different language and living in a totally different civilization.

Evolution of Iran's role

During the Sassanid era, Iran and Mesopotamia had been a single unit. The capital of the new empire was at Seleucia-Ctesiphon, in Aramean territory, but there had already been all kinds of exchanges (alphabet, vocabulary, techniques, ideas) between the two regions. The Arab conquest was a headlong dash in pursuit of the last Sassanid sovereign along the major route leading from Mesopotamia through Iran to central Asia. After occupying the cols and passes of the Zagros Mountains, the armies captured the oasis towns along the caravan route running through the Diyala Valley. Then came the Battle of Nihavand in 642 and the assassination of the last Sassanid, Yazdagird III, at Merv, in 652.

The period of the Umayyad Caliphate saw the establishment of the new conquerors in the form of a military colonization, carried out by the *jund*. These were bodies of men organized along military lines, who settled initially in quarters which they built for themselves next to the older cities, genuine little towns alongside the others, complete with fortress, mosque, and market. The result was the growth of dual towns made up of the old original Iranian town with its four gates (in Persian *shahristan*, in Arabic *medina*) and the new suburb close by (in Persian *birun*, in Arabic *rabad*), which was the conquerors' town. This duplication of cities was quite marked, particularly in Khurasan and Ma wara' an-Nahr, at Merv, Bukhara, and Samarkand; this clear preference for segregation even led to complete separation, as at Balkh where a second town, Baruqan, grew up some miles away from the old town.

The earliest supporters of the Abbasid dynasty and the counsellors of its first caliphs in the mid eighth century, came from northwest Iran, from Khurasan and Ma wara' an-Nahr. Military colonization was over; a movement in the opposite direction was developing. Iran became a powerful centre for the spread of influences which were felt throughout the Muslim East. There was a revival of Persian language and literature; at the turn of the tenth century Firdawsi wrote his *Book of Kings* (*Shah-name*). There was even an attempt at 'Persianization' by means of the language, on the part of the Turks of central Asia and India, which was to continue until the era of the great Moguls.

This process of Iranization of the Semite conquerors could be observed at the urban level. Segregation was over and the two towns formerly existing side by side were now joined. The *Shahristan* became once again the centre of government, the administrative centre (governor's palace, offices), the economic centre (markets, *suqs*), and the religious centre (great mosque). Round about this old, but newly discovered, centre were built new and populous suburbs which were subordinated to it. The dynasties of amirs, more or less independent of Baghdad, became, with their brilliant courts, centres of Iranization. From that time it was possible to speak of a genuine 'Iranian diaspora' along the caravan routes to the west, the east, and the south.

Geographical regions

Iran is a vast country of salt deserts or arid steppes, and bare mountains with occasional fertile spots, or oases where flower gardens bloomed and urban life flourished. Compared with the steppe this was *firdaws* or 'paradise'. At the centre of the oasis the main town within its walls was surrounded by a garden suburb irrigated by a system of underground channels (*qanat*) to prevent evaporation in these lands of torrid sunshine. The Abbasid era, continuing these major engineering achievements of the Sassanid era, saw a considerable expansion of land under irrigation, which enabled urban growth to continue and to increase. The technique of this Iranian irrigation system was to travel via the desert route and via the oases as far as southern Algeria (Foggara) and southern Morocco (Khattara). The Tauregs called these irrigation techniques 'Persian waterworks'.

These Iranian oases were scattered at the foot of the inner slopes of the surrounding mountain regions or at the foot of the central diagonal chain which splits the country into two arid depressions. The water running down from the mountains was collected on the spot and with great care for dwellers on the periphery, a string of towns serving as staging-posts along the caravan routes. These routes were traversed by the huge Bactrian camels (with two humps), reared in the region of Balkh, one of the capitals of Khurasan. They were also used by the powerful Iranian horses, strong enough to carry the heavily armed cataphracts (*asawira*) which are such a feature of Sassanid bas-reliefs. The Kurds and Lurs, who bred these horses, lived on the edge of the plateau which slopes down towards Mesopotamia, in Kurdistan and Luristan, nomad countries which always remained independent of the great administrative and bureaucratic States of the plain: those of the Achaemenids, Seleucids, Parthians, Sassanids, caliphs. These Kurds and Lurs, though held in check by the civilized organization of the lowland region, still posed a continual threat of invasion. This explains why there was, and still is, a broad strip of pastoral, wild territory between the Mesopotamian Plain and the Iranian Plateau.

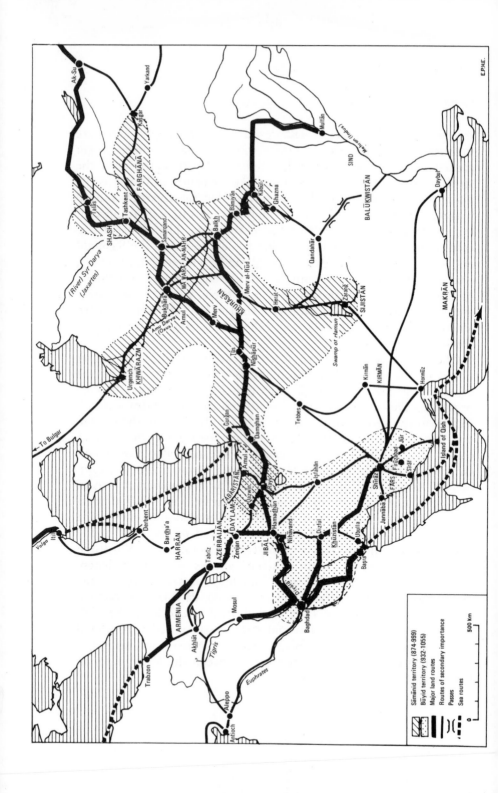

There were three possible openings through which this area could be entered, three major routes guarded by the forces of order. First there was the road into Armenia, where the valley of the Tigris and the Bitlis, via Jazira Ibn 'Umar,. led to Bitlis and Akhlat: then, towards Iran, the great route leading from Baghdad through the Diyala Valley to Kirmanshah and Hamadhan (Ecbatana), and from there, to Zanjan and Azerbaijan, Armenia, and Trabzon or to Arran, Derbent, and Itil; or else, after crossing the Jibal (the 'Mountains'), to Rayy (Teheran) and from there via Khurasan to central Asia; finally, there was a route leading from Baghdad to Khuzistan (Dizful) and to Fars (Shiraz).

A similar strip of land inhabited by wild, mountain-dwelling nomadic tribes, Afghans and Baluchis who had been brought there by the Sassanids from central Asia, bounded Iran to the south-east. There too the trade routes and the links between civilized communities were no more than narrow strips guarded by fortresses: Balkh, Herat, Kandahar, Ghazna, and Kabul.

The main geographical features of Iran are the mountainous ledge with its central ridges inhabited by nomadic shepherds, the arid depressions, and a string of peripheral oases stretching towards the interior. At the foot of the mountainous ledge, or else outside it, lay the 'outer Irans': Khuzistan, Arran (Transcaucasia), Tabaristan (south shore of the Caspian Sea) or oases of central Asia such as Ma wara' an-Nahr and Khwarizm (Oxus Delta on the Aral Sea).

On the marches, the Sassanid Empire had set up four important civilian or military governments (*ispehbed*). They were Azerbaijan (Atropatene) in the north-west; Fars (Persis) in the south-west; Sijistan (Sakostene) in the south-east; and Khurasan in the north-east. They pointed in four major directions: the Azerbaijan gateway opened on to Armenia and the Caucasus; the Zagros gateway on to Mesopotamia; the Kandahar gateway on to India; and the Khurasan gateway on to the Turanian Steppe, central Asia, and China. These major divisions of Iran were retained under the Abbasids.

Azerbaijan

Azerbaijan is a mountainous country which is a continuation of
Armenia and forms a transition region towards the Iranian Plateau.
These mountains are arid on their inner side, but they direct mois-
ture to the hollows lying in the steppes, which are fertile when
irrigated. The region was also a transit area crossed by the routes
to Armenia and as far as Trabzon, to Hamadhan and Mesopotamia, to Rayy and central Asia. Its commercial role was most
important. Great trade fairs were held at Tabriz. Further north,
Bardha'a in Arran formed with the Derbent Pass Iran's defensive
outpost in the west. The Bab al-Abwab, the 'Gate of gates', was set
in a wall with lead joints which was built to resist the incursions of
the Khazars and the peoples of Turan.

South of the Caspian

A high, narrow barrier separates Iran from the south of the Caspian Sea. This is the Elburz range of mountains, where a volcano
superimposed on foldings reaches a height of more than 18,000
feet at Demavend. The southern foot of the Elburz has a string of
oases which were staging-posts on the road through Zanjan, Kazwin, Rayy, Damghan, and Bistam. The most important was Rayy.
A watercourse, the Kizil Ouzen, flows down into the Caspian,
crossing the mountain chain along which runs the road from the
plateau to the port of Amul on the Caspian. Rayy was a great
storehouse set at the departure- and arrival-point of the caravans
to and from Khurasan, Baghdad, and Fars. The town was famed
for the splendour of its ceramics and was of considerable importance. In the thirteenth century, after the Mongol invasions, it
ceased to exist and was replaced by its suburb, Teheran; but from
the eighth to the eleventh centuries it played a vitally important
role, to which Ibn Khurdadhbeh bears witness in the mid ninth
century. It was to Rayy that Rus merchants, i.e. Slav or Scandinavian merchants, brought swords, furs, and slaves. These Rus or
Majus also pushed south and carried out pillaging raids, as happened in 913 and 944, against Bardha'a.

To the north of the Elburz runs a narrow alluvial border along
the shore of the Caspian, where sandbanks prevented the building
of good ports. The damp, hot, unhealthy climate made Tabaristan
'the fever country'. The same was true of Jilan, Mazandaran, and
Daylam. The lush vegetation of forest and jungle was inhabited by
tigers and leopards. Daylam continued for some time to supply
manpower in the form of slaves or mercenaries for the caliph's
guard. Not until the late ninth century did Islam begin to gain a
solid foothold there, mainly as a result of 'Alid propaganda. From
the close of the Sassanid era certain new crops appeared: rice,
cotton, sugar-cane, orange trees and mulberry trees (for silkworms). The Muslim Caliphate gave a fresh impetus to the cultivation of food crops and the supply of raw materials for industry,
thereby encouraging the trend towards urban development. It
must be remembered that this region was one of the points where
silkworms were reared, along a line running from central Asia to
Azerbaijan, Arran, and Armenia, while another route carried the
technique to northern Syria, in the sixth century under Justinian,
and from there to every suitable area in the Mediterranean during
the Muslim era.

Khurasan

Khurasan includes several mountain chains stretching from the
Elburz to the Pamirs, but at considerably less altitude (under
9,000 feet). There are very many hollows lying between the folds
in the mountains, which are easy to cross, especially along the
main silk route leading to central Asia, which was also the main
route taken by the invaders from the east (Turks, Mongols). Khurasan shields Iran in the east as it does Azerbaijan in the west.
There was a firmly established military organization (*merzban*),
which later became the starting-point, in the mid eighth century,
of the Abbasid movement supported by a Khorasanian army. At
the foot of the mountains was a string of oasis towns surrounded
by richly cultivated land, bearing in particular rice, cotton, and
cereals. West Khurasan, the region of Nishapur and Tus (Meshhed),
was the granary for the whole of eastern Iran. Cities played an

important role; according to Iranian traditions incorporated by Firdawsi in his *Book of Kings*, they included the first three cities which were created by Ormuzd: Balkh (Bactra), Merv (Margiana), and Herat (Aria). To these three must be added Nishapur (Naw Shapur); 'the New city of Shapur').

Balkh faced the crossing-points of the Oxus (Tirmidh, Kalif), and the 'the-other-side-of-the-river' (Ma wara' an-Nahr), and the foot of the Hindu Kush passes (Bamiyan, Kabul, Peshawar) which afforded access to India via Gandhara and Kapica, Graeco-Buddhist kingdoms where Indian and Iranian influences met. Along these passes, between Iran on the one hand and Turan and India on the other, ran the trade routes, but they were also the routes taken by missionaries and influences of every kind. This was, in particular, the major route which brought Buddhism from India and in the opposite direction it was the route taken by pilgrims from China like Hiuantsang (629–645). In the Bamiyan Col there are huge Buddhas carved out of the rock-face. Also on this route, at Balkh, there used to be a genuine community of Buddhist monks, the Novaia Viraya or 'New Monastery', under the direction of a superior or *paramaka*. After the Muslim conquest, this *paramaka* embraced Islam and secularized all the property of his monastery. This was the origin of the Barmekid family, members of which were counsellors to the first Abbasid caliphs: customs from east Iran, India, and China reached Baghdad through them. Paper was officially introduced into the offices of the civil service by Ja'far, the Barmekid who founded the first paper-factory in Baghdad, in 794–795, under Harun ar-Rashid; it was the first of a long chain of factories throughout the Muslim World. The earliest mention of Egyptian paper was in 796.

Merv (Antioch of Margiana), an oasis in the middle of the desert, was an important staging-post on the caravan route between Iran and the Oxus, rather like Palmyra. The Amu-Darya, the 'river of Amul', was crossed at Tachardjui (Amul) on the way to Bukhara and Samarkand.

Nishapur, the gateway to Iran in the east, like Tabriz in the west, was similarly a great trading city. After Baghdad shrank in size in the eleventh century, it became economically more important and had a larger population, becoming the capital of the new Seljuq rulers. It was sacked by the Mongols in the thirteenth century and today is merely a modest town of 10,000 inhabitants. It was supplanted by Meshhed (Tus) where the tomb of the Iman Rida is preserved, the sanctuary of Persian Shi'ism. The mountain lying between Nishapur and Meshhed contains considerable metal deposits — silver and more particularly lead.

A series of rivers run down to the west of the Paro Pamisus Range, arid mountains rising from the desert on the western side of the Hindu Kush, and drain the rainfall into fertile valleys. On the River Hari Rud, Herat (the Asian Alexandria) was a very big trading town on the semicircular trading route which passing through Balkh, Merv, Herat, Kandahar, and Ghazna skirted the west side of the Hindu Kush to join, downstream, the basins of Kabul and the Indus Valley. This region too was important because of its metal deposits, iron in this case, which was found near Herat where it was processed by the Indian method of tempering steel. From it were obtained ingots and weapons for export.

Sijistan

Sijistan (Sistan) falls into two parts. First there is the southern side of the Hindu Kush along which ran the route linking Kandahar to Herat, Merv, and Balkh an area enjoying most favourable communications, in that Kandahar, watered by mountain streams, was the starting-point of the route which, in the south-east, led to India and ended in the Kandabil Plain, an important region for the rearing of Bactrian camels. The second part was the desert basin round a central lagoon (Hamun) which made irrigation possible and into which flowed two rivers forming a constantly shifting delta. This meant that the population had frequently to move their homes. The area contains remarkable archaeological remains submerged by alluvial deposit; and some significant discoveries have been made there. The fertility of the region depended on a vast network of hydraulic arrangements. Corn was the main crop and this oasis was the granary for the south-east part of the Middle East. Extensive pasture-land made it possible to rear the Indian humped ox. The country was prosperous and well populated round Zaranj, but in 1384 Tamerlane sacked the town and destroyed the hydraulic system. The country suffered immediate decline and is an object-lesson in the precariousness of prosperity based on an irrigation system requiring regular maintenance by the whole community under responsible control.

Makran

At the extreme south, on the Gulf of Oman, Makran is almost impassable desert country. A range of nearly unscaleable mountain ridges cuts off from the hinterland the handful of little fishing ports which acted as ports of call for shipping between the Persian Gulf and northern India. These coastal oases, producing palms and cotton, played an important role as stages in the spread of sugar-cane-growing from India to Mesopotamia. In the interior, behind the mountain rampart, ran the route leading from Fars to the Lower Indus Valley, through an arid and unfrequented region inhabited by wild and uncivilized tribes (the Baluchis). Even so, the earliest Muslim armies took this route when they invaded the Indus Valley. After the conquest of Kirman and Sijistan (634–644) an initial, fruitless attack was launched against Daybul. But in 712 a victorious expedition under the command of Muhammed ibn Qasim, who was sent by Hajjaj, the Umayyad governor of Iraq, took the route from Makran to Daybul, and followed the Mihran (Indus) up to Multan. In 872, the Government of Sind was added to the area already ruled by Ya'qub ibn Layth the Saffarid in Ma wara' an-Nahr, Khurasan, Sijistan, and Kirman, a grouping which, as a result, included the whole of eastern Iran, Transoxania, and Sind, now for some time under the control of a dynasty almost independent of Baghdad.

Kirman

Between Makran and Fars, the mountain folds forming the southern face of the Iranian Plateau draw together and become lower, thus affording easy access to the interior — Kirman, a region separated from Oman, a corner of the Arabian tableland, by the Strait of Hormuz, which are dotted with islands and contain many ports. Kish (Qais) was the major port in the Persian Gulf, particularly from the eleventh century onwards, when it took over from Siraf, which was destroyed at the beginning of the century by a terrible earthquake. Roads led from Hormuz into the interior, to Shiraz and Fars, to Kirman and beyond Tabas and Nishapur to Zaranj, and further still to Herat and Balkh. The eleventh century was the period of greatest prosperity for Hormuz and Nishapur. Aden in 1513 and Hormuz in 1515 were to become the strategic points used by the Portuguese in their trade with the Indian Ocean.

Kirman, known to Ptolemy and Strabo as 'Karamania', still presents the same pattern of oases strung along the foot of the extensive mountain ridges which run diagonally across the Iranian Plateau. They were typical of oases in torrid zone, where the crops grown under the shade of the palms were rice, henna, and indigo. The date-palm spread as far north as the Tabas oasis, which could then boast 100,000 palm trees. There camels were reared, which were moved from their winter grazing in the desert to cooler regions in the hills in spring. Deposits of ore in the mountainside produced a burst of creative activity with the extraction and processing of iron, lead, and copper. Tamarisk-stumps provided the necessary fuel for braziery and the production of Indian steel which was carried out, for example, at Herat. Marco Polo later spoke of the 'ondanique' mines (*hindawani*, 'Indian steel'), which he saw at Kirman, where weapons were manufactured. The textile centres of the region used lamb's-wool and goat's wool. The cloth was printed by means of carved wood-blocks, according to a Sino-Indian process also used in the important neighbouring centres at Fars.

Fars

The mountains of Fars are a continuation of the Zagros Mountains, but are lower and less complex. Closed longitudinal valleys are enclosed by parallel ridges traversed by high passes. There are three distinct regions in Fars: first, the coast, appallingly hot, humid, and unhealthy, with an unpleasant beach covered either with pebbles or oily sand. There were one or two ports used for trade in the Persian Gulf, but poorly linked with the interior: the port on the Island of Kish (Qais), Siraf, and Jannaba. Of the three Siraf was the most important, being a major depot between Meso-potamia and India, an important equipment centre where great merchant ships were built with imported wood, namely teak from the west coast of India. The fleets which sailed along the Persian Gulf, south of Arabia, in the Red Sea, and to some extent the Egyptian fleets were made from this teak. The port of Siraf saw its most active period in the tenth century, after Basra and before Hormuz flourished. The shift of the major ports away from the Persian Gulf, the Basra—Ubulla—'Abbadan group, then Hormuz, then the Island of Kish, was bound up with economic and political vicissitudes: the Qarmat movement, the struggle between Sama-nids and Barluks, the decline of Baghdad, and the rise of Nishapur.

Above the coastline rises an area cleft with gorges which was inhabited by hill-dwelling nomads, who bred horses and camels and worked as caravaneers, but also kept sheep and sent the wool to supply the textile centres of Fars. There too the flocks regularly sought fresh pastures according to the season of the year, leaving behind the hot coastal belt for the cooler regions of Fars itself, via the area intersected by gorges. Fars is composed of sheltered hol-lows at a high altitude, which form a contrast with the desolate plateau because of the idyllic appearance of their well-irrigated oases. The Shiraz oasis was praised by the thirteenth-century poet Sa'di in his *Gulistan* or *Rose Garden*. It had cool gardens planted with flowers and vegetables, orchards, and vines producing famous wines which, when transplanted to Spain and acclimatized, would later yield the famous wine known to us as 'sherry'. In this area there flourished, from the remotest antiquity, settled civilizations in the towns of Persepolis and Pasargadae. It was here in this more genuinely Iranian province of Persis, that the earliest movement towards Iranization originated, under Sassanid leadership. The sec-ond came from Khurasan, in eastern Iran, with the Abbasids, but it contained other elements, Indian and Chinese, and was less pure than the first.

Fars was pre-eminently a textile centre, the most important in the entire Muslim World, including those in Khuzistan and the Egyptian Delta. In it the old Iranian traditions were maintained, particularly the technique of hand-embroidery embellished with metal coins, precious stones, and pearls — the *susanjird*. But new techniques were imported from Egypt and Armenia during the Muslim era: *dabiqi* material (from Dabiq, in Egypt) was made here, and also carpets from 'Arminiya'. Round Shiraz were scattered a series of smaller textile centres: Fasa, Darabjird, Firuzabad (Jur), which also produced a kind of rose-water known as *Juri* which was exported all over the world.

Jibal

We return to our point of departure, the edge of the Zagros Mountains, via a broad mountain region over 1000 kilometres long by 200 kilometres wide, a kind of thick, continuous pad made of huge parallel ridges which was known as 'Jibal province' ('the mountains') under the Abbasid Empire. One single river, the Diyala, follows a course straight through the middle of the mountain range along a saddle which played an important role as a line of communication between the Iranian Plateau and the Mesopotamian Plain. At the end of this natural route stood Baghdad, an Iranian bridgehead in Aramean territory, just as Seleucia-Ctesiphon had been, but of greater dimensions. The city, circular in shape, had four gates named after the four main centres to which they pointed. In the north-east was the Khurasan Gate; in the south-east the Basra Gate; in the south-west the Kufa Gate; and in the north-west the Syrian Gate. The Khurasan road was the triumphal route taken by the new Abbasid dynasty. It was the old historic route going through Kirmanshah, Behistun, and Nihavand, where the Muslims engaged in the decisive battle against the Persian troops which enabled them to press on to Hamadhan (Ecbatana). After leaving Kirmanshah it crossed a pass, the Zagha Col (2340 metres), then ran down the mountainside towards Hamadhan to reach a plateau from which roads branched off to Rayy and Zanjan. Stony, desolate slopes form the inner rim of this mighty wad of mountains. However, one or two oases existed at the end of watercourses which ran down the mountain, such as Hamadhan and Isfahan, linked by caravan routes with Fars in the south, and in the north with Rayy and Hamadhan, both of which were on the major route leading to Khurasan and Mesopotamia.

Jibal was a province of crucial importance for communications between the Abbasid Caliphate and Iran. Ibn Khurdadhbeh, who was Postmaster-General (*sahib al-barid*) of Jibal under the Caliph al-Mu'tamid (870–892), described stage by stage in his *Kitab al-masalik wa'l-mamalik* or *Book of Roads and Provinces* the major roads radiating from Baghdad. The Postmaster-General was an important official who was of necessity very well informed. He kept a check on the official couriers, spied on the other officials, and maintained direct contact with the central administration. The work of Ibn Khurdadhbeh, compiled for the use of his subordinates, enables us to retrace very accurately the road network of his day.

Boundaries and roads

The crossroads of central Asia

The crossroads of central Asia formed the background to the civilization and the economy of the Abbasid era. This system of roads all radiating from one point conferred importance on a region which played no part in the spread of Islam but simply broadened its economic scope. Its oasis towns with their carefully maintained irrigation systems, already flourishing under the Sassanids in Khurasan and also in Khwarizm, were inhabited by wealthy merchants who had a wide network of commercial contacts and spoke a commercial language, Sogdian. Their activities were stimulated still further by the establishment of Muslim domination. Colonies of merchants settled in Balkh, Merv, Bukhara, Samarkand, and Kashgar. The exchange of personnel, merchandise, ideas, and techniques, was intensified. Various influences came together, and then merged in these Iranian oasis towns, isolated pockets constantly exposed to raids by the nomads of Turan. Long defensive walls several hundred kilometres in circumference had been thrown round the entire oasis, including the crops, at Bukhara, Samarkand, and Derbent, ever since the Sassanid era, just as the Great Wall of China was built, or the wall in the Crimea under Justinian. But these walls could not fend off major invasions. Islam set up in front of these towns isolated *ribats*, advanced outposts for attack and defence, rather like monasteries for champions of the Faith. These outposts gave the impetus to the Islamization of the steppes by blood and the sword, in the manner of the Teuton campaigns in Slav countries. Farghana was for a long time under the dominion and influence of the T'ang, who introduced paper and wood-engraving into the area. But the Battle of Talas in 751 put an end to Sinization. At the same time Turkish tribes began to infiltrate, and in fact later on they gained the ascendancy. But there was already a genuine and progressive Turkization by means of the language.

There were, briefly, three influences at work in central Asia: Chinese in the form of techniques, Muslim in the form of religion, and Turkish in the form of language. In the eighth and ninth centuries the Turks became established in the region of Talas, in Shash, Farghana, and Kashghar. In the eleventh century they invaded Transoxiana, then the whole of eastern Iran; they pushed forward into Syria and Anatolia and founded the Seljuq Empire. But these Turks had absorbed Iranian influences, and what they took with them to the most westerly parts of their conquered territory was Iranian civilization, yet again with a few additional elements of horsemanship which were purely Turkish. One can quite confidently assert that the Turks continued the process of Iranization.

In matters of religion the invaders were until the end of the ninth century Shamanist or Manichaean (the Uigurs), or even Nestorian (Karaites at the beginning of the eleventh century). They were tolerant towards the religions of former Iranian cities which still adhered to Buddhism, Mazdaism, Manichaeism, Nestorianism, or Judaism. But from the middle of the tenth century the Samanids began the process of Islamization.

Between Iran and the Turkish Steppe, in the region where, after the Battle of Talas, Chinese influence yielded to Islam, there were many considerable shifts of population. The Buddhist Tibetans moved northwards, the Turks went south; Manichaean Uïgurs, Shamanist Qarluqs and Ghuzz, all advanced as far as Khwarizm. These tribes had not yet been Islamized and constituted an almost limitless source of slaves, the Bilad al-Atrak where merchants went to buy, but where raiders were also sent from the *ribats.*

At the end of the tenth and the beginning of the eleventh centuries a Ghuzz clan from the banks of the Syr Darya embraced Islam, and formed the first Muslim Turkish dynasty, the Kara-khamids. At the end of the eleventh century a second clan was converted to Islam and formed the Seljuq Sultanate which seized power in Khurasan after the fall of the Samanids. Another Turkish clan, the Kipchaks, occupied southern Russia (1054) and drove the Pechenegs into the Balkans. In their rear, the Polovtsians cut off the Russian river routes.

Routes leading towards the Eurasian Steppes

Contact with the Eurasian Steppes was made chiefly by means of the Volga, which was held by the Khazars, with Itil on the Caspian Sea as the starting-point, and the Dnieper which was held by the Rus (Kiev). These rivers led to the great Nordic forest, on the fringe of which dwelt the Bulghars, a Turkish tribe which was still not completely sedentary, in that they used their wooden town, Bulghar, set at the confluence of the Volga and the Kama, on the edge of the forest, only in winter. Later on Kazan was built close by. Bulghar, the main city of Greater Bulgaria, became Islamized at an early stage.

Like the Bulghars, the Burtas were semi-nomadic. The beginnings of Islamization were evident in the Muslim quarter of Itil (near the site of Astrakhan). Khaqan of the Khazars embraced Judaism. Like Bulghar, Madina al-Burtas was a town set at the confluence of two rivers, the Oka and the Kama, on the edge of the forest. This was the site of Nijni-Novgorod.

Inside the forest, Finnish, Finnish-Ougrian, and Slav tribes made up what the Arabs called the 'Bilad as-Saqaliba', the 'Slav country', the second vast source of slaves, stretching as far as the Germanic and Illyrian forest. The area provided, apart from slaves, furs, honey, supple Bulgarian leather for the manufacture of riding-boots, and maple wood (*Khalanj* wood). From Burtas via Bulghar and from Kiev, the road followed the rivers, and reached Itil and the shores of the Caspian, then Tabaristan and Rayy. Another road ran directly across the steppe and linked Burtas and Bulghar with Khwarizm and Khurasan. These two routes rivalled each other.

Relations with India and China

The Muslim conquest of Sind from the south took place as early as 712. But penetration into India by the Hindu Kush passes was effected only gradually from 751 onwards after the Battle of Talas. The region behind Balkh, Tukharistan, a difficult mountainous area populated by savage tribes, was progressively taken over in the ninth century by the Tahirids and then by the Saffarids who finally settled in Kabul. This town initiated the Islamization of the mountain-dwellers of Kafiristan (*Kafir* means 'Infidel'; cf. the Kaffirs in Africa), rebellious tribes who also provided a constant supply of slaves. But gradually, valley by valley, the communication corridors came under Islamic domination, for example the Ghazna Pass on the route leading from Kabul to Kandahar. The Turks settled here and it was here that the Ghaznavids founded, in 962, the first Islamized independent Turkish dynasty in Iranian territory. Between 1014 and 1025 they conquered and Islamized northern India, and it was to India that they withdrew later on, when they were driven out of central Asia and eastern Iran by the Seljuq advance.

There were two possible ways of reaching China from Iran, one in the north via Tashkent, Talas, and Aqsu, the other in the south via Farghana, Kashghar, Yarkand, and Khotan. They joined at Touen-houang to form a single road leading to the Great Wall and the T'ang capital. In the eighth century, trade along these routes was disturbed by Tibetan (T'ou-fan) raids on the oases lining the northern route. But by then the main route to China was by sea, from the Persian Gulf to Canton, where colonies of Muslim and Jewish merchants had flourished since the eighth century. In the ninth and tenth centuries order was restored along the land routes. The Tibetans dropped their aggressive tactics when they embraced Buddhism. The Turkish nomads acted as convoys and protectors of the caravans plying between the Muslim and Chinese civilizations, and trade was resumed. Mas'udi puts the time taken to reach China from Iran at four months. It was at this period that Muslim communities began to be set up in northern China.

The importance of the road nexus: the Samanid Emirate

Before the Samanids came to power, the unification of eastern Iran had already been attempted by the Tahirids (820–872) who occupied Kirman and Rayy, and by the Saffarids (867–903) who, with Ya'qub ibn Layth already governor of Sijistan, succeeded in uniting the region of Herat, Transoxiana, and Fars, but failed in the last resort. During this time the Samanids fought against the Buyids. This unremitting rivalry between the four dynasties, of little intrinsic or even factual interest, was aimed at the caravan termini and was connected with the domination of the Asian land routes. The Samanid Emirate (875–999) was a State relying entirely on roads and on slaves.

The ancestor of the Samanids, a noble Iranian family, was Saman Khudat, who founded the town of Saman near Balkh. The new dynasty reached out beyond Islam and attempted to draw closer to the Sassanids, which was indicative of a Persian revival, whereas the western dynasties which followed all strove to follow the Prophet. The descendants of Saman embraced Islam and offered to serve the Abbasids. There were four brothers, all of whom were made provincial governors in 820 by al-Ma'mun at Samarkand, Farghana, Shash, and Herat. The only one left in 892 was Isma'il ibn Ahmad, and his capital, Bukhara, eclipsed Samarkand. In 893 he captured Talas in a campaign against the Turks; in 900 he entered Khurasan; in 902 he seized Tabaristan (Rayy, Kazwin) which opened up the road to the Caspian and Baghdad. The dynasty reached its highest point in the reign of Nasr II (913–942) whose Emirate stretched as far as Talas in Farghana, and as far as the Kashghar region in the east, Khwarizm and Bulghar in the north, Rayy and the Caspian in the west, and Sijistan and Kandahar in the south. Stabilization, followed by incipient decline, came with Nuh I (943–954), who fought with the Buyids for the possession of Rayy.

The Buyid Emirate can also lay claim to a Sassanid origin. It relied on Daylamite mercenaries and also strove for mastery of the central Asian routes. One of the emirs captured Rayy, Isfahan, Shiraz, Siraf, occupied Jibal and finally, in 945, entered Baghdad where he remained as *amir al-Umara'* ('Emir of the emirs') until 1055 and the arrival of the Seljuqs.

The loss of the routes, first in the west, then in the south, marked the decline of the Samanids. The Ghaznavids, who were local chieftains, captured Kabul and Tukharistan in 977 with the help of Turkish mercenaries. Under their rule the State was no longer Iranian but rather a Turkish State which offered protection to Persian writers and carried on the Samanids' activities on the intellectual plane. It was also a State on the move, which seized the Hindu Kush and Khurasan passes, then, in 1030, conquered Khwarizm, Jurjan, and Rayy which it took from the Buyids. Finally the Ghaznavids occupied northern India where they took refuge after the Seljuq thrust.

The great wealth of the Samanid cities was based on the slave-trade. Merv, Nishapur, Rayy, Balkh, Bukhara, Samarkand, and Herat, all trafficked in Slav slaves who came via Khwarizm, Indian slaves who came via Kabul, and especially Turkish slaves brought in via the frontier posts. Many of them were resold after undergoing castration or completing military training, and subsequently rose to positions of authority in the Samanid Empire, until the rebellious *mamluks* brought about its downfall. It had been an Iranian custom to surround oneself with slaves and Turkish guards. The Barmekids, in particular Fadl ibn Yahya, were partly responsible for launching this fashion whereby the Muslim World became more and more receptive to Turkish influences. Under al-Ma'mun the Tahirid Emir of Khurasan was obliged to pay to Baghdad a tribute of 2,000 Turkish slaves who formed the caliph's personal guard. Under al-Ma'mun they were not given command, but under al-Mu'tasim (833–842) they were allowed to become officers. The disturbances provoked by 70,000 Turks in Baghdad obliged the caliph to found Samarra in 836 as a means of escape; later on, al-Mu'tamid returned to Baghdad, once more a prisoner of the Turks. Ahmad ibn Tulun was the son of a Turkish slave from Bukhara; he founded the Tulunid dynasty in Egypt. In 935, al-Ikhshid, a Turkish slave from Farghana, became in turn the founder of the Ikhshidids in Egypt. The importance of Farghana slaves in the royal guard was the same at Byzantium as it was at Baghdad.

With the establishment of the Samanids, the process of Turkization gained breadth and momentum. Turks formed the guard at Bukhara. Turkish slaves were purchased in enormous quantities from rival clans along the frontiers. Raids were launched from the *ribats* against neighbouring tribes. There were volunteers too: indeed mercenary and slave were virtually indistinguishable. Both were employed within the country or were sent westwards, with all customs dues paid, to the crossing of the Oxus. During his first year, the slave served as a foot-soldier and lived in barracks; in his second year the general (*hajib*) gave him a horse; in his third year he received a special belt, the rough equivalent of 'stripes'; in his fifth year he had a saddle and more ornate weapons; in his sixth year, a parade costume; in his seventh, he was put in command of a tent and was entitled to wear distinguishing marks (tall fur hats). He could become a high-ranking *hajib* at the head of a government. But in practice this career was often thwarted by intrigue. The Samanid Emirate was an Iranian-Turkish society, but its civilization was Iranian. The tenth century in eastern Iran and Transoxiana, under the Samanids, was a vital period of Iranian renaissance in language, literature, and science.

Continuity of the Iranian element

The earliest known texts in which the Persian literary language appears in a completely developed form were found in Khurasan.

This language, Farsi, was not based on a local vernacular, but on an imported Fars dialect. Opinions differ on the date at which this Fars language reached Khurasan. Christensen maintains that it came when the Sassanids were in power, but it seems more likely to have arrived during the first centuries of Muslim rule. Tahir ibn Husayn very probably contributed towards the adoption and development of this language. The Sassanids created a vast library in their capital at Bukhara and attracted to their court men of letters and scientists. Under Nasr II (913—942) lived Rudaki, the earliest Persian poet of whom anything is known, fragments of whose writings have come down to us: the old Hindu fable *Kalila wa-Dimna* translated into Persian verse. It had already been translated into Middle Persian by Chosroes Anushirwan and into Arabic by the Persian Ibn al-Muqaffa' under the first Abbasids. Though lyric poetry in Persian had already been composed under the Tahirids and the Saffarids, it was particularly under the Samanids that the Persian language reached its full flowering.

A further problem is the origin of Persian poetic form. The Iranian syllabic metre is governed by the Arabic quantitative prosody based on long and short sounds, which is pre-Islamic, and therefore Arabic in form. Under al-Mansur (961—976), the Vizier Bal'ami translated into Persian *The Annals* written in Arabic by Tabari, a Persian from Tabaristan. This marked the beginnings of Persian prose. At Bukhara, Ibn Sina (Avicenna) wrote in Arabic his great scientific works (Arabic was still the language of science, as was Latin in Europe up to the eighteenth century) but composed a summarized version of his philosophy in Persian.

The Samanid emir, Nuh II (976—997), did much to promote Persian epic poetry. Ancient Sassanid annals written in Pahlavi which are partly legendary accounts, but of great importance for the varied information they contain, had been translated into Persian. Nuh II commissioned the poet Daqiqi to recast this translation in verse, but Daqiqi was assassinated before he had advanced very far. His work was continued by Firdawsi, who was born about 932—934 in a suburb of Tus, the ruins of which city may still be found near Meshhed. The first version of *Shah-name* (*Book of Kings*) was made about 994 and it underwent alterations and

additions until 1010. The total length of the work was 50,000 dis-
tichs: eight times as long as the *Iliad*. But these were troubled
times: the Samanid Emirate collapsed. Firdawsi turned then to the
new 'head' of Iranian civilization, Mahmud of Ghazna, and offered
him the homage of his 100,000 lines. Mahmud could not bring
himself to listen to them all the way through, whereupon Firdawsi,
smarting under this ungenerous treatment, prefaced his work by an
epigram instead of the adulatory dedication he had intended, and
fled. He died at Tus in utter obscurity between 1020 and 1025.
This literary anecdote is significant, showing as it does that the
Iranization of the new Turkish masters was only skin-deep. Even
so, it was the Ghaznavids who spread Persian influences into
northern India.

It is, therefore, possible to point to several stages of Iranization.
The earliest Iranian diaspora took place before and after the Arab
conquest. It received scant attention from subsequent historians
and geographers. Parsee communities settled on the west coast of
India, particularly from the eighth century onwards, in Gujarat
and Bombay. Iranian settlements became established on the east
coast of Africa before the Arab conquest and were reinforced after
the conquest by Persian migrations. The second Iranian diaspora
occurred after the Abbasid movement. It went beyond the Muslim
Empire as far as China and also the West. Persian pilots (*nakhudha*) were transferred to Syria, to the coastal towns, where they
handed on the maritime techniques of the Indian Ocean. The
writer al-Ya'qubi and particularly Rustam, who founded the
Rustamid dynasty of Tahert, in North Africa, were both Persian.
The third diaspora was brought about by Iranized Turks, first
Ghaznavids then Seljuqs, and spread as far as Anatolia.

CHAPTER 3

The Muslim West

In the older countries of the Levant, i.e. Iran, Syria, Mesopotamia, and Egypt, with ancient civilizations, there was no perceptible break between the Byzantine-Sassanid period and the Muslim era (eighth to eleventh centuries) as regards the continuity of cities, workshops, or the arts. The East was a power-house radiating influences: Islamization (religion), Arabization (language), Semitization and Iranization (mental concepts, methods, techniques, and also sets of ideas and art forms). By contrast, the Muslim West which was to receive these ideas — Ifriqiya, Maghreb, Sicily, and Spain — was composed of countries which had lapsed into barbarism, ruralism, or nomadism, countries in which memories of their Punic or Roman past had faded or in many places been totally obliterated. The urban decline which followed the great crisis of the Late Roman Empire was further accentuated by the barbarian invasions. There were, however, still some urban centres which survived: Carthage, Volubilis, Tingis, Septem, Gades, Malacca, Hispalis, Cordoba, Toletum, Caesarea Augusta, and Panormus. But these cities, already on the decline, were further reduced by the development of rural patterns of life, both in Spain and Sicily, and also by the growth of nomadism and the development of zones traversed by camel-drivers in North Africa. The limited extent, the weakness, the precariousness of Justinian's reconquest were soon to become evident.

In comparison with the older civilized countries of the Levant, which were exhausted by the protracted exploitation of their resources, these younger — or rejuvenated — Muslim countries to the West offered fresh economic possibilities, a still untapped human potential, and a wealth of untouched resources. These new countries attracted Muslims from the East, prominent among whom were the Umayyads in Spain, the Idrisids in the Maghreb al-Aqsa, Rustamids in the Maghreb al-Awsat, and Aghlabids and Fatimids in Ifriqiya. They came to seek their fortune in these distant colonies, and their courts were besieged by adventurers of every kind, merchants and scholars alike, drawn by the fat pensions to be earned, by the places waiting to be filled, in these new Islamic States in the West. This was especially true of the court at Cordoba, where there was no autochthonal intellectual flowering such as existed in the East. These adventurers were the pioneers who transmitted Eastern culture to the West.

North Africa

In North Africa the centuries preceding the Muslim conquest had witnessed the retreat of urban development and the advance of nomadization. This process had not been arrested by Justinian's reconquest: just over a century of union with Byzantium (533–647), and only a small part of the country at that, was not enough to halt the progressive stifling of urban life. The land near the towns, the surrounding countryside on which they depended for food, the approaches to the *castella* or little fortified outposts, were progressively encircled by Berber nomads. Raids and punitive expeditions alternated. Byzantine military campaigns became restricted to the communication corridors between mountain ranges, where Berber settlers asserted their independence with more and more determination; they steered clear of the high plateaux or the deserts where the tribes of camel-drivers wandered far and wide.

This restriction of the area open to urban influences was, of course, matched by an acceleration and extension of the process of de-Romanization and by the resurgence of the distant Berber past, an evolution similar to the one observed in Syria and Egypt where, after de-Hellenization, the old Aramean and Coptic ways of life reappeared. But whereas in the Mediterranean Levant it was the old, civilized, urban past which came to life, here it was a barbarian and nomad past which rose to the surface, with one notable difference: the dromedary was used as a mount. This process, which had been going on for some time, was not interrupted by the Byzantine reconquest either. An ever-increasing number of Berbers ceased using Latin or Punic, which were in any case predominantly urban, literary languages, and returned to Berber, a Shamitic language, an ancient Libyan tongue which is preserved for us in one or two ancient inscriptions. It had no connection with the Semitic or Indo-European languages, had a mainly oral tradition, and had no written literature. Not only did the Berbers revert to their former language, they also returned to their age-old customs (*Qanun*), their own social habits, namely a tribal structure with democratic and egalitarian tendencies. Their taste for independence, their traditionalism, their savage individualism resulted in the establishment of separate little conservative mountain republics, or nomadic clans.

However, Punic and Latin continued to be used in urban areas. Punic held its ground in some parts of Ifriqiya, which may explain the rapid victory of Arabic in the eastern towns. Latin continued to be spoken for a long time in the towns. The latest Latin inscriptions in Volubilis date from the end of the seventh century. Ya'qubi, at the end of the ninth century, refers to the 'Afariqa' or 'Africans' who speak *ifriqi*. But Latin subsequently developed into a genuine Romance dialect and, even in the twelfth century, Idrisi stated that the inhabitants of Gafsa in the south of Tunisia spoke a specific 'Latino-African' language.

The towns welcomed the conquerors; it was in the mountains, on the plateaux, in the desert, that they encountered resistance. After the Muslim conquests, the townships and the corridors of communication between the mountain ranges adopted Arabic, whereas the hill-dwellers and desert tribes went on speaking Berber.

Parallel with the decline or urbanization and Romanization,

Christianity lost ground. The African Church, which had played an important role in the fourth century during St Augustine's lifetime (and he was a Berber), was as it were decapitated by the persecutions of Arian Vandals. Moreover, evangelization had never reached certain regions of the interior. Sixth-century Byzantine texts speak of many tribes which were still pagan or had relapsed into paganism. The Berbers possessed a great fund of religious feeling which found satisfaction in magico-religious practices of old African cults existing long before the introduction of the Phoenician or Roman gods, and so before Christianity and Islam. Many of the specific characteristics of Berber animism derive, no doubt, from the Negro World; or perhaps the contrary is true. In remotest antiquity the Berber World had contacts with Nigritia which extended to the south of Jazirat al-Maghreb and retreated further and further into the Sudan before the Berber camel-drivers. These animist anthropolatrous beliefs were never completely overlaid either by Christianity or Islam.

On the other hand there were in Roman Africa Jewish communities which had collected round an original core of Punic or Punicized elements in towns converted to Judaism. By means of these urban centres and the migration of more and more mobile tribes since the dawn of modern times, Judaism reached the interior of Berber territory, in the high plateaux and mountain ranges, and also in the Sahara. It reached Jerawa of the Aures, Nefusa in south Tunisia, and several tribes in the Atlas Mountains and in south Morocco. The progress of Judaization may be traced across the Sahara. In line with Muslim tradition, these Jews were already artisans and traders. With the eclipse of African Christianity, Judaism persisted and re-established its links with the Eastern centres of the official Synagogue which were also the centres of wider world trade. The itinerary followed by the Radhanite Jews in the ninth century passed through the colonies in India and China, the staging-posts of Judaized Khazars in the loops of the Volga, and also the Judaizing communities in the northern Sahara.

The great masses of the Pagan World embraced Islam. Any remaining urban centres became the earliest centres of Islamization and Arabization, just as they had been the centres of Punicization and Romanization. Having won over the towns, both old and new, which reached their greatest prosperity in the eighth and ninth centuries, Islam gained ground along the roadways and addressed itself to the mountains. Even so, part of the mountainous region remained outside its influence until the nineteenth century when Islamization was at last achieved by the French colonial system in its anxiety for administrative uniformity. But even when the Berbers were converted, they renounced the faith on many occasions: at least twenty times, according to Ibn Khaldun, particularly during the first two centuries of the Muslim conquest. The African version of Islam was quite unlike any other. It welcomed heresies like Kharijism which was opposed to the Sunnism of the established, central, organizing powers, but was well suited to Berber particularism (Mzabites). Sunni Islam itself, adopted by the Berber masses after prolonged resistance, became overlaid by superstitious practices such as saint-worship or anthropolatry, marabouts, and belief in *baraka*.

The picture, then, is of the persistence of the old African origins and background, which emerged more and more insistently between the fourth and seventh centuries; the fragility of the Roman and Christian veneer in North Africa; the slow spread of Islamization, but in many places the depth attained by Islam once it had fused with older African beliefs.

The economic regression, a direct result of the shrinking of areas under cultivation (olive trees, corn, vines) and the atrophy of trading interchange, was not eradicated by the Byzantine reconquest, which failed in the very area in which Muslim domination later succeeded, namely the reintegration of North Africa, in a period of regression, into the main currents of the world economy.

Despite its urban decline, the resurgence of the old, uncivilized Berber character, and the economic regression, the Maghreb did possess two great potential strengths. First, its vast manpower. During the early struggles considerable consignments of slaves were sent east, then, after the more accessible regions had been converted to Islam (and thus closed to the slave-trade), Barbary began supplying soldiers and mercenaries who helped to conquer Spain, Sicily under the Aghlabids, and Egypt under the Fatimids, and who colonized the Sahara as far as the Sudan. This demo-graphic advance by the Berbers in the Early Middle Ages may, or may not, have been a consequence of the *Pax Romana*; the ques-tion must remain open because it is still the same today. In the eighth and ninth centuries North Africa was a storehouse of mili-tary power, like Daylam in the West (see above, p. 35).

The other potential which Islam succeeded in translating into reality was the opening up to the Berber World towards the Sahara and the Sudan. The incorporation of Sudanese-Berber trade into the Islamic World led to the diversion of both gold and black slaves towards the Mediterranean and the East. Gold conferred trading power and black slaves constituted the labour force to work in the plantations; their warlike qualities also helped to strengthen the power of Berber North Africa.

The regions of the Maghreb

The 'island of the Maghreb' (Jazirat al-Maghreb) is exceptionally well situated between the Muslim East and Muslim Spain, and also between the Sahara-Sudan and the Mediterranean. The three main regions of the Maghreb, which the Muslim invaders arriving from the east tried to control, were Ifriqiya, the Maghreb al-Aqsa, and Tingitania on the edge of the Sahara.

Ifriqiya or Afriqiya (Africa proconsularis) looks out on to the Sicilian Strait. It was an old Punic centre, a strategic point held by the Vandals, then by the Byzantines. The cities, particularly Carthage, had Levantine inhabitants. They grew olive trees, corn, and vines. The Maghreb al-Aqsa ('the most distant' or 'the Far West'), to the north of Tingitania, commanded the strait of the Pillars of Hercules. On either side were cities: Tingis, Septem, and Lixus, with Malacca, Gades, and Hispalis opposite, inhabited by Levantine colonies and Jews. This, too, was an old Punic trading centre. In the interior, Volubilis (Ulili, Walila) would later become the first Idrisid capital before Fez (late seventh to early eighth centuries). These two zones, Africa and Tingitania, with their ancient urban centres, first Punic then Roman, transit areas on the way to Italy or Spain, were very quickly Islamized and Arabized.

The same was not true of the edge of the Sahara at the foot of the Atlas Mountains, a vast zone running from east to west from which the trans-Sahara routes branched off, so that along its entire length were to be found the northern termini of the caravan routes which passed through the Sudan and the Sahara. This region was also the desert refuge of the Berber nomads living on the high plateaux. Since it was vital to deny them this access, the Arab conquerors made this their immediate task. Sidi 'Uqba led several raids from the Jerid against Ghadames (the former Cydamus) even going as far as Sus al-Aqsa ('the remotest Sus'), towards the Oued Draa and the tracks running along the Atlantic. There is a story that 'Uqba rode his horse into the sea and regretted he could go no further.

The relief of the Maghreb consists, in the central area, of terraced ridges running from east to west, which are, taken from north to south, from the Mediterranean to the Sahara, as follows: the Coastal Sahel, broken up by chains of mountains, the Little Atlas, the High Atlas, the Saharan Atlas, and the desert. On either side, littoral plains stretch as far as Ifriqiya (Tunisia) and the Maghreb al-Aqsa (Morocco). This fact explains the difficulties placed in the way of invaders tackling the relief frontally as did the Romans and the French, and conversely the ease of access enjoyed by conquerors coming from the west like the Vandals or from the east like the Arabs, who were able to travel along the natural lines of communication between and along the foot of the mountains.

There were two major routes. The first, along the high plateaux, starts at the Jerid, runs round the Aures, through the Hodna Gate and reaches the Taza Gap and north-west Morocco. After the pacification of the mountainous region in central Ifriqiya and the creation of Kairouan, a road linked Kairouan to Tahert via the Tarf Basin and the Hodna. The second route, the 'Qsours' route (the form *qsur* is the plural of *qsar*, 'a fortified place'; hence Spanish *alcazar*), takes over at the Jerid the route coming from Egypt through Cyrenaica and Tripolitania. It follows the southern foot of the Saharan Atlas as far as south-west Morocco. It is easy to appreciate the importance of these valleys which broke the

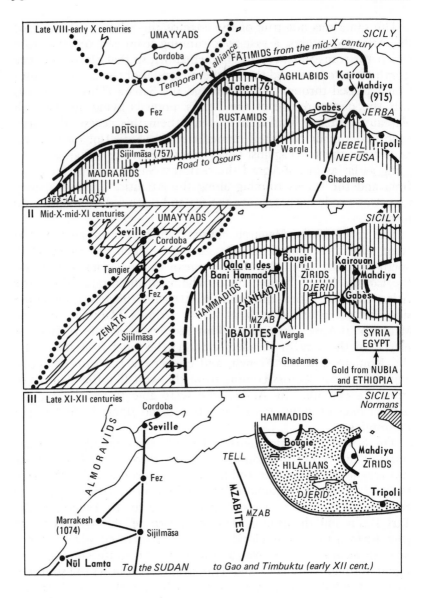

Fig. 4. The Maghreb.

continuity of the east–west chains and made it possible for roads to run from north to south and link the 'Qsours' route, the route from the high plateaux, and the shores of the Mediterranean. The intercommunication points, which were also the sites of towns, were mainly the Ifriqiya Sahel, the Hodna Depression (Tahert, Wargla, Sedrata, the Mzab), and the passes of the Moroccan Atlas: Tizi n'Telghemt (Fez, Sijilmasa), Tizi n'Teluet (Aghmat, Marrakesh, Sijilmasa), Tizi n'Test (Fez and Marrakesh towards the Lower Sus and Nul Lamta).

The northern termini of caravan routes to the Sudan fall into three major groups: the Jerid; Sedrata, Wargla, and the Mzab; and Sijilmasa and Nul Lamta. These were the points at which gold and black slaves were delivered and from which they were redistributed to the Mediterranean and the East. These staging-posts were founded from the mid eighth century to the mid eleventh century, and were one of the features of the urban development taking place in Barbary at that period. The three sets of roads – east, centre, and west – were the prize for which successive conflicts were waged in North Africa. There was the struggle between the Idrisids, the Rustamids, and the Aghlabids in the ninth century; the struggle between the Idrisids and the Fatimids in the tenth century; the struggle between the Fatimids and their clients the Sanhaja and the Umayyads and their allies the Zanata in the eleventh century; and finally the struggle of the Hilalians in the east, the Mzabites in the centre, and the Almoravids in the west, in the eleventh century.

North Africa was an area of vital strategic importance in the Muslim World. It opened up so many new horizons and was in touch with other civilizations. It was a staging-post between the East on the one hand and Spain, Sicily, the barbarian West, and the Sudan on the other. It linked civilized countries with those still unexplored. Under Muslim rule it experienced a fresh demographic and urban development, a fresh economic and commerical prosperity.

The Saharan region

In 761 Rustam founded Tahert and became independent of the

Caliphate. The Kharijite or Ibadite dynasty of the Rustamids occupied the whole of the central Maghreb, included the Jabel Nefusa and the Island of Jerba, and even extended to Tripoli. In the south-west at Sijilmasa, founded in 757, the Midrarids belonging to the Kharijite sect of the Sufrites advanced as far as Sus al-Aqsa. The two Kharijite dynasties were united by family ties and formed a great empire dominating all the routes from the south. The Zanata, nomad merchants who were engaged in large-scale trade despite their rigorist doctrines (the *imams* never touch money), used the network already existing between North Africa and the Sudan. Tahert was then known as 'little Basra'. After the destruction of the Rustamid State by the Fatimid conquest, the *imams* withdrew to the Mzab. The Zanata maintained good relations with the Umayyad emirs of Cordoba and drew up an alliance with them against the Sanhaja (clients of the Fatimids) in the struggle to gain control of the major caravan-route termini.

During the first half of the tenth century the Shi'ite Fatimids captured Kairouan and marched on Sijilmasa. They took possession of the routes leading to the Sudan and, thanks to the gold and the slaves it produced, built up war funds and an army for their grand design: the conquest of Egypt. In 915 they founded a new capital, Mahdiyya near Kairouan, and controlled North Africa, except for its north-western point where the Idrisids were in power. In 944 came a great danger, namely the revolt of Abu Yazid, a Kharijite of the Jerid, a caravaneer by trade. But the revolt was crushed. The Fatimids were once again in control of all the southern routes. In the mid tenth century 400,000 dinars a year were minted at Sijilmasa. In 972, Jawhar led his army along the oasis route to achieve the conquest of Egypt for which his propaganda had prepared the way. The Kutama, black mercenaries, together with gold from the Sudan, were what he relied on.

From this time the Fatimids abandoned North Africa to the Zirids and the Bani Hammad (Sanhaja). The Umayyads launched their Zanata clients on the western route termini and they seized Sijilmasa. The Idrisids of Fez, who were allies of the Sanhaja, lost Tangier and the caliphs of Cordoba seized Morocco by using their Zanata clients. Two blocs emerged, the Umayyads controlling the western termini and the Fatimids controlling those in the centre and the east. There was a continuous naval and land war between the Sanhaja and the Zanata. At the beginning of the eleventh century the Ibadites of Sedrata and Wargla, caught in the crossfire, fled to the Mzab.

From now on the stream of gold from the Sudan flowed in two directions, to Cordoba and to Cairo. In Cordoba it maintained the supply from which dinars were coined, it kept the court in luxury, paid for the huge mosque, the Madinat az-Zahra', and contributed to the patronage of the arts. It was Sudanese gold which maintained the brilliant Andalusian civilization of the eleventh century. In Cairo, Sudanese gold joined gold from Nubia and Ethiopia and also gold removed from the tombs of the Pharaohs, to create great wealth for the Fatimid caliphs, and enabled them to maintain the holy cities as befitted them. When Nasir-i-khusraw was in Cairo he admired the fine dinars from the Maghreb. Indeed, they supported an expansionist policy towards the Indian Ocean as well as a magnificent court and considerable urban development (building of palaces, mosques, and great *suqs*).

In the mid eleventh century the Hilalian invasions of Ifriqiya, in the east, obliged the Hammadids to take refuge in Bougie and the Zirids in al-Mahdiyya, while in the west the great Almoravid Empire was built, stretching from the Sahara to Spain. In the centre, the Mzabites, who were already engaged in modest trade with Tell, began to take part in the busier Sudanese trade. In the twelfth and thirteenth centuries, Barbary was finally severed from the East by the Hilalian and Norman invasions, and exploited by Christendom. Ships from Genoa put in at Mers al-Kebir or Massa to take on gold cargoes. In the thirteenth and fourteenth centuries the Venetians in Tunis revived the easterly routes, and in the fourteenth and fifteenth centuries the Genoese opened up the caravan trails of the western Sahara. Later people from Dieppe and other ports, and then the Portuguese, carried out sea raids to capture Sudanese gold.

The coast

In this connection it is essential to bear in mind the general picture

of the relief of North Africa, arranged in ridges running from east
to west, and also the way the ridges fan out at each end: in the
east the Ifriqiya Sahel and in the west the Atlantic plains of
Maghreb al-Aqsa. It took only a few hours to reach Sicily or Spain
by sea from one of these two points. The favourable position and
economic importance of these two regions had long been known.
The cities facing the Sicilian Strait and the Strait of Gibraltar
were linked by lively trade. The eastern and western ends of North
Africa were to be the springboards for the Muslim conquests of
the barbarian West. They were shipbuilding areas, thanks to the
forests on the mountains along the coast, and in Barbary from the
Khoumir area to the Rif; they passed on Eastern influences which
came from the Mediterranean Levant and spread westwards. They
were also redistribution centres of Sudanese products: the Ifriqiya
Sahel sent goods to Sicily and the Muslim East, the Strait of
Gibraltar sent goods to Spain, and, further still, to Bilad al-Ifranj
(the Carolingian Empire) which had remained untouched by the
advance of Islam.

These two regions enjoyed one privileged maritime activity –
they were fishing zones. Unlike the north coast of the Maghreb
where the sea becomes very deep almost at once, the littoral plat-
form of the Strait supported water rich in fish, and salt production
for export was made possible by sea-salt and by rock-salt found
inland. Moreover it was an easy matter to reach the opposite coast
from Madinat al-Majus at the northern point of Cape Bon to
Sicily, and from Qasr al-Majus between Ceuta and Tangier to
Tarifa and Algeciras. Berber fishermen and Levantine merchants
formed ready-made communities long prepared to play an active
part again as soon as favourable circumstances arose; their chance
came when the creation of the Muslim World opened an immense
horizon for trade.

The sea route linking the Muslim Levant via the Libyan coast
with Ifriqiya and Sicily, then via the north coast of the Maghreb
and the Strait of Gibraltar, with Spain, was twofold. There was
first of all the normal system. Great ports were built, complete
with docks, jetties, towers, cables, and arsenals, as at Alexandria,
Mahdiyya, Tunis, and Bougie. Powerful vessels put in there and

unloaded massive cargoes. The process gained momentum from the eighth to the eleventh centuries. This was the period when the typical large trading vessel was developed from the Mediterranean ship with raised hull and two masts flying so-called 'lateen' sails. It was a development of the merchant ship of Mediterranean antiquity plus additional new techniques from the Indian Ocean, and it was the ancestor of the Venetian and Genoese ships of the eleventh and twelfth centuries. But the sailors also coasted from anchorage to anchorage, at times no more than sheltered spots such as creeks or estuaries, places where one could beach a boat, in ships of less tonnage, like the *paranzella* which even today redistribute water-coolers from Nabeul, maintaining the ancient practice of coastal navigation. These two networks of sea routes combined but took on characters of their own; for example every town on the coast of the Maghreb was matched by a corresponding town on the Spanish coast opposite.

The conquest of Ifriqiya was almost complete by the second half of the eighth century, but the safety of the garrisons had still to be ensured, together with the protection of the country against the threat of attacks from outside in the form of raids by Byzantine fleets. In the interior the old fortresses were repaired and brought back into service. Along the coast a complete system of defences was set up to forestall any landing attempts by the Rum or Byzantines. A string of *ribats* stretched from Syria to Morocco and they were particularly concentrated in the Tunisian Sahel. They were look-out and signalling posts, coastal defence forts for the protection of seafaring activity and the vitally important opening on to the sea. The garrisons were manned by marabouts who divided their time between prayer and the defence of Bilad al-Islam against the Infidel. Not only were these *ribats* used as bases for expeditions and raids, but also as cores of resistance and Islamization, like those in central Asia and also those on the Anatolian frontier and along the Spanish Marches. They were foundations with a dual function, both military and religious, and were defended by soldier-monks who were the prototype of the medieval Christian military Orders in the Holy Land or in Spain after the *Reconquista.* They were to be found at Alexandria, Sfax,

Monastir, Sousse, Tunis, Rabat opposite Sale on the other side of
Bu Regreg, and as far as the west coast of Africa.

Two *ribats* of the Tunisian Sahel have been preserved and studied. They are Monastir, built in 796 by the Abbasid governor,
Harthama b. A'yan, and enlarged for the first time in the ninth
century and for the second time about the beginning of the eleventh century; and Sousse, built in the last quarter of the eighth
century by the Abbasid governor, Yazid b. Hatim, and completed
in 821 by a watchtower constructed by order of the third Aghlabid Emir. They consist of a square of buildings set round a central
court flanked by round crenellated towers. This is the usual plan
of Byzantine *castella*, but several improvements have been introduced. Their gates have defence systems, a grating, machicolations,
or successive fall-traps along an entrance corridor. This system,
which was already known in Mesopotamia and Sassanid Armenia,
was subsequently adopted by the Crusaders. In addition, these
fortifications have a semicircle of merlons, and, at one corner, a
square tower carries a round watchtower several storeys high.
These merlons and towers are seen in the ancient monuments of
the East and it may reasonably be supposed that an engineer from
the East who was conversant with the buildings of Iran and the
ribats of central Asia influenced the choice of the Abbasid and
Aghlabid governors.

Just as caravan towns were strung out along the 'Qsours' route
in the south, so there grew up along the coast of North Africa
ports of call which constituted a line of urban development coinciding with the network of general interconnections. These new
ports or newly revived port installations sometimes retained a cor-
rupt form of their former Punic or Roman names.

This is how Tunis developed. After the capture of Carthage in
698 by Hassan, the old city was abandoned and became a heap of
rubble used as a stone-quarry. The new urban centre was built on
the site of Tynes (a suburb of Carthage); a channel which Hassan
caused to be dug across the lake linked the town with the sea and
turned it into a lagoon port. Several thousand Copts, specialists in
shipbuilding, were requisitioned in Egypt and taken with their
families to work in the Tunis Arsenal. Nakhudha from the Persian

Gulf had already been serving in the naval dockyards in Syria; now Coptic workmen came to the Tunis Arsenal; later on Syrians, Egyptians, and Ifriqiyans came to the Spanish coast to work on that mighty achievement of the Emirate of Cordoba, Almeria. And so, men moved from east to west, taking with them the techniques and the terminology in which to describe them, Persian or Greek words in Arabic dress on which was based a whole technical vocabulary, later to be taken over by the Romance languages and to influence the Germanic tongues.

The Fatimid era was to see the foundation on the coast of Ifriqiya of al-Mahdiyya ('the Mahdi's town'), built in 915 by 'Ubayd Allah when he wished to move out of Kairouan, a large and turbulent centre containing few adherents of Shi'ism. The new town grew up on a rocky peninsula projecting into the sea and so easily sealed off. It had a large mosque in the centre, two palaces for the Mahdi and his son, and an audit office (*dar al-muhasabat*); it was enclosed by ramparts with iron gates; 360 vast cisterns dug deep in the rock, walled round and supplied with lifting gear, supplied the town with water. The Zawila suburb included *suqs* of freestone and houses. Along the coast of the peninsula, the port of Mahdiyya consisted of a rectangular dock carved out of the rock and measuring 26 by 57 metres, with a channel of about 15 metres. According to al-Bakri it could accommodate thirty vessels. It was protected by the ramparts of the town in which were set a water-gate: two towers connected by an arch under which ships could pass but which could easily be blocked when a chain was stretched across it. Mahdiyya was later the refuge of the Zirid princes in 1057, after the Hilalian invasions and the abandoning of Kairouan.

These Ifriqiyan centres engaged in active trade with the Mediterranean Levant, Sicily, and Spain. Tunis was the first port, from which one could sail direct to Tortosa on the Ebro Delta. Gabes, a 'Saharan town' and a Mediterranean one, was the coastal outlet for the Jerid and the Sudan routes. Sfax, Mahdiyya, and Sousse were the exporting centres for the oil produced by the large olive groves in the Tunisian Sahel. From there and from Tunis itself the local products (corn, oil, coral from Marsa l'Kharaz) were shipped to

the East, together with the produce of the Numidian hinterland
(wool, leather, wax, and horses). North Africa was to become,
with Syria, the remounting centre for the cavalry of the Egyptian
sultans up to and beyond the campaign of St Louis. Ifriqiya also
traded in Sudanese products such as gold and black slaves, and it
imported products from the East: cloth, ivory, pearls, and luxury
goods; and also products from the West: slaves, furs, and swords.

Other ports, often rebuilt on the site of former installations,
lined the coast of Maghreb al-Awsat from Tunis to Morocco. Near
Tunis were Benzert (Hippo Diarrythus, Bizerta); Marsa l'Kharaz,
the 'trinket port'; and La Calle, where there was coral-diving with
a whole fishing fleet devoted to it, equipped with nets fastened to
St Andrew's crosses made of metal-tipped wood. Red coral was
supposed to bring good luck and there was considerable demand
for it in the countries of the Indian Ocean which had only white
coral. Further west was Buna (Hippo regia, Hippone, Bone) which
exported iron from Edugh; the coast of Little Kabylia which exported wood along the shore to the naval dockyards of Ifriqiya;
and Skikda (Rusicada, Philippeville). Other parts, from east to
west, were Bougie, whose arsenal used resources close at hand —
wood, iron, pitch, and wax — for caulking; Algiers ('the isles',
al-Jaza'ir); Bani Mazghanna, founded about 946 by the Zirid
Bologgin, which was a market used by tribes from the interior;
Cherchell (Iol, Caesarea); and Tenes, founded in 875—876 by a
band of Andalusian adventurers who organized a market with the
Berbers in the region, setting up tents, building a small fortress,
then a town. Oran owes its origin to similar circumstances: Andalusian adventurers established relations with the Berber tribes
about 902—903, then the new centre was burnt down by the
Berbers in 910 and rebuilt in 911, remaining prosperous until 954,
when it was laid waste by the Bani Ifren, to be restored some years
later. Finally, in Maghreb al-Aqsa, on the shores of the Strait of
Gibraltar (al-Zuqaq) there were older towns, Septem (Ceuta)
Tingis (Tangier), and also new ones, Qasr Masmuda. Facing the
Atlantic were Arzila (ninth century), Shammish (Lixus, al-'Ara'ish,
Larache), Sale, and Rabat at the furthest limit of Roman Morocco.
Further south, ports in southern Morocco such as Afis, Mazagan,

Agadir, and Massa were a direct result of a general move south and of the new importance of the termini of the caravan route to the Sudan. These ports of Maghreb al-Aqsa engaged in vigorous trade with the Atlantic ports on the south of the Iberian Peninsula, such as Cadiz (Gades), those at the mouth of the Guadalquivir, and even Seville and Cordoba using river-craft, as well as Saltes and Alcacer do Sal in the Algarve. To these Andalusian ports went grain, cattle, wool, leathers, wax, and honey from the Atlantic hinterland, and also ores, iron, silver, and especially copper from the Moroccan Atlas.

The route along the high plateaux

The earliest Arab attack on Ifriqiya came in 647. As we have seen, the cities held by Byzantine garrisons were quickly reduced. The citizens welcomed the conquerors, who brought with them strong rule, an administrative organization which was urban in nature, and protection against the nomads. It was the Berbers of the interior who put up resistance, both the mountain-settlers and the nomads of the plain. Kairouan, founded in 670 by 'Uqba b. Nafi' in the middle of the steppe, behind the Tunisian Sahel, was a bridgehead, a camp, a *ribat* in fact. The very name, 'al-Qayrawan', means 'staging-post' and 'parade-ground'. Its situation at the end of the main route from Egypt made attack and retreat easy. At the time of the great Kharijite rebellions in the mid eighth century, the city was captured on several occasions by insurgent Berbers and its fortifications were destroyed. In 772, Yazid b. Hatim defeated the heretics and repossessed Kairouan where he rebuilt the great mosque, erected brick walls 12 cubits (about 5 metres) thick, and built a *suq* for every trade guild. He was the town's second founder. With the conquest of the entire Maghreb, or at least the major communication corridors running between the Berber mountain ranges, Kairouan became the starting-point of the high plateaux route, running from the Tunisian Sahel via the Tarf Basin north of the Aures, the Chott al-Hodna, with roads leading off to Bougie on the one hand and Biskra and Wargla on the other, then along the high western plateaux and the Taza Gap, until it reached Maghreb al-Aqsa and flat plains once again.

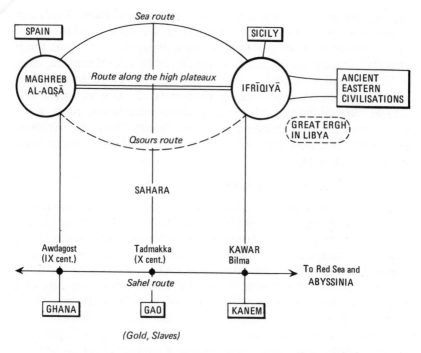

Fig. 5. Commercial routes and influences in North Africa in the eighth and ninth centuries.

Under the Aghlabids (800–909), an Eastern dynasty of Abbasid governors who were almost entirely independent, and then under the Fatimids, the original city assumed much greater proportions. In the ninth and tenth centuries, three satellite towns were created one after the other: al-'Abbasiyya, ar-Raqqada, and finally Sabra Mansuriyya.

Like Fustat-Cairo and Cordoba, Kairouan derived its importance from this proliferation of towns, based on the expansion of trade. The layout and the monumental appearance of the town bore witness to influences originating with the Irano-Mesopotamian territory of the Abbasids. Writers, lawyers, and scientists from the East, drawn by the wealth of these new courts, settled there and made disciples. The Berbers came and learned from them just as their forebears had learned from their Roman masters. They became to some extent Islamized, and even Iranized. The new religious, artistic, linguistic, and literary influences, the customs and mental attitudes, were first of all adopted by the new capital, then they spread to its environs. Later they were carried into the interior along the high plateaux route as soon as the remaining Berbers broke up and were driven back into the mountains where the original language was still based only on oral tradition. Along this route new towns sprang up at those points at which the high plateaux route was intersected by roads coming from the south, from the caravan termini of the trans-Sahara trade.

We must now examine the points of intersection in this enormous criss-cross of trade routes in the Maghreb al-Awsat. There was, first, Tahert, lying west of the Chelif Valley, on the mountainside, commanding the tracks along the high plateaux. It was founded in 761 and remained until 908 the residence of the Persian Rustamids and the main centre of Berber Kharijism, which preserved links with the Kharijism of the Persian Gulf. Its trade flourished; very many men of letters flocked to it from the East; the impressive Rustamid library acquired books bought in the East, particularly books of astrology and astronomy. When the Rustamids sought a refuge they found it first near Wargla, at Sedrata, then in the Mzab, along the road running from north to south. At the end of the eighth century, Tobna in the Chott al-Hodna was fortified by Abbasid governors; in 927, the son of the first Fatimid caliph, 'Ubayd Allah, founded Msila to the north of Tobna.

In their turn the Sanhaja Zirids, clients of the Fatimids, who left them behind to take charge of the Maghreb after they moved to Egypt, founded a series of cities. Even before the Fatimids' departure in 935, Ziri b. Manad, the Zirids' ancestor, had founded Ashir on the mountainside between the Chelif Valley and the Chott al-Hodna. The carpenters and masons were found locally, but the Fatimid Caliph had been asked to supply an architect. The town developed rapidly. His son, Bologgin b. Ziri, founded Medea, on the plateau to the east of the Chelif, Miliana on the right bank

of this river, and al-Jaza'ir (Algiers), centres which line the road to
the sea all the way from Ashir. Bologgin's younger son, Hammad,
founded in 1007 the Qal'a of the Banu Hammad, on the mountainside north of the Chott al-Hodna, the capital of the Hammadid
State. There are still considerable ruins of this town remaining: the
palace was planned along the same lines as Samarra, and the same
plan may be seen in the Alcazar at Seville. Its population increased
rapidly, and included merchants, artists, and scholars. Its woollen
cloth was famous throughout the Maghreb. Caravans converged on
it from all directions. The town maintained trading connections
with Egypt, Syria, and Iraq. During the second half of the eleventh
century Qal'a benefited from the destruction of Kairouan and
Ifriqiya, which was overrun by the Hilalians, until it was itself
extinguished by the nomads' westerly advance, when the
Hammadids sought refuge in Bougie.

To the west of Sanhaja territory (Zirids and Hammadids) lay
Zanata territory, which corresponded to western Oran and
Maghreb al-Aqsa. The main towns were Tlemcen (formerly Pom-
aria) and Oudjda, which was founded by a Zanata chieftain in 994
on the road running west from Taza to Fez. When he reached
Morocco in 788, the eastern chieftain, Idris, the son of a *sharif* and
a descendant of Muhammad, sought refuge at Ulili (Volubilis) with
the Awraba tribe. His brother Sulayman, who joined him shortly
afterwards, went to Tlemcen. They founded two principalities,
one at Tlemcen, the other at Fez. The Idrisids excelled at restoring
and founding cities. Those based on Tlemcen breathed fresh life
into the town which had in the ninth century, so Ya'qubi tells us,
a very dense population and palaces and residences inside a double
stone wall. They constructed its ports, such as Arashgul (Island of
Rashgun) and Hunayn (Cape Noah near Nemours), and a series of
smaller centres, townships which attracted economic activity and
which bore a name formed from the word *suq*, followed by the
name of its founder, as in Suq Ibrahim and Suq Hamza.

Idris I abandoned the Roman ruins of Volubilis and founded, as
did all the eastern monarchs, his own capital. Fez took over from
Volubilis, just as Tunis took over from Carthage. The site was well
chosen; it was on the road leading west to Tlemcen and south to

Sijilmasa, in a fertile region blessed with stone and wood for building, and drinking-water in plenty. In 789 a city grew up on the right bank of the river (the Oued Fez, today Oued Sebou). This original Madinat Fez was at first a Berber-type town, a collection of tents and *ad hoc* dwellings, enclosures for cattle with a mosque and possibly a collective shop (*agadir*), the whole protected by a defensive wall made of reeds and tree-trunks. It was, in fact, a very modest settlement, which served Idris I as his headquarters when he was not at Ulili. He died in 791.

His posthumous son, Idris II, who was brought up by his father's loyal freedman, Rashid, was joined in 805 by 500 men from the East lured by the prestige of the descendant of the Prophet and by the attraction of unfamiliar territory. Others came from Ifriqiya. They formed an unruly bodyguard (*Jund*) round Idris II, an Eastern court requiring an Eastern setting. And so in 808 the new town of Fez was founded, on the left bank of the river, upstream of the first town. This was the official town with the sacred mosque said to belong to the 'Chorfa' (*Shuraf'*, 'descendants of the Prophet'), and next to it the palace, the markets, and the mint where coin was struck as early as 801. It was known as 'al-'Aliya', 'the Lofty one'. Ya'qubi calls it 'Ifriqiya'. Subsequently one district was called 'the Kairouan quarter'. The Berbers remained in the older Madinat Fez on the right bank, which retained its rural character. After the uprising of the suburb (*rabad*) of Cordoba in 814, some Andalusians emigrated to Egypt (Alexandria) and then to Crete, while 8,000 families were offered shelter by Idris II in that part of Fez on the right bank which became known as 'Adwat al-Andalus', with its mosque, its markets, and its mints.

A similar urban development took place in the south of Maghreb al-Aqsa: Aghmat and Naffis grew up on the passes leading to the Sus al-Aqsa (Igli) and to Tafilelt (Sijilmasa) and 1077 saw the creation of Marrakesh by the Almoravids who had made their way from the Saharan *ribats* along the caravan routes. First it was an assorted jumble of tents and houses, then a rampart and monuments were built. It evolved in the same way as Fez from a Berber encampment to an Eastern city. This great southern capital was to give its name to the whole area — Morocco.

Thus, a new kind of city was introduced into the western Maghreb, which had until then known only the Berber type of rural settlement and the Roman city. Urban civilization reappeared in a fresh guise, that of an Eastern town engaged in trade, with its walls and gates, separate districts, markets and industries. With it emerged a new kind of people, the middle class or *fasi*, consisting of Berbers who had been Islamized to a considerable degree, which ensured the spread of urban activity.

The Iberian Peninsula

The Iberian Peninsula offers wide variations. It has coastal plains, where the Muslim conquerors first became established, for example the Levante Plain (*Campus juncarius*), a new area with relatively virgin soil, and the Algarve, a zone of forests and oases; in the interior are plateaux covered with steppes and farmland where movement is easy; finally there are mountainous areas used as refuges and remaining aloof from the mainstream of events such as Estremadura. It is a country of sharp contrasts. The north-west corner of the peninsula, inhabited by Asturians, Cantabrians, and Vascons, was never overrun by the Visigoths or by the Muslims. It was always used as a withdrawal zone; later on it was the Asturian kingdom which served as a base for the *Reconquista*.

The northern frontier of Bilad al-Andalus was a no-man's-land, an area open to raids (*algaradas*) and guarded by a series of front-line fortresses. The towns behind this line were the chief towns of these marches ('ath-Thughur): the upper march (ath-Thaghr al-a'la) with Saragossa; the middle march (ath-Thaghr al-awsat) with Madinat Salim (Medinaceli); the lower march (ath-Thaghr al-adna) with Coria. Roads crossed these border areas at certain specific places. The major median road ran from Saragossa via Toledo to Cordoba and Seville where it joined the river traffic on the Guadalquivir. Cordoba was at the centre of a whole system of communications. For example there was a route along the Ebro from Tortosa via Saragossa and Tudela to the Vitoria Pass. The main sea routes were along the east coast, from Narbonne to

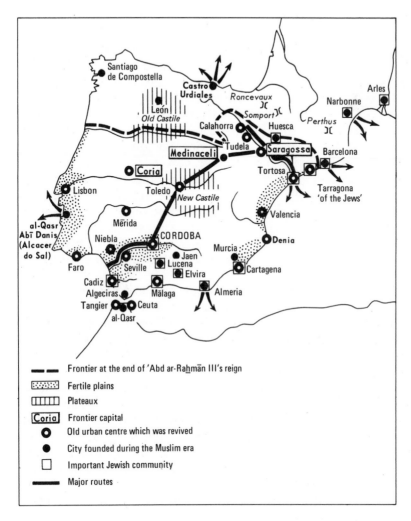

Fig. 6. Spain.

Almeria and the Guadalquivir, and along the west coast from Castro Urdiale on the Bay of Biscay to Alcacer do Sal and the Guadalquivir.

The Iberian substratum

Apart from the Basque element in the north-west, Spain was, at the time of the Muslim conquests, inhabited by old Iberian populations together with Germanic and Levantine elements (Syrians and Jews). The more or less Romanized — or, more accurately, de-Romanized — Celtiberi, lived scattered over desert or near-desert areas. The Levante, or swampy lagoon region, was important only because of the coastal route; during the Muslim era the route shifted to the interior. The Algarve, covered with pine groves, was very thinly populated. The mountain regions and the *mesetas* in the interior were also thinly populated or indeed deserted. There was no demographic growth in Spain before the Muslim era, as was the case in Barbary. The populations witnessed a revival of their old pre-Roman, Celtic, or Iberian identity during the general disturbance and economic regression attendant upon the collapse of the Empire.

The arrival of the Visigoth hordes, who had not yet advanced beyond a primitive stage of economic and social organization, greatly accelerated this process. The old Iberian society knew the strength of emotional and personal ties binding one person to another; it was the *devotio iberica* mentioned by Latin authors recounting the Roman conquest of Spain, and using the same term — *devotio* — which they used in describing Germanic societies. Standards and ways of life both of invader and invaded underwent modification. Family and tribal grouping, which was pre-eminently the primitive arrangement of the Germanic peoples, was also the norm with the Iberians. Each clan clung fiercely to its independence. It was a tight, yet anarchical organization, entirely comparable with the pattern followed by the Berbers of the Maghreb — which may well explain the subsequent collapse of the Reyes de Taifas (*Muluk at-Tawa'if*).

And so the clock was turned back in the fifth century and there was a return to older, pre-Roman practices, made possible by economic conditions, the collapse of the State structure, and the establishment of Germanic domination. The general process of de-Romanization would have gone even further than it did, but for the Church which preserved tradition, together with the Latin language. The Spanish episcopate had from the very beginning been rich and powerful. The bishops were drawn from the great landowner class, and gifts from the faithful further swelled their lands. The acceptance of the Catholic faith by the Visigoth royal line, in place of Arianism, strengthened the position of the bishops, particularly the Metropolitan of Toledo, who was always regarded as an important figure by the caliphs. At the time of al-Hakam II (961–976), when the king of Leon, Ordono IV, came to Cordoba, the Matran (Metropolitan) of Toledo was one of the Christian dignitaries sent to meet him to familiarize him with the etiquette of the Muslim Court.

This powerful hierarchy of the Church in Spain explains the continued existence of lively, active, sometimes turbulent Christian communities, particularly at Toledo, Seville, and Cordoba. The cities were the centres where Romanization and Christianity were preserved, just as they later became centres of Islamization and Orientalization. Christians enjoyed the status of *dhimmi* (protected), sometimes guaranteed them by a genuine treaty of capitulation, like the one signed by Theodemir for the region of Murcia. The conquerors undertook to respect the religion of the conquered, and to safeguard their churches. Tolerance was extended to all, except apostates from Islam and Christians seeking martyrdom. The Christian Mozarabs (*musta'rib*, 'Arabized') were organized under the authority of leaders chosen by themselves, to be responsible for good order and the collection of taxes, in accordance with Eastern practice. They elected a *defensor* or *comes*, to represent the community, a bishop (*episcopus, al-usquf*), an *exceptor* to collect taxes, and a *censor* (*qadi an-nasara*) or judge. They had their own liturgy – the Mozarabic rite. The strong cohesion of the Christian Church also explains the retention of the Latin language, which evolved into a Romance language with the addition of Arabic words, mainly technical terms. *The Cordoba Calendar*, in 961, was written in two languages, Latin and Arabic. The Christian Church was to persist with its main characteristics unchanged from the Visigothic era until the *Reconquista*, and its relations with the rulers of the northern Christian States grew closer until the close of the tenth century.

The Levantines

Another important feature of Spanish life during the Visigothic era was the Levantine element, which was further strengthened during the Muslim era by fresh arrivals from the East. Most of these people were Jewish merchants and 'Syri' or Syrians, and they were concentrated mainly in the major transit zones in the south-west and north-west of the peninsula: in the south, near the Strait of Gibraltar, near the old Carthaginian territory where Punic was still spoken in the second century of the Christian era; round Malacca ('the royal'), which Strabo had found to have a Punic look about it; on the coast, at Gades (Cadiz) and Cartagena; and in colonies inland, namely Lucena between Malaga and Cordoba and Elvira (the Jewish Granada). The Judaization of the old Levantine diaspora is one of the most important facts of Mediterranean ancient history. In the north-east, the Levantines were grouped in the Pyrenean passes (Puertos secos) which were the means of communication between Spain and France or Ifranga. On either side of the mountains, whether in Septimania or Catalonia, the population was the same. Tortosa, Saragossa, Tudela, Tarragona, Barcelona, and Narbonne were all stages on the route taken by the Radhanite Jews which ultimately reached Lyons via the Rhône and then continued along the Rhine.

In the Visigothic kingdoms the Jewish element was not assimilated by the Iberian and Germanic populations. There was little friction under the Arian rulers, but under Catholic monarchs like Reccared the Jews suffered persecution. It was hardly surprising that they gave a warm welcome to the Muslim invaders, particularly if they lived in the south; indeed, they could almost be accused of 'connivance', though in fact the ground had been prepared by Muslim prisoners and by the Orientalization of the Roman World and of the part of the Mediterranean inhabited by barbarians. It was the Jews who were put in charge of the Andalusian towns conquered by the Muslims. From the eighth century onwards there was a steady flow of Jews from the East into Spain. The most important Jewish community in the whole of Muslim Spain was Cordoba, an economic and political centre with a synagogue (eleventh and twelfth centuries). Toledo had two synagogues (tenth and eleventh centuries), which later became Christian churches and may still be seen today. The Jews also figured prominently at court, for example the doctor, Hasday b. Shaprut, who was Vizier to 'Abd ar-Rahman III. In the eleventh century they organized the kingdom of Granada.

The Jewish or Judaized element facilitated interchanges between Muslim Spain and the East, particularly in cases of opposing powers (Umayyads and Fatimids). It also facilitated relations between Muslim Spain and the Christian countries of the north. A network of Jewish communities covered the Rhône Valley and the Rhineland which were actively engaged in a large-scale slave-trade extending from the banks of the Elbe to Bilad al-Andalus. Indeed this network extended from Spain to Maghreb al-Aqsa, to Sus al-Aqsa, to the Sahara, and to the Sudan, and it kept in being the trade in gold and black slaves despite any struggles and political rivalries which might rend North Africa. The letter sent by the Vizier of 'Abd ar-Rahman III, Hasday b. Shaprut, to the king of the Khazars, who were a Judaized people living on the Volga, sheds light on the relations between one community and another, along all the routes of major world trade.

But the Jews did not merely play a major role in the history of trade relations. The Jewish schools of Cordoba and Toledo attracted and received currents of thought originating in Mesopotamia. Cordoba possessed a school of Talmudic studies which enjoyed a high reputation. Apart from their Hebraic culture the rabbis were deeply versed in classical Arabic literature; they read the works of the scholars, doctors, astronomers, and astrologers. Maimonides of Cordoba was the most eminent of these twelfth-century rabbis. Similarly at Toledo, a Mozarab Christian and also Jewish city, there was an important centre where translations were made from Arabic into Hebrew and from Hebrew into Latin. At the time of the *Reconquista* in 1085 these translations found their way to the Christian West. It is possible to trace the spread of Aristotelian thought, translated from Greek into Syriac, then into Arabic, into Hebrew, and into Latin, by the tangible signs of this process at clearly defined stages of its journey: there were the Syriac monasteries in northern Syria and Mesopotamia; al-Ma'mun's translation establishments in Baghdad; from there the way led to Egypt, North Africa, and Spain (Cordoba, Toledo), and the Jewish centres of Languedoc, and finally, in the thirteenth century, it reached the Sorbonne in Paris.

The invaders: Berbers and Arabs

The Muslim conquest was swift (711–714) and failed to provoke strong reactions in the rural populations. After the military collapse of the Visigoths on the Rio Barbate in 711, the towns under siege surrendered and Jews were put in charge of them. By 714 Muslim troops had reached Septimania; these invaders were Berbers and Arabs. Tarif's preliminary reconnaissance, then Tariq's expedition, were carried out with the help of almost exclusively Berber troops. Tariq was himself a Berber, a client of the Governor of the Maghreb, Musa b. Nusayr, and his expedition numbered only 7000 men. The following year in 712 the governor, Musa, entered Spain himself with entirely Arab troops some 10,000 strong. Not one of these soldiers of the invading force went back to Africa. And so the first influx of 17,000 Berbers and Arabs was entirely military in nature. However, it was soon followed, during the eighth century, by sizeable immigrations of Berbers from the Maghreb who were attracted by the wealth of the conquered territory. This infiltration went on quite regularly until the close of the Middle Ages and enabled the kingdom of Granada to survive into the fifteenth century. The important fact is that the vast majority of the immigrant Muslim population was Berber.

The year 741 saw the revolt of the Berbers in Spain against their Arab leaders, which was a consequence of the Berber revolt in the Maghreb, an explosion of Kharijism. They had maintained links with their African brothers, and kept the same ideal of independence within anarchy. They elected a leader, held meetings, and shaved their heads to avoid being confused with the enemy. Their revolt was crushed by the Arabs already settled in Spain, backed by a fresh contingent from Africa, the Syrian troops of Balj, emir of Barbary, numbering several thousand men. After inflicting a bloody defeat on the Berbers, these Syrian troops settled in the southern areas, the Damascus 'contingent' (*jund*) at Elvira, the Jordan contingent at Malaga, the Palestine contingent at Sidona, the Emese troops at Seville, and the Qinnassrin troops at Jaen. The Syrians introduced the breeding of silkworms and silk-weaving into the region.

The Arabs scorned working on the land and instead they settled in the towns and lived off rents paid them by smallholders. In Spanish place-names the Arab influence shows in the plains, especially in the Levante, in areas beginning with 'Beni', as in Benifayo near Valencia, Benicasim near Castellon de la Plana, Beniganim near Jativa, and so on. The Berber immigrants in Spain behaved quite differently, in that only a minority of them seem to have chosen city life. These Moroccan mountain-dwellers found the Spanish mountain areas the only places fit to live in, so they chose the south-east massif, the Serrania de Ronda and the Sierra Nevada, and to the north of the Guadalquivir Plain, the Sierra d'Almaden and the Sierra de Guadarrama. Almost all the Berber colonies seemed sited away from the plains and great valleys of Andalusia. Wherever the terrain looked promising, small groups of mountain-dwelling Berbers came together. The names of the original tribe are still traceable in Spanish place-names; for example, between Granada and the sea, the massif where the Jazula lived is called the 'Sierra de los Gazules'. The greater part of the south and west of Spain, apart from the plains, was Berber country. The Berbers raised stock on a communal basis, from which the *mesta* later developed, and they grew olive trees. The eastern part (the Levante) of this area was more specifically Arabized. Ibn Sa'id, as late as the thirteenth century, notes that in the mountain regions the inhabitants wear the African head-dress, the turban, while at Cordoba and in the Levante they wear the *qalansuwa*, a tall cap of Iranian origin.

The development of the Guadalquivir Plain during the Muslim era was merely the continuation of the amazing growth of Roman Baetica. The specific achievement of Andalusian Islam took place in more or less desert regions; the Levante and the Algarve became populated and were then fully reclaimed and developed. To this achievement must be added the organization of the *mesta*. Let us first consider the placing under cultivation of the Levante (sharq al-Andalus, ash-sharq), which involved the transformation of the *campus juncarius* into *huertas*, irrigation systems making it possible to grow Oriental crops like rice, cotton, sugar-cane, and orange and banana trees. There was also silk manufacture, a luxury industry of which Spain kept the monopoly in the West for some time. And finally there was the great urban foundation — Almeria. To put under cultivation the Algarve (Gharb al-Andalus, al-Gharb) meant clearing a pine forest and turning it into a tropical garden, with olive groves at ash-Sharaf west of Seville. The second arsenal in the Cordoba Caliphate was founded at Qasr Abi Danis (Alcacer do Sal) near the large salt-marshes of Setubal. Fishing and maritime trade were made possible by extensive shipbuilding yards using timber from the neighbouring forests.

The northern Berbers brought with them into Spain their communal methods of raising sheep, which involved guarding the flocks and organizing a regular change of pasture along specific itineraries. In fact the *meshta* became the *mesta*, and was operated on the plateaux in the interior and the mountain ranges surrounding them, regions which in Roman times were repellent deserts. The *Reconquista* set the seal on this system and made it a 'national' organization. The amount of wool Spain produced contributed to her national prosperity. The *merino*, with soft, flexible wool, whose name figures in twelfth-century Spanish texts, was introduced alongside the *churro* with a coarser coat. There was also a great increase in horse-breeding. The barb, the Berber horse from North Africa, was crossed with another species to give the Spanish jennet (Spanish *jinete*, from 'Zanata'), and it seems likely that this development in breeding was connected with the introduction of a fresh type of fodder, particularly lucerne, a plant of Persian origin still known in Spain under its Arab-Persian name *alfalfa*.

The Orientalization of Spain: the Cordoba Emirate

In Spain, as indeed throughout the Muslim Empire, the period running from the eighth to the eleventh centuries brought very considerable urban development, beginning with the revival of older centres. There were far more of these than in North Africa because the urbanization of Phoenician and Roman Spain, though not more advanced than in North Africa, was denser, and in addition the nomad Visigoths settled in the towns. During the Muslim era the towns expanded tremendously, out of all proportion to their growth under the Roman Empire: in particular Cordoba and Seville, the two major centres in Baetica; Malaga and Gades, the ports of the Strait of Gibraltar; and then Toledo and Saragossa. Apart from these old centres which took on a new lease of life, only two cities were genuinely new creations. Both were ports, one on the Mediterranean, Almeria, founded in 756; the other Qasr Abi Danis on the Setubal Lagoon, of about the same date.

Cordoba, a city of some size, was essentially a palatine centre. The Umayyad 'Abd ar-Rahman I, who made it the capital of an independent Emirate in 756, was an Oriental prince, a refugee like the Rustamids, the Idrisids, and the Fatimids, fleeing from the Abbasid regime into the Muslim equivalent of the 'Far West', namely the Maghreb. He felt homesick for Syria and could not forget the Damascus of the Umayyads. He and his successors, particularly 'Abd ar-Rahman II (822–852), tried to reconstitute the setting they missed so much, an Eastern-style court. One of the palace cities nearby bore the name 'ar-Rusafa' as if in Syria. The new emirs aped the fashions of Baghdad, the great, dazzling capital, a rival caliphate but even so a renowned metropolis. They called on men of letters, wits, musicians, poets, scientists, and lawyers from the East, and offered them places at court coupled with fat stipends. A satirical play by Ibn Bassam depicts the snobbish courtiers on the look-out for changes in fashion taking place in the East. "If a crow starts cawing or a fly starts buzzing in the depths of Syria or Iraq", he says, "they fall flat on their faces as if before an idol."

Cordoba was an immensely wealthy city. Gold from the Sudan enabled her to buy Slav slaves which she redistributed throughout the Muslim Empire in exchange for good Eastern currency. And so, at this end of the Empire as in the Samanid Principality at the other, a vigorous system of exchange was set up. The Cordoba Emirate also held a strong attraction for men of letters and artists.

The adoption of Eastern fashions in Umayyad Cordoba seemed to crystallize round the arrival of the musician Ziryab from Baghdad about 230 of the *hijra* (*c.* 845). He is reputed to have introduced all the latest fashions. Ziryab, a pupil of Ishaq of Mosul, was a singer and musician, trained in the Medina chant. With the help of a group of educated slave-girls, known as 'Ziryab's girls', he undertook the cultural education of Cordoba's polite society. They introduced to the public a new type of music, the five-stringed lute (*al-'ud*), and other kinds of stringed instruments (*citara*), as well as the Medina chant, from which developed *cante jondo*.

New dishes made their appearance, Oriental recipes based on rice, sugar, and spices, such as confectionery, marzipan, and nougat. Here too the West was enabled to learn from the East through the agency of Spain. At the same time polite society in Cordoba started to use crystal glasses, 'Iraq glasses' (*'iraqi*), which became current in the West in the tenth century, according to the sources we possess. There was furniture covered with leather, goffered and gilded according to a technique which had made its way along the 'Qsours' route. This was Cordoban leather; it was also used for interior hangings. New styles of dress were introduced, elegant and luxurious Oriental costumes made of materials with broad stripes of Persian inspiration, coats made of transparent materials originally from Khuzistan and the banks of the Nile but later woven in Andalusia. The *Cordoba Calendar* of 961 notes that with the arrival of colder weather in October, white clothing is being discarded in favour of dark-coloured woollen garments, an innovation attributed to Ziryab. It was 'Abd ar-Rahman II who first introduced into Spain the idea of the *tiraz*, a palace workshop making goods only for the court and producing cloth of superb quality with the sovereign's name and various eulogies upon him woven into the material. This was a workshop with the most complicated administration, rivalling a department of State, with its own head, the *sahib at-tiraz* ('grand officer of the palace').

In these various ways the mode of life of the wealthy class at court and in town was transformed. A new and different Oriental influence reinforced the link with the East forged by the early Syrian immigrants and the Jewish communities in touch with the cities of Mesopotamia. Thus the most westerly point of the Muslim Empire, Bilad al-Andalus, was exposed to various influences emanating from the East. These influences, whether Semitic or Iranian, profoundly modified urban society in the course of its development and helped to shape what is known as 'Andalusian civilization,

Muslim Spain lay between the African coast and the barbarian West which comprised the Iberian kingdoms in the north of the peninsula, and 'Firanja', first the Carolingian Empire then the Capetian kingdom. Arab texts refer to this as *al-ard al kabira*, the 'great land' by which is meant the mainland as opposed to the 'islands', namely Sicily and the Spanish Peninsula. In the south the 'transit ports' ensured a link across the Strait of Gibraltar. In the north there were roads crossing the passes in the Pyrenees and a vigorous coastal trade linked Almeria with Barcelona and Narbonne. The greater part of Spain's trade with Africa consisted of gold from the Sudan, black slaves from the Sudanese Sahel (Senegal as far as Chad), and gum from West Africa for use in manufacturing silk. These products were bartered for assorted wares and for mercury used to produce gold amalgam. From the Christian kingdoms in the north came Slav slaves who had been conveyed from the Elbe across Germania and Francia, mainly by Jewish merchants. Along the same route came furs from the great Nordic forest, together with 'Frankish swords' (*sayf al-Firanja*) with imitation Damascus blades which the Carolingian Empire exported in great quantities. In exchange Muslim Spain offered one or two luxury products such as the cloth known as *spanisca*, but its chief export was gold and silver currencies. Dirhems were minted first by the emirs of Cordoba, though the main stream of Sudanese gold flowed into the Fatimid Empire, and dinars originated in the Muslim East. After the rulers in Cordoba had, through the good offices of their Zanata clients in the western Maghreb, become involved with the production of gold in the Sudan, gold coins were struck in Cordoba. The definitive victory of the Umayyads of Cordoba over the Idrisids of Fez, who stood in the way of their policy of expansion, occurred in 974.

It was the consumer demand of the cities of the Cordoba Emi-

rate which provoked a considerable flow of commerce and caused
the establishment of a road system running both north and south.
It is worth noting that these same roads were later used as invasion
routes in the eleventh century: the 'barbarians' were spurred into
action by commercial expansion, and simply advanced along existing trade routes. From the north came invaders from the Iberian
States, supported by Norman and Burgundian horsemen, and by
the monastic Order of Cluny. This was the great movement known
as the *Reconquista* by Christian Spain, or the 'Western Crusades'
by the Christian West. From the south came the invasion of the
Almoravid Berbers of the great Nigerian Sahel, following the trade
routes to Sijilmasa and, through Morocco, into Spain.

With the *Reconquista* a whole section of Islam came under
Christian rule, just as Syria was later conquered by the Crusaders. At
first the fanaticism and plundering instincts of the northern barons
destroyed part of the brilliant Andalusian civilization, but in time
they developed an understanding of it. Artisans and artists went
on with their work and continued to develop their techniques,
though now under the rule of the 'Infidels' (*mudejar* art). The
Muslim influence was strengthened by this process and its spread
throughout the West facilitated. The *juderias* and the *morerias*, the
areas in cities inhabited by Jews and Moors respectively, continued
their activities as before. The harmonious development of Andalusian civilization suffered a similar setback initially with the arrival
of the Almoravids. The rigorist approach of these conquerors, who
were rough desert camel-drivers, made them disperse the courts
and burn down the libraries. But gradually they accepted this
civilization which, because of links forged by one and the same
political rule on both sides of the Strait of Gibraltar, finally spread
throughout the Maghreb and into the Sudan (Almoravid Empire).
The Berber camp south of Morocco grew into the city of Marrakesh (1077); Timbuktu was founded in the twelfth century; this
was the era of the travelling marabouts.

Sicily

After Spain we must now turn our attention to another sphere of

Berber expansion, Sicily, which occupies a central position between the two Mediterranean basins. The bases used were the ports
on Cape Bon, namely Tunis, Nabeul, Kelibia, and Sousse. The
Punicized Berbers who inhabited the region spent their time fishing, trading, and privateering. They provided the crews of ships
made from timber which was unobtainable in the area and had to
be procured either from the Maghreb or by means of raids on the
coast of Sicily, southern Italy, or even Dalmatia. By the end of the
seventh century expeditions were being sent to Sicily to bring
back timber from the mountains of Aspromonte and Sila, which
were still thickly wooded. But the Byzantine fleet based on Sicily
organized surprise raids on the coast of Ifriqiya, which the *ribat*
garrisons were not always strong enough to repulse. It therefore
seemed imperative to occupy the island. In 700 Pantellaria was
occupied by the Berbers, then in 703 occurred the first attempts
to gain a firm foothold on the coasts of Sicily. Even so, it was over
a century later that the victorious expedition of the Aghlabid
emir, Ziyadat Allah took place. Palermo was captured (827–831)
and then Syracuse (878). These towns were at opposite ends of
the island and were formerly battlefields between Greek colonizers
(with Syracuse facing Graeca Major) and Carthaginian colonizers
(with Palermo facing Carthage). Just as Byzantine Sicily had had
Syracuse as its main city, so Muslim Sicily witnessed the revival of
Palermo, where there was, as in Carthage-Tunis, a very ancient
Phoenician background. In the early ninth century Byzantine
Sicily was very markedly Hellenized. Though both Latin and
Greek were spoken, the only written language was Greek. The
Church was attached to the Patriarchate of Constantinople and the
monasteries followed the rule of St Basil. Arts and architectural
and decorative techniques were derived from Byzantium (mosaics); they were subsequently adopted by the emirs of Sicily along
with contributions made in the Muslim era. Under the rule of the
Aghlabids of North Africa, then of the Fatimids, very many buildings were erected, of which nothing has been preserved except a
few fragments of a palace, the Favara (from *fawwara*, 'a fountain')
at Palermo. All that remains today of Muslim art in Sicily dates, in
fact, from the Norman era, namely the Cuba, the Ziza (al-'Aziza,

'the glorious'), and the Cubola. The plants, decoration, and epigra-
phy all derive from formulae imported from Ifriqiya, Egypt, or
Baghdad. Sicily was by then a piece of Muslim territory under
Christian rule, where there was no break in techniques or production, a situation paralleled by the *mudejar* art of the Iberian Peninsula. Both Sicily and Spain were older civilizations now under
fresh rule. This superimposition of one civilization on another
made easier the handing on and the spread of creative processes
and decorative methods, and also encouraged new syntheses. The
Christian reconquest played the same role in the West as the Muslim conquest: as it spread across the territory of older Oriental
civilizations it absorbed features of these civilizations into the barbarian West which had hitherto made no direct impact there. The
following is the pattern governing the spread of agricultural and
industrial techniques: the irrigation of the *huertas* (like that of the
Conca d'Oro near Palermo), the cultivation of cotton, sugar-cane,
rice, orange trees, then silkworm-breeding, the setting up of textile
industries (cotton goods and silk), the production of glazed ceramics, and so on.

The importance of urban development during this period should
also be noted. It was the Muslims who fixed definitively the capital of Sicily at Palermo. Today the city numbers about 400,000
inhabitants, whereas Syracuse numbers only 40,000. In the tenth
century, Ibn Hawqal counted 300,000 inhabitants in Palermo. It
was one of the most important cities in Islam by virtue of its many
mosques. It was second only to Cordoba in the Muslim West and,
as Arab authors observed, the rhythm of growth of these two
metropolises was comparable. The ports on the opposite coast of
the Tyrrhenian Sea — Amalfi, Salerno, Naples, and Gaeta — were
economically within the orbit of Palermo and Muslim Sicily,
which was itself the cornerstone of the Fatimid Caliphate. Fatimid
currency was in use throughout southern Italy. Dinars and particularly quarter dinars (*rub'*) were in circulation and were imitated
(*tarin*), a phenomenon similar to that observed in the Christian
kingdoms in northern Spain and the county of Barcelona which, in
the eleventh century, imitated the Muslim gold currencies in use in
the south of the peninsula.

After the Norman conquest of 1061–1089 incorporated Sicily into the Christian Empire of the West, exchanges of skills and ideas increased. Techniques such as silkworm-breeding and silk manufacture reached northern Italy (Lucca, Venice), and this trend was strengthened at the same time by influences which came more directly from the Frankish principalities of Syria, a direct result of the Crusades. It must be added that Sicily and southern Italy, like Spain, had acquired every kind of knowledge during the Muslim era, especially in the fields of medicine, philosophy, astrology, and science. This educat nal process went on under the Normans and the Hohenstaufens, especially at the Court of Frederick II. Together with Spain, Sicily was one of the points at which Oriental influences penetrated to the West. They contributed to the synthesizing achievements of the Italian Renaissance of the fourteenth and fifteenth centuries, a period in which they both attained their fullest development.

CHAPTER 4

The linguistic factor

We have described the Muslim World as a melting-pot in which a number of varied and hitherto foreign components were mixed together resulting in a fusion which incorporated older traditions instead of discarding them. An examination of the linguistic factor, expressed in problems of language and alphabet, will help to clarify one aspect of this phenomenon.

Before the Muslim conquests the situation was roughly as follows: apart from the group of Semitic languages spoken over one area, there were also the Indo-European languages, the Turco-Mongol (or Uralo-Altaic) languages, the languages spoken in the Coptic area and, lastly, those of the Berber area.

The effect produced on these ancient territories by the expansion of the Muslim Empire was the spread of Arabic, which split into two main groups as a spoken language, namely western and eastern. Finally, on the fringe of the Muslim Empire appeared composite commercial languages, Sogdian in central Asia, Swahili on the east coast of Africa, Azer in the Sudan, and the lingua franca in the Mediterranean.

Semitic dialects

The dominant feature of that part of the Semitic area where no

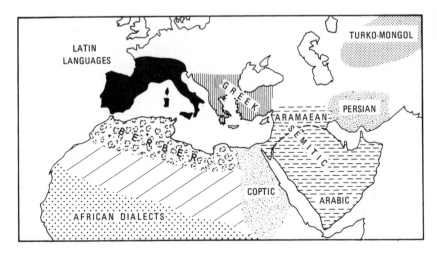

Fig. 7. Distribution of languages before the Muslim conquests.

Arabic was spoken was the important phenomenon of the Aramaic synthesis. As long ago as the sixth century BC Aramaic had in fact absorbed, at least at the spoken level, almost all the Semitic languages in the area except Arabic.

Before the Arab conquest, the official languages were Greek in Byzantine Syria and Pahlavi in Sassanid Mesopotamia, but the living, spoken language was Aramaic. It included two dialects, firstly western Aramaic in the Byzantine Empire, which was both a spoken and a written language and was used in the fourth to sixth centuries in the composition of the so-called 'Jerusalem' (*yerushalmi*) Talmud, and secondly eastern Aramaic in the Sassanid Empire, which in turn consisted of two sub-dialects, Babylonian, spoken and written by the Jews, in which was written, in the fifth and sixth centuries, the so-called 'Babylon' (*babli*) Talmud, and Edessanian Syriac, a written language which later became the literary and ecclesiastical language used in all Christian Churches, whether Jacobite or Nestorian, from Palestine to Mesopotamia and Persia, and which flourished from the fourth to the fourteenth centuries.

The linguistic situation at the time of the Arab conquest was that the Bedouin vernaculars and the Meccan modes of speech used by the conquerors developed into the language of the Koran, the type of written Arabic known as 'literary'. The subject peoples of Syria and Mesopotamia spoke Aramaic (both western and eastern) and wrote it, or else they wrote Syriac in its two alphabetic forms, Nestorian or Jacobite. All these languages were closely related, indeed their consonantal structures often overlapped. As a reaction against the fluidity of the vernaculars several attempts were made to vocalize writing with the aim of giving a definitive form to the sacred Hebraic texts. This work went on in the centre for linguistic studies in Tiberias, where grammarians assembled; their studies of linguistic archaeology took them as far afield as Mesopotamia in their search for documents, with the result that the hitherto separate dialects, eastern and western Aramaic, met and finally merged so as to form one mixed spoken dialect. This syncretism was made possible, or rather, suggested, by the unification of the Muslim World.

At the same time, and with the same end in view, i.e. the establishing of a definitive version of the sacred texts, Syriac writers were trying out methods of vocalization. The Jacobites (late seventh to early eighth centuries) placed Greek vowels on or under the line. The Nestorians, from the eighth century onwards, indicated vowels by dots placed under and above the line. Also at this time the Koran underwent a similar process: the short vowels, 'a', 'u', 'i', were placed over or under the line of writing. The unified Aramaic dialect which was spoken for a time in Syria and Mesopotamia also disappeared, at the latest by 800. It was overlaid and replaced by a new Semitic language, Arabic. Both Aramaic and Syriac, the languages of the sacred texts, were now used solely as vehicles for writing.

Ancient Hebrew was now studied almost entirely as a dead, sacred language, in rabbinical centres in Palestine and Mesopotamia. This is how the literature of the Talmud ('Study') developed in its two forms known as *yerushalmi* (of Jerusalem) and *balbi* (of Babylon). The Talmud itself can be divided into the Mishnah, which is strictly speaking teaching written in Hebrew and completed in the second century, and the Gemara, which is a commentary on the Mishnah and was completed in the sixth century and written in Aramaic, both eastern and western, corresponding to the two versions of the Talmud. It is obvious that all peoples of the Jewish faith were obliged to be bilingual.

In the Graeco-Latin World, Syria possessed four languages, namely a spoken language, Aramaic, a written one used by the Jacobite Christians, Syriac, a second written, sacred language, Hebrew, studied in the schools in Palestine, and lastly Greek, which was restricted to administrative procedures and foreign relations. In the other direction, within the orbit of the Sassanid Empire, Mesopotamia possessed the same languages except that the Persian language, Pahlavi, here fulfilled the function of Greek. Hebrew and Syriac also displayed certain specific characteristics in Mesopotamia. Jewish culture had spread and flourished in this area, indeed the 'Exilarch', the Resh Galutha, the 'leader of the Exile', was to be one of the leading figures at the Abassid court, Syriac found its expression in the Nestorian Church; here, too, the leader of the community, the Nestorian Catholicos of Seleucia-Ctesiphon, was to play a considerable part at the court in Baghdad.

Syriac eventually went beyond the regional framework and became the instrument whereby a fusion of Greek and Persian thought was achieved. The content of many Greek and Persian writings was translated into Syriac, a written language, an aristocratic, cultured tongue, which made possible an extraordinary blend of vocabulary and ideas. Syriac, with its distinctive linguistic patterns, developed a composite civilization based on contacts with other civilizations. These contacts constitute one of the most marked cultural characteristics of early Eastern peoples.

Let us now examine the situation in the area where Arabic was spoken, still within Semitic territory. The languages spoken by the populations of the Arabian Peninsula can, in fact, be divided into three groups which were later unified linguistically by the style of the Koran from the seventh century onwards.

First of all, southern Arabic, which may be subdivided into Himyarite, Sabean, and Yemenite, covered the south-western part of the peninsula, Arabia Felix, with its great port of Athana (Aden), a region of vital importance because of its trading relations and also as a point of intersection between the seagoing trade of the Indian Ocean and the network of caravan routes from western Arabia, which led from Mecca to Mesopotamia and the Mediterranean. This language spoken in southern Arabia has come down to us in the form of inscriptions covering the period from the eighth century BC to the sixth century AD.

Omani was the language of the south-east coast, another major centre of maritime trade commanding the approaches to the Persian Gulf route. It is hardly surprising that here the spoken language had a strong admixture of Persian under the influence of the neighbours across the water.

Nabatean, which was spoken in the north, was linked with the memory of Petra, the great caravan city of the first centuries of the Christian era. It has come down to us in the form of inscriptions dating from the first to the sixth centuries.

Lastly, people living in the centre of the peninsula spoke either the city dialects of Hijaz, particularly that used in Mecca, the focal point of the large-scale caravan trade between the Sabeans in the south and the Nabateans in the north, or else the dialects of the nomad Bedouin of the Nejd, who were camel-breeders. These dialects were not written; pre-Islamic poetry was recorded in writing only after the advent of Islam, and had been preserved hitherto by oral tradition. The Arabic used in the Koran was, in its essentials, borrowed from a kind of poetic language current throughout central Arabia; this was the core of the subsequent classical Arabic, which, in the seventh century, spread across the whole Arabian Peninsula.

It is clear that the Semitic area rested on two linguistic elements, namely Aramaic in Syria-Mesopotamia and Arabic in the Arabian Peninsula. The two languages were, moreover, closely related in that they shared a triliteral consonantal structure, nondelineated vocalic inflexions, and the same basic alphabet derived from the old Phoenician alphabet. When the Muslim conquest was launched it was Arabic which won the day. From the early ninth century the Aramean World, helped by the linguistic similarity, began to speak Arabic throughout what had been the territories of Syria-Mesopotamia. But Aramaic was not the only casualty; the eighth century saw the beginning of a process of Arabization of the civil service, at the expense of Greek and Pahlavi. Syriac, which had grown rigid because of the exclusively written and literary uses to which it was put, was, by the end of the tenth century merely a learned language, and Christian writers used Syriac or Arabic equally. Even so, Syriac did not quite die out, indeed it even enjoyed a certain expansion because of the activities of Nestorian missions in central Asia and China.

Non-Semitic vernaculars

We must now turn our attention to the area of non-Semitic vernaculars, still at the time of the conquest.

Coptic, the language of the Nile Valley, derived ultimately from Ancient Egyptian, and was written down in a modified form of the Greek alphabet. Here too Coptic and Greek were progressively replaced by Arabic, although less swiftly. Some dates enable us to trace the history of this process. The conquest of Egypt took place from 639 to 641, and the first bilingual papyrus (Greek and Arabic) is dated 693 and the last 719, while the last papyrus written entirely in Greek is dated 780 and the first one entirely in Arabic 709. Literary and epigraphic sources yield further indications, for example the fact that Patriarch Michael (728–752) knew no Arabic, and that the Abbasid Caliph al-Ma'mun was accompanied by interpreters when he visited Egypt in 832. On the other hand there is every reason to assume that in the ninth century the Christian clergy was familiar with Arabic, in that 909 is the date of a Christian stele in that language. It is true that popular verse in Coptic could still be heard at the close of the ninth century, but by the tenth the Coptic clergy wrote in Arabic if they wanted to be sure of being understood. Even so, Coptic was far more than just a liturgical language, and even when it had given place to Arabic it still persisted for a considerable time. In the twelfth century, cultured members of the Christian clergy were still familiar with it, and the patriarchs of this period wrote it as elegantly as they did Arabic. The latest Coptic inscriptions date from the thirteenth century. The foregoing remarks apply to Coptic as a written, learned language. As a spoken language it disappeared more swiftly; it gave way to Arabic in the tenth century, which was even so a whole century after the Aramean World had become Arabic-speaking.

Although Arabic became the predominant language in the central regions of the Empire, the same is not true of its eastern and western extremities, where despite the adoption of Arabic by the urban and intellectual centres, two linguistic blocs persisted: Persian in the east and Berber in the west.

We are concerned here only with Middle Iranian, derived from an old Persian dialect cognate with the dialect in which the *Avesta* was written. This Middle Iranian, or Pahlavi, the direct ancestor of modern Persian, continued to be used alongside Arabic. The Iranian influences in the Abbasid era were, certainly, transmitted by means of Arabic. But in the tenth and eleventh centuries there was a revival, this time in Persian, under the Samanid princes of Khurasan, then under the Ghaznavids. One of the monuments of Persian literature, the *Shah-name* by Firdawsi, dates from this time, 990–1020.

Berber was spoken from the hinterland of the Nile Valley and of Cyrenaica to the 'Far West' (the Maghreb) on the one hand, and to the Nigerian Sahel (Sudan) on the other. Here, Arabic affected mainly the towns. Since it was a religious language, a language of urban civilization, it made only very slow progress in the Berber hinterland. In so doing it encroached on the former urban possessions of the Carthaginian colonies. St Augustine, and later on Procopius in the sixth century, show that Punic was still spoken round the old Romanized Carthaginian centres. This may have provided a base which explains the speed with which Arabic was adopted in the Roman towns of North Africa — at least this is S. Gsell's hypothesis.

However this may be, the sudden change from Latin to Arabic can be explained in any case by the need felt in urban centres to adopt a genuine written language, as used in administration and commerce, which was obviously superior to the loose regional spoken language of the Berber dialects. Also, Arabic penetrated to some extent into the mountains of Little Kabylia (Kutama area) in the tenth and eleventh centuries, along with the Fatimid movement. Similarly in the eleventh century the Hilalian irruption involved some degree of Arabization of the nomad tribes of Ifriqiya, and the Algerian high plateaux were affected in their turn in the fourteenth and fifteenth centuries. But this was a slow process and only really affected the towns and their immediate environs.

We must finally examine the linguistic situation in Spain, at the western end of the Muslim Empire. Latin still persisted and was evolving into a Romance language, itself destined to become the origin of Iberian dialects. Alongside Latin were some Berber elements, particularly in the mountainous regions in the south-east which were populated by groups originally coming from North Africa. Aramaic was spoken by the Jewish communities, and then there was the new arrival, Arabic. The hypothesis has been advanced that there was a block of western Arabic dialects, including those of the town-dwelling populations of Muslim Spain and of the Maghreb, Malta, and Sicily. This western Arabic was to be known as *al-gharbiyya*, in Spanish *algarabia*, from which French later derived the word *charabia* (gibberish). Together with this dialectal Arabic there existed, of course, classical Arabic, the language of literature and philosophy, identical throughout the Muslim Empire. It was also the language of religion, administration, trade, and civilization, and fulfilled the same function as Latin had formerly done in Western Christendom, or as Greek had done in the Byzantine Empire.

The languages of commerce

Not only did Arabic attain a position of almost exclusive supremacy within the Muslim Empire, it was also taken across its frontiers by the Radhanite Jewish merchants of the Narbonnaise or the Berber traders settled in the Sudan, and it even travelled as far as the Arab-Persian counting-houses in the Indian Ocean, Indonesia, Indo-China, and southern China — in Canton there was eventually a large colony of merchants who came originally from the Muslim

World. It also spread to the north where Muslim colonies had settled in the *emporia* on the Russian rivers (Itil, Bulghar, Kiev); Byzantium itself eventually possessed a mosque for the use of the Muslims living there.

To complete this linguistic picture, mention must be made of the composite languages which developed on the fringes of the Muslim Empire. These languages, though they arose at this period, underwent considerable modification later on. They are Swahili, an African language spoken in the ports along the Indian Ocean, loaded with terms borrowed from Arabic, Persian, and the Indian languages; Azer, the language of the counting-houses connected with the trade in gold and slaves in the Sudanese Sahel, which borrowed from Arabic, Berber, and the African languages (Soninke and Songhai in particular); Sogdian, already the language of large-scale commerce during the Sassanid era, an Iranian language which had assimilated various words taken from neighbouring tongues; and finally the lingua franca of the Mediterranean, which persisted for a very long time — in fact the last person to speak it died in the mid nineteenth century at Ragusa. Later a certain kind of Malay, the sort spoken in the ports of the Indian Archipelago, played a similar role.

These linguistic areas, though they appear marginal on a map, were in fact of great importance, because they were the melting-pot in which technical vocabularies, especially maritime or commercial terms, underwent change before moving on into neighbouring languages. The importance of this process must be stressed, in particular the entry into Romance languages of technical terms derived from the Muslim World.

This brief survey of the languages spoken within and on the fringes of the Muslim World makes it possible to define more accurately the term 'Muslim' and to establish the vital distinction between the Arab World and the Arabic-speaking World. The expression 'Arab World' should be suppressed. As was stated above, the ethnic element which was strictly Arab was unimportant and soon absorbed by far more compact, civilized, and urbanized populations. The expression 'Arabic-speaking World', though less unfortunate, is still not entirely satisfactory. In fact the outlines of this world were not stabilized, nor did its territory enjoy much uniformity. The cities and the urban network contrasted with the country and in addition, at either end of the territory there persisted and developed, as has been seen, two very important languages, Persian and Berber, both destined to continue for a long time.

* * *

The expression which certainly should be retained is 'Muslim World'. It is probably the least unfortunate one, provided one agrees on what the term implies. Here too we are dealing with a spatial unit in evolution. Here too the skeleton was formed by cities and links between them, and their influence spread gradually over the surrounding rural or nomad areas. But apart from such areas Islam was sometimes slow to advance. For example in certain corners of the Berber mountains the religion of Islam, with the rights and the customs it involves, took root only very recently in the nineteenth century under the influence of an external phenomenon, namely French administrative centralization. Another reason was that this Muslim World, in the eighth and ninth centuries, did not yet include the Ganges area of India, or Indonesia. Lastly, within the Caliphate itself were many people who had not embraced Islam, for instance Christians, Jews, 'atheists' (*zindiq*), Mazdaans, idolaters, Buddhists, Gnostics, and so on.

It would, all things considered, be best to refer to the area 'which had come under Muslim domination'. If we do retain the expression 'Muslim World' it will produce a similar effect to 'Hellenistic World' or 'Roman World'; it will conjure up a picture of diverse peoples united by a common civilization, or better still, peoples caught up in the network of urban relations which was the essential feature of this syncretic civilization.

Defined in this way, the Muslim World may be described as follows: it was first and foremost a vast economic territory, and next an area of civilization with very diverse roots drawing from Greek, Semitic, Iranian, Indian, and of course Arabic sources. It was above all a synthesis. Its art also bore witness to the most varied origins: Persian, Mesopotamian, Byzantine, and even Visigothic. Islam's great achievement was to fuse all these elements into one single civilization, in which the original elements were sometimes very hard to detect. A Muslim work of art, for example, will often conceal its origin, the archaeological province to which it belongs. If the question is not decided by an explicit inscription it is impossible to tell whether it comes from India or Spain, Egypt or central Asia. The Arabic language has this same universal character, since it is the language of religion, administration, commerce, and culture.

The Muslim World, a world of synthesis like the Hellenistic and Roman worlds, had one quality they lacked — size. It was bigger than both of them put together. If the boundaries of Alexander's Empire, the Roman Empire, and the Muslim Caliphate could be imagined as superimposed on each other, it would become clear that the human elements of the Caliphate were taken from both the Hellenistic and the Roman worlds; that is, it included the populations of the East and of the Mediterranean. For, geographically speaking, the possessions of the Caliphate cover not only both the Middle East and the eastern basin of the Mediterranean, as the Hellenistic World had done, but also the eastern and western basins of the Mediterranean, as the Roman World had done. The world of the Abbasid Caliphate lay wide open, far more than the Hellenistic World, to the Indian Ocean, India, central Asia, and China; in the other direction it lay open to the Atlantic and the north-west, as had the Roman World. But in addition to all this it opened out on to the region of the great Russian rivers, the routes to the Caspian or the Baltic, and also towards the Sudan and Central Africa via the trans-Sahara caravan routes. The advent of the Muslim Empire, in fact, meant a widening of the commercial horizon and the elaboration of an economic domain which was more extensive, more varied, and more powerful than anything which had preceded it.

PART II

MONETARY POWER AND URBAN RHYTHMS

CHAPTER 5

Monetary problems

I have so far adopted the geographical approach and worked on a regional basis. We must now turn our attention to some of the more important aspects of power in the Muslim World as a whole, beginning with its mainspring, currency. Then we shall consider urban growth and the social disturbances which were bound to accompany economic upheavals.

The monetary situation on the eve of the Muslim conquests

If a map is drawn of the currency distribution in the Ancient World before the establishment of the Muslim Empire, three quite separate areas, corresponding to three distinct economies, appear.

The barbarian West was almost entirely drained of gold, and relied on silver, an indigenous metal. All that has come down to us of this silver currency, usually of most inferior quality, is the Merovingian *triens* (a third of a *solidus*), a silver, thinly plated, very light-weight currency of very low standard. Major commerce had left the country. Trade in luxury imports was in the hands of the Levantines ('Syri'), who drained and indeed exhausted the gold reserves of the barbarian West. Once it had lost its gold, the basic currency of major Mediterranean commerce, the West became an area organized on predominantly rural and domanial lines, with increasing urban decay and a tendency to a closed economy.

Meanwhile the Byzantine Empire experienced serious gold shortages. First the supply of new mined gold was scant and irregular; the northern barbarians cut the supply routes to the Ponto-Caspian Steppes, while in the south the Blemmys of Upper Egypt closed the African routes. Access to the Indian Ocean area was similarly blocked because it was not dominated by the Sassanids.

This gold shortage was aggravated by hoarding, particularly on the part of the Church, which thus removed from circulation a considerable proportion of precious metals for the benefit of monasteries in Syria, Egypt, and Constantinople. This impoverishment was the more serious in that it occurred precisely when the flow of minted gold coming in from the barbarian West was dwindling to a trickle, drained, as we have seen, by the 'Syri' and their trade. All these phenomena taken together made for even greater restriction and sluggishness of monetary circulation.

However, there were large gold reserves in the eastern provinces, Syria and Egypt, former transit areas, 'buffer countries' between the barbarian West and the Sassanid East. Thanks to these reserves, Byzantium succeeded in overcoming her monetary crises and retaining her *nomisma* (Constantine's denarius, *chrosous, solidus aureus*), which still remained the sole instrument of exchange in the Mediterranean and one of the trump cards of Byzantine diplomacy.

Even so, the Byzantine Empire still suffered monetary embarrassment. Major commerce slowed down and became progressively smaller in volume until it was not much more than a circuit operating within a limited area localized in the eastern Mediterranean, namely the circuit Alexandria—Antioch—Constantinople—Alexandria. Concurrently with urban centres which continued to thrive, a kind of domanial paralysis appeared and spread, as is revealed in the case of Egypt, by sixth- and seventh-century papyri, and for the Empire by the imperial rescripts which tried to ward off the increasing encroachments of the great landed proprietors.

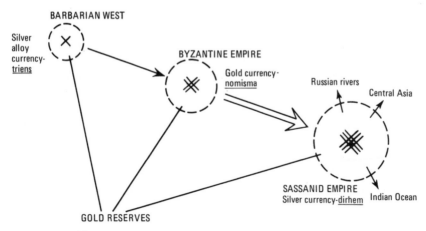

Fig. 8. Monetary movements before the Muslim conquests.

The Sassanid East had no gold in circulation. This was the area of silver monometallism, based on the dirhem (drachma). But vast gold reserves in the form of jewels or costly furnishings accumulated in the palaces of the Persian sovereigns and nobles. These stocks made the Sassanid East appear to swallow up gold.

On this basis of silver currency, which dominated the markets of the Middle East and the Indian Ocean, and to some extent central Asia and the area of the great Russian rivers, there developed in the Sassanid East very powerful economic activity involving urban development. Rural and domanial characteristics tended to be overshadowed by mercantile and urban considerations. The older landed gentry grew weaker as commercial activity spread towards the countries of the Indian Ocean, the Red Sea, central Asia, and the Russian rivers. Moreover, the Sassanids now controlled, as unavoidable intermediaries, Byzantine's supplies of precious objects from Asia. At the head of the Persian Gulf the Ctesiphon-Ubulla group (which took over respectively the function of the Hellenistic cities, Seleucia and Apologos) already foreshadowed the commercial role of the Baghdad-Basra group.

This economic pre-eminence of the Sassanid area was expressed on the artistic plane by the spread of the technical, architectural, iconographic, and decorative formulae of Mesopotamia and Iran, eastwards (the Ajanta grottoes in India, and frescoes at Khotan, Kucha, and Turfan in central Asia), northwards (cloisonné-work of the steppe tribes), and westwards (particularly Byzantine fabrics).

Having defined the areas covered by these three monetary regions we must now discover in what direction these currencies flowed. The direction of the flow was, in the last analysis, from west to east. The West lost its gold to Byzantium and Byzantium lost it to the Sassanid East. Before the Muslim conquests there was, therefore, a linear movement from west to east which exhausted the West and the Mediterranean to the benefit of the Middle East and the Indian Ocean area. All this gold was swallowed up by the Sassanid and Indian treasure-chests.

At the beginning of the seventh century there was a more and more serious imbalance in the distribution of the total volume of gold, as between hoarded gold and gold in circulation. The barbarian kingdoms, whose reserves were nearly exhausted, suffered from a dearth of monetary gold; the circulation of gold in the form of currency also dwindled in the Byzantine Empire, despite still considerable reserves; while the Sassanid Empire combined a lack of minted gold in circulation with an over-abundance of hoarded gold. The trend was, therefore, towards a restriction of the volume of gold in circulation in the form of currency, and towards a geographical shrinkage in the size of the gold area as the silver area grew.

The area of gold circulation, where the *nomisma* was in current use, was more or less restricted to the eastern basin of the Mediterranean, Byzantine territories which were thus enclosed between the barbarian silver area which appeared in the West, and the area of Sassanid silver which was gaining ascendancy in the East. The three causes of this over-all movement were, briefly, hoarding, weakness and irregularity of supplies from the mines, and the linear, one-way west to east direction imposed on monetary trends by the trading balance.

The Arab conquests and the formation of the Muslim World were to affect these three factors and transform the monetary map.

Monetary metals in the Muslim World

The two essential factors were the inflow of gold to be used to mint the dinar (denarius), and the exploitation of other mineral resources, partly to produce silver, a metal which formed the basis of the dirhem (drachma), and partly copper and tin, metals from which smaller currency was struck (*fals*, from the Byzantine *phollis*).

The flow of gold took three forms: a return into circulation of hoarded gold, the arrival of new gold, and progress in processing techniques. The return into circulation of hoarded gold was accelerated by plunder, first from the Sassanid palaces and, later, from the time of the Caliphate of the Umayyad 'Abd al-Malik (685–705), from Syrian and Mesopotamian churches. Indeed, this particular Caliph vigorously encouraged the process of Arabization by introducing Arabic into the civil service and by minting a Muslim-style dinar, and he abolished the privilege of the clergy, who had hitherto been exempt from the poll-tax (*jizya*). They were in future required to pay one gold piece per head, and their property was checked and subjected to a harsh land-tax (*Kharaj*).

And so the treasures of the churches and monasteries fulfilled the function, in the Muslim World of the eighth to ninth centuries, of reserves of precious metal into which the sovereign dips in times of crisis, just like the treasures of the temples of the Ancient World which Constantine had tried to mobilize by creating the *solidus aureus*. It should be noted that the earliest steps taken by the Umayyad caliphs to recover the gold from church treasures date from about 700; that in Byzantium the earliest measures taken by the Isaurian 'iconoclast' emperors date from 726; and that in the West Charles Martel embarked on his policy of despoiling the churches in 730–731. This is a movement apparently spreading from east to west, from the Muslim World to Byzantium, then to the Frankish West, and it brought to an end a cycle of treasure-hoarding.

Lastly, there was the gold hidden away in the tombs of the Pharaohs, and then rediscovered. The Muslim conquests spelt the end of funerary treasures hoarded in Egypt. There is mention in the texts of important and numerous discoveries made by the treasure-seekers, the *ashab al-matalib*, from *talaba*, 'to look for', a veritable guild which paid the government one-fifth of all its finds and worked in close co-operation with the Mint (*Dar as-sikka*). It was a similar situation to that obtaining in the America of the *Conquistadores*, where the *guaqueros* were specialists in seeking out ancient Peruvian tombs (*guacas*), or again in the Middle Ages in the West, although the French tomb-robbers (*larrons fossiers*) with far less wealth at their disposal, cut a sorry figure in comparison with their Egyptian and Spanish equivalents.

To return to the gold of the Pharaohs, we know that the weight of pure gold removed from the tomb of Tutankhamun amounted to several thousand kilogrammes and represented double the gold held by the Bank of Egypt. But Tutankhamun was a minor monarch; it is difficult to conceive of the value of the gold stored in all the tombs of the Pharaohs, most of which were violated! Nowadays we preserve what we find, indeed we substitute scientific hoarding, symbolized by the Museum of Antiquities in Cairo, for funerary hoarding; in medieval times the discovery of gold was followed by its return to circulation, because this rediscovered gold was minted as currency.

The arrival of new gold, the second form in which gold flowed in, was based on mine-working. New gold from the mines was, because of the size of their empire, practically in the hands of the Muslims. Either they actually possessed the sites of these mines, or they controlled the routes carrying gold from abroad. In this way they held, directly or indirectly, the mines of western Arabia, the Caucasus and Armenia, the Urals and the Altai, which supplied the trade of the nomadic Turkish tribes; they held the mines of Tibet and Dekkan, the gold from which found its way into the counting-houses of the Indus and the coast of Malabar; and the mines of East Africa which created such wealth for Sofala, the 'golden Sofala', Sufalat ad-dhahab; and finally the mines of Nubia and Wadi 'Allaqi of which Ya'qubi tells us, and which produced gold eventually reaching Aswan.

In addition to all this, the Muslim World gained a new and far more important source of gold, which was to provide the main

flow of new gold to the Mediterranean from the ninth to the
fifteenth century. This was the gold of the Sudan. The gold was
extracted by black gold-washers whose descendants are still active
today. The metal collected was transported by the trans-Sahara
trade of the Berber camel-drivers, from the storage centres of the
Senegal-Niger area to the major caravan termini of the north, on
the northern edge of the Sahara, such as Nul Lamta, Sijilmasa,
Wargla, and the Jerid, all of which were Maghreb gold ports.
Sijilmasa in particular, founded in 757 in the Tafilelt, ranked as a
major port of entry to the country of the Negroes, Bilad as-Sudan,
also called Bilad at-Tibr: the word 'Tibr' meant 'native gold',
which had been melted down and formed into plaited threads.

The third contributory factor in this flow of gold was the progress made in techniques for treating the ore, by the general use of
amalgam, the *amalgama* of the alchemists' Latin, itself derived
from an Arabic form which was a corruption of the Greek *malag-
ma*, or else, more simply, from the Arabic *al-majma'*, meaning
'joining' or *'amal-al-jam'*, 'a joining operation'. The process always
makes use of Spanish mercury (*az-zawq*; Spanish *azoque*). A thousand workers were active at Almaden (from *al-ma'din*, 'the mine'),
and mercury already fulfilled the function here that it later assumed for precious metals in America. It was, moreover, exported
from Spain to Morocco and the Sudan, to Egypt and Nubia, to
Mesopotamia, central Asia, and the Indian Ocean, in other words
the gold-producing countries. The term for a wash-trough, a tool
used in gold-washing, has come down to us in Spanish as *batea*,
from the Arabic *batiha*.

Not only was the area rich in gold, but in silver too. The major
silver-producing areas of the Muslim World were the same as in the
Ancient World, primarily southern Spain, the ancient Tartessos
region, visited by the Phoenicians, the Carthaginians, and the
Romans, before the Muslims went there. Their arrival ended the
period of inactivity under the barbarians, which had reduced or
even brought to a standstill all mining activities, and led to a
powerful revival. The silver-mines of the Moroccan Atlas, which
were worked by native labour, kept up a strong flow of exports,
handled by the Phoenicians of Lixus. They were still active in the
sixteenth century.

A more important group of mines existed in Armenia, northern
Iran, and central Asia, forming a large silver-bearing zone which
the Sassanids had already drawn on considerably to mint their
dirhem. The two major mining centres were Ma'din Benjhir, in the
mountains of Kabul, with 10,000 labourers, and Ma'din ash-Shash,
in Transoxiana, north of Farghana. Silver currencies of Harun ar-
Rashid and the Saffarid dynasty (ninth century) bear an impress
'Ma'din Benjhir' and 'Ma'din ash-Shash', which confirms that it
was customary for a mint to be installed close to the mines.
Lastly, the region of the Cilician Taurus, north of Syria, is famous
for its site, Bulghar Ma'din, already exploited by the Phoenicians
who exported its silver to Egypt under the Pharaohs.

And so the Muslim World included two major silver-bearing
zones, namely the western tip of Spain and central Asia together
with the eastern point of northern Iran. These two areas supplied
respectively the workshops of the West and the Muslim East
where dirhems were produced (*dirham*, plural *darahim*).

And finally there were copper resources, as is obvious when one
reflects on the countless works of art in copper, bronze, or brass
(copper and zinc), which have been preserved. The extraction of
copper made possible the minting of small change (*fals*, plural
fulus), local currencies, and alloys. The metal came from Cyprus
and more particularly from the Arghana Mine (Ergani-Ma'din), in
Upper Mesopotamia, which even today supplies all the Levantine
artisans producing copper goods and inlaid copper and exports
copper to Mosul and Damascus. North Africa was represented in
the production of copper by the mountainous region of the
Kutama, in Kabylia of the Babors, which loyally supported the
Fatimids. Central Morocco, with the Dai region, on the middle and
upper course of the Oumm er-Rebia, exported its copper to Fez
and the south, in the direction of Sijilmasa, and from there to the
country of the Negroes. The Sus al-Aqsa, meanwhile, exported to
the Sudan copper in ingots and also in the form of bowls and
rings. Spain had been renowned since ancient times for her rich
copper deposits. Finally copper from the Caucasus and central
Asia supplied materials for Turkish copperware.

Tin which, mixed with copper, yields bronze, came from two

main sources some distance away, whose economy was thereby linked with major world trade. The first source was the 'Cassiterid Islands', which gave their name to the Arabic word *qasdir*, 'tin', and the second was the 'Kalah country', namely the Malay Peninsula; this kind of tin was known as *qala'i*. Tin from Britain crossed the sea and entered Muslim Spain. It entered the countries of the Muslim Mediterranean via Gaul and Narbonne, and the Muslim East via the passes of the Alps and Venice. Tin from Malay entered the Muslim World by way of the Persian Gulf and through the Arab-Persian trade of the Indian Ocean and the Red Sea.

Minting and circulation

The steady flow of gold and the abundant supplies of silver and, to a lesser degree, copper and tin, offered immense possibilities to Muslim coining and minting. Coining workshops sprang up, the minting of gold became decentralized and was undertaken in every town of any importance in the Muslim World, thus releasing on to the market considerable quantities of gold and silver currencies minted by the caliphs and, after the collapse of the Caliphate, by all the sovereigns of the various Muslim States. Quality, moreover, went hand in hand with quantity, for the dinar, like every dominant currency, was minted with extreme care.

The geographer Ibn Khurdadhbeh (*c.* 850) bears witness to the existence and extent of this money circulation, and to the abundance, even in the tiniest communities, of metal coins of gold and silver. He uses currency terms when giving tax figures or sums spent by caliphs on buildings, which reveal a considerable degree of urban development.

These typically Muslim coins, the gold dinar and silver dirhem, were not evolved all at once. The early days of the conquest brought no modification in the types of coin in circulation, in that Sassanid dirhems in the eastern provinces, Byzantine denarii in the western provinces, continued in use, and the earliest Muslim mints merely went on reproducing them up to the Umayyad Caliphate of 'Abd al-Malik. The reason for this delay in replacing the older currency must be sought in the traditional, routine character ascribed by the world of trade to its instruments of exchange, and its instinctive mistrust of any innovation in the monetary field. Change comes about only after modifications taking place in the economy itself have made it inevitable.

This delay, then, in establishing a Muslim currency was a direct reflection of economic evolution. The currency used in large-scale commerce was still, up to the end of the seventh century, the Byzantine gold coin and the Sassanid silver coin ('Abd al-Malik's reform took place in 693–695), because the older trading circuits of the Byzantine World and of the Sassanid World were still in existence. But from the seventh century onwards these two systems had fused into one economic whole, and the new conditions made possible a transition to a unified currency based on the gold dinar and the silver dirhem.

It is possible to trace accurately the stages of this evolution. The caliph 'Ali was the first to attempt a reform, at Basra in 660, by introducing a Muslim dirhem with the inscriptions in Kufic script, but his attempt failed. Forty years later it was again introduced and this time it succeeded. These forty years, therefore, saw a change in the money situation which reflected a change in the economic sphere. Muslim currency failed, then passed, the searching test to which any new form of currency is exposed when it appears on the market and has to contend with currency already in existence.

The Muslims carried through their first monetary operation during the Caliphate of 'Umar (634–644), namely a standardization of the weight of silver currencies. Whereas gold currency was based on a single system, the *nomisma*, there were in the Muslim World three different systems of silver currency, namely the *bajli* dirhem in Persia, the *rumi* dirhem for exchange with Byzantium, and the *tabari* dirhem in central Asia. The desire to create one large unified area of silver currency caused the weight of the dirhem to be fixed at an average of 14 *qirats* (from the Greek *keration*, from which we have the term 'carat'), that is to say, about 3.96 grammes. It should be noted that the weight of the legal dirhem was defined in a term inherited from the Greek, the *qirat*, and not the Persian measure, the *daneg*. This was done so as to link the new silver currency with the gold currency, itself derived from the Greek system.

Not until the reform of 693–695 instituted by 'Abd al-Malik was a truly Muslim currency created by the striking of a gold dinar at Damascus. This gave the movement the necessary impetus: in 694–696, a governor of Iraq struck silver dirhems, also of the Muslim pattern, at Basra. Then all the provinces were won over; in 696–697, the governor of Egypt, 'Abd al-'Aziz, the father of 'Abd al-Malik, struck dinars at Fustat. This new kind of dinar carried on the obverse the date of issue running round the rim, thus: 'In the name of God, this dinar was struck in the year . . .', to which was added, from the Abbasid Caliphate of al-Ma'mun (813–833) onwards, the name of the town where it was minted. In the field, still on the obverse, was a pious formula set in three lines. On the other side was a circular legend in praise of Muhammad and in the field a pious formula arranged in three lines. The dirhem was similar in appearance, but was of greater dimensions; the silver coin was indeed much larger and thicker. Finally, the *fals* bore legends in Arabic of very varied kinds. I must repeat that this was merely a localized, accessory currency, not subject to regalities, and was struck by a local authority. Moreover, no legal connection existed between bronze and other monetary metals.

The monetary type thus created was characterized by its inscription in square Kufic letters and by the absence of any effigy. A portrait on a coin, for example the representation during the Abbasid period of al-Mu'tasim on a throne in the Sassanid manner, remained the exception. Along with the standardization of its outward appearance went the careful regulation of the weight of this new currency. While the weight of the silver dirhem followed the norms fixed by 'Umar, the weight of the dinar was fixed according to an average arrived at on the basis of a fairly wide sampling of Byzantine gold coins in circulation, the weight of a Constantinian gold coin being 4.25 grammes. But because these coins had been in circulation for some time, and had therefore become somewhat lighter, the result was that the new Muslim gold coins weighed slightly less than the Byzantine ones. Since weak currency always drives out strong currency this slight difference in weight between the two rival coins certainly contributed to the rapid spread of the new currency throughout the Muslim World. The older currencies were gradually withdrawn, so that bankers and money-changers found themselves obliged to give all such coins in their possession to the official authorities, who melted them down and minted them afresh. The dinar, the major gold currency of the Caliphate, also extended its zone of circulation beyond Muslim territory, particularly in those countries where it was in conflict with the Byzantine *nomisma*, namely southern Russia and the barbarian West.

Thus it will be seen that the Muslim dinar and dirhem, derived respectively from the Byzantine *nomisma* and the Sassanid drachma, brought together two hitherto watertight monetary systems, as is shown in the following diagram:

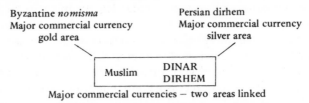

On a basis of one dinar to twenty dirhems, gold currency was geared to silver currency (Mediterranean bimetallism) and the former Byzantine and Sassanid monetary areas became progressively merged. The result was the victory of the gold standard and the extension of the circulation of gold, both eastwards in the former Sassanid territories and westwards in the barbarian West and in Spain.

It remains to indicate the precise stages of this extension of the gold area within the Muslim World. The actual minting of money was supported by a steady influx of metal arriving in successive waves corresponding to the acquisition of plunder and the return to circulation of hoarded gold, and finally the arrival of new gold from the world at large and particularly the Sudan. As a result of this influx, the value of gold, and consequently the purchasing power of the currency it underpinned, tended to fall. And, since

no one holds on to a currency which is steadily becoming de-
valued, but instead reinvests it immediately in business, in re-
sponse to an expanding economy with ever-increasing profits, it is
hardly surprising that a rush to grow rich motivated the Muslim
World after the conquests, particularly the merchant class.

Let us examine for a moment the gold from the Sudan. This
gold, which had been the main source of supply of precious metal
from the end of the eighth century and particularly from the ninth
century, reached the Muslim World, as we have seen, via the little
caravan towns in the southern Maghreb, indeed the entire political
and dynastic history of North Africa is governed by the desire to
control the arrival-points of the gold caravans. This gold did not
stay in the Maghreb, but merely passed through it, just as in the
sixteenth and seventeenth centuries the gold and silver from
America unloaded at Cadiz was taken to the centres of trade,
banking, and industry, which were the nerve centres of the economy at that time.

Thus, Sudanese gold made its way to the major producing areas

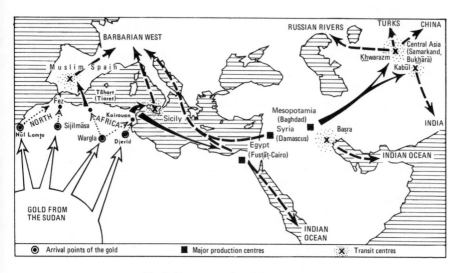

Fig. 9. Movement of gold from the Sudan.

engaged in the export trade, i.e. Egypt with its corn, papyri, and cloth, and Mesopotamia with its sugar-cane and fabrics. It also made its way to the transit areas receiving merchandise entering the Muslim World from outside; it went to Spain together with slaves and other products in demand in the Christian West; it reached the centres in Egypt, Syria, and Mesopotamia which bought Asian products, particularly spices; it went to the trading centres of central Asia — Samarkand, Bukhara, Khwarizm — which commanded the route to the Russian rivers, the country of the Turks, China, and India. And finally Sudanese gold made its way to the political centres, the courts of kings, for example the Tulu-nids of Egypt who, in the ninth century, paid an annual tribute of 300,000 dinars to the Abbasid Caliph of Baghdad.

However, this gold was not evenly distributed. It reached areas remote from the major exchange routes in the form of a thin trickle, but it accumulated in major commercial and banking cen-tres in urban and palace markets. It was in these major centres that gold and silver, and to a lesser extent copper, coins were minted, and from which they were redistributed. And so, by this intricate pattern of monetary flow, Sudanese gold injected fresh life into the Muslim economy; the role of the Maghreb was to redistribute this gold to the major economic centres.

Five distinct sources of information enable us to appreciate the extent to which gold currency circulated throughout the Muslim World, the prime source, of course, being the coins themselves which are preserved at the Hermitage in Leningrad, in museums in Cairo, Damascus, and Baghdad, at the British Museum in London, at the Cabinet des Médailles in the Bibliothèque Nationale in Paris, and elsewhere. These currencies enable us to specify the places where coins were minted, and to pick out the mints on a map. These were, first, Damascus under the Umayyads, then, from 763, Baghdad. Under al-Ma'mun (813–833), minting became decen-tralized. From 827, gold currency was minted in all the main towns, both in the West and in the East. But the uniformity of monetary procedures as regards minting maintained the fusion of the two areas, that of the gold standard (*ahl adh-dhahab*, literally 'gold folk') and that of the silver standard (*ahl al-warq*).

Another source of information is the evaluation in gold of the taxes paid in the Abbasid Empire as a whole. Until the closing years of the ninth century, the budget of the Caliphate of Baghdad was expressed in dinars for the West and in dirhems for the East, but from the beginning of the tenth century it was expressed throughout in dinars, a fact which bore witness to monetary unification at the administrative level.

Muslim Spain is another example of the spread of gold currency. Until the ninth century the Umayyads of Cordoba only minted silver coins, but then they began to mint gold currency too: a symbol of power which was confirmed in the tenth century by the adoption by the caliph of the title 'Emir of the Faithful'. In addition there were very many gold coins from the East in circulation in Spain. Part of this gold reached the barbarian West as payment for slaves which were then re-exported to the East, a traffic which cast Spain in the role of transit country. Lastly, Spain was no stranger to Sudanese gold and she intervened from beyond the seas so as to control the northern arrival-points of the trans-Sahara trade. This gold, minted at Cordoba or Madinat az-Zahra', entered circulation again in the former silver area of the barbarian West.

Another instance of the spread of gold currency is the minting of this metal by the Fatimids. In the tenth century the Fatimids acquired the monopoly of Sudanese gold, thus amassing great wealth and a war treasury which enabled them to conquer Egypt, already won over to their cause by an active dinar policy. The Fatimids went on to intensify their minting of gold, and huge quantities of gold were produced on their territory, from Syria to Sicily. They also created the gold quarter dinar (*rub'*).

Our final source of information on gold circulation comes from the figures provided by Arab historians or geographers. One or two examples will suffice to establish an order of magnitude. In Spain, on the death of 'Abd ar-Rahman III in 961, the Treasury contained 5,000,000 dinars, or 250 hundredweight of minted gold. Under his successor, al-Hakam II (961–976), the total moneys paid into the Public Treasury (*Khizanat al-mal*) amounted to 40,000,000 dinars. In Egypt, on the death of the powerful eleventh-century Minister, al-Afdal, his treasury was found to contain 6,000,000 dinars, representing 300 hundredweight of minted gold. At Baghdad under Harun ar-Rashid (786—809) the Public Treasury (*bayt al-mal*) received annually 7,500 hundredweight of minted gold, that is 150,000,000 dinars. The caliph al-Wathiq (842—847) presented to the merchants of al-Karkh, a district of Baghdad destroyed by fire, 500,000 dinars, which represents 25 hundredweight of gold.

These figures, picked out at random from many others, in the writings of authors who had access to contemporary archives, bear witness to the size of the movement. They must not, of course, be accepted as entirely accurate (even modern statistics are often unreliable), but at least they give an order of magnitude and fully justify the assumption that there was a prodigious increase in gold currency throughout the whole Muslim World. This is even more remarkable when one takes into account the relationship between

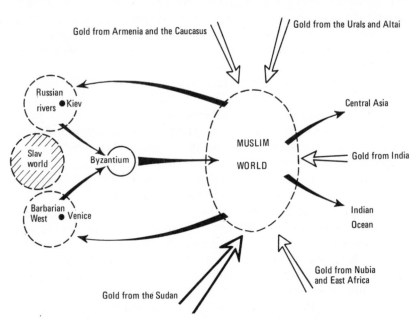

Fig. 10. Monetary movements after the Muslim conquests.

the volume of gold in circulation and the population figure, which was far lower than it is today.

To sum up: in the history of world currencies the Muslim World is remarkable for its steady supply of precious metal, the sources and operation of which have just been examined. Thanks to an abundance of that privileged instrument of exchange, gold, great urban centres in mid-expansion were able to call on any materials they might need, however distant; their need was the more pressing for being linked with the wealth and climb to power of certain strata of society. And so, within the Muslim World and outside it, fresh monetary currents appeared along the great trade routes. There was no longer, as there had been before the conquest, a linear displacement of the mass of metal, but a completely new pattern, in fact a genuine circuit.

CHAPTER 6

Urban expansion and consumer demand

Urban rhythm before and after the formation of the Muslim World

From the eighth to the eleventh centuries the Muslim World was the scene of prodigious urban expansion. This expansion was characterized, at first, by the creation of towns, some of which rapidly became the largest in the world. Sao Paulo has been called 'the most rapidly growing city in the world'; it had 60,000 inhabitants in 1888 and 2,000,000 in 1950. But what is one to think of Baghdad, which in an even shorter time, 762–c. 800, grew from a town of a few hundred souls before the Arab conquest, when the site was occupied by a Sassanid castle and a few Nestorian monasteries, to a city of nearly 2,000,000? Alongside these urban areas, most of which are still large cities even today, older urban centres acquired a new lease of life with a consequent increase in surface area, population, and influence of hitherto unknown proportions.

In this way a vast urban network grew up, linking one town with another and forming as it were the material framework of the Muslim World, as well as a circuit carrying the main currents of civilization. This development, which is of major importance and has hitherto received scant attention, was far greater in scope and effect than the trend to urbanization in the Roman Empire and ranks equally with the great period of urban development in the

Hellenistic era, or the growth of cities in western Europe, at least in the early stages.

At this point it is imperative to take stock of, and indicate the direction followed by, urban evolution before and after the construction of the Muslim World. Before, i.e. in the first half of the seventh century, we find as we did when examining currencies, three areas in which urban activity and rhythm develop along roughly the same lines. We have seen that the barbarian West was characterized by an almost complete lack of money circulation. The trading network had shrunk and was functioning in isolation on a piecemeal basis, while urban slavery had been replaced by rural servitude; as a result urban ways of life were lost. The city of antiquity disappeared, overwhelmed by economic crises, invasions, and brigandage. The town was now merely a cramped *castrum* intended to offer defence and refuge. This period marked the triumph of the large estate and of rural economy. Barbarization and ruralization spread over almost the whole of the Western World, and nomadization prevailed in North Africa.

The Byzantine sphere of influence in the eastern Mediterranean was characterized by an increasingly sluggish circulation of money, and by exchange restrictions which reduced the trading circuit to a very short radius, so that it revolved round the three cities of Alexandria, Antioch, and Constantinople. The Byzantine Empire also suffered a falling-off of slave labour and stagnation leading to the decline of urban activity. The rigid domanial system which, according to evidence in the papyri, affected Egypt, also gained ground in Syria and Asia Minor, together with a pastoral way of life. Activity was concentrated in one or two cities, Hellenistic foundations such as Alexandria or Antioch, or Constantine's more recent foundation, Constantinople. Strictly speaking these cities were mere islands.

The Sassanid Empire, which enjoyed an actively circulating monetary system based on the silver dirhem, accumulated gold stocks, a very large supply of slave labour, and trade wide open to central Asia and the Indian Ocean, witnessed a decline in the power of its large landowners, the *dihqan*, and a parallel expansion of its towns which were springing up in great numbers. Some of

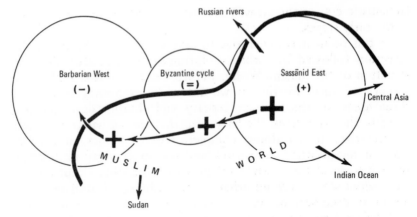

Fig. 11. Directions of urban evolution before and after the Muslim conquests.

their names, ending in the suffix -abad, suggest prosperous inhabited territory.

We have seen, then, that urban rhythm, the intensity of the urban movement, decreased from east to west, in relation to the shrinking of gold reserves and slave manpower and the general structure of world trade. The establishment of the Muslim World in the seventh to early eighth centuries created a vast integrated area, a huge common market stretching from central Asia to the Indian Ocean, from the Sudan to the barbarian West and the region of the Russian rivers. This large unit which overlapped the three former areas, the Sassanid Empire, Byzantine Syria, and Egypt, and the western, barbarized Mediterranean, enjoyed an influx of gold, a plentiful supply of slaves (Turks, Africans, Slavs), and a network of major trade routes which stretched from China to Spain and from black Africa to central Asia and encouraged tremendous urban expansion. In the former Sassanid territories of Mesopotamia and Iran the urban movement already begun during the preceding era continued with greater vigour; the most famous examples of this were Baghdad and Samarra. In the former Byzantine terrritories of Syria and Egypt urban development, which had suffered a check in the preceding era, now forged ahead, which explains the wealth of Damascus and Fustat-Cairo. Lastly, the

former territory of the barbarian West (North Africa, Spain), witnessed the reintroduction of large cities; Kairouan, Fez, and Cordoba had a symbolic value in the great urban movement spreading
from east to west.

The urban movement between the eighth and eleventh centuries

In each of the main regions of the Muslim World, namely the
former Sassanid East, what had been Byzantine Syria and Egypt,
and in the erstwhile barbarian West, I shall try to explain the
over-all movement, then I shall deal specifically with Baghdad,
Fustat-Cairo, and Cordoba.

The former Sassanid territories: Mesopotamia and Iran

Mesopotamia is a country with a very old civilization, a 'place of
cities' where the rhythm of urban life has always depended on the
irrigation carried out in the rich alluvial soil (the Sawad or 'dark
earth') and on the extensive reclaimed marshland (the Bata'ih or
'marsh') where it was possible to grow food crops. These crops
made possible the gross overcrowding of cities. Wheat, barley, mil-
let, and rice had come long ago from the Indian deltas to the
marshy zones of the Lower Euphrates. More recently, in the sixth
century towards the close of the Sassanid era, sugar-cane came
from India and reached Khuzistan, i.e. the former Susiana, then
the Karun area round Tustar. The date-palm came originally from
the Persian Gulf, but refused to grow on the site of Baghdad until
acclimatized by a gardener from Basra. The orange tree was introduced from India to Basra and Oman, and then planted in Baghdad. The importance of this agricultural economy is abundantly
attested by Arab sources describing the foundation of Baghdad.
Every conceivable specialist was called on, including technical experts in hydraulic installations and gardeners with experience of
acclimatizing new species.

But men must not only be fed, they must also be clothed. The
textile materials available were flax from the Sawad and cotton

which came originally from the west coast of India and had become acclimatized in Upper Mesopotamia, in the Great Khabur Basin. Cotton was grown along with sugar-cane, and the plantations required slave labour, the 'Zanj', black slaves from the east coast of Africa. This same threefold association was later repeated in the Mediterranean and the Caribbean.

And, finally, men must be housed. The main raw material for building was clay from alluvial land, dried in the sun or baked in the oven. Baghdad, for example, had a massive triple rampart made of unbaked earth, except for the foundations and the trenches carrying the water from the irrigation channels which were made of baked clay. Varnished or enamelled baked clay provided the materials for earthenware, ceramics, and brightly coloured wall-coverings, which were masterpieces of Mesopotamian art. But it is a fragile medium, and as a result all these old capital cities are now piles of rubble. Wood was a scarce commodity; the boats plying up and down the Tigris and the Euphrates were shaped like round baskets and made by plaiting osiers and painting them with pitch from the Kirkuk area. Wood had to be imported, and was floated downstream from Armenia and Syria in the form of rafts which were dismantled on reaching their destination. Even today the *kellek* of Armenia go downstream to Lower Mesopotamia. Other woods came from India, particularly *saj* or teak which was brought from the coast of Malabar to all the towns of the Persian Gulf and the Red Sea.

We must now examine the impact of the Arab invasions on Mesopotamia, a country whose urban life rests on accumulated reserves of tradition, on a way of life, a technology, an aesthetic, which are all town-centred.

The Arabs entered by the south-west where the desert runs right up to the Euphrates. They built their earliest towns on the west bank of the river, the 'Arab' bank. They became established in the desert at the end of the pilgrims' routes to Mecca and Medina, on the outskirts of the grazing area, the steppe, and the land under cultivation, represented by the river-valley with its waters and canals. These early towns were originally fortified camps. Soon they became focal points, densely populated cities. Near Hira, the former Lakhmid capital, a little upstream from Qadisiyya, where the decisive encounter with the Persian troops took place, Kufa was later built, while Basra was built on the Mesopotamian sea coast on the neck of land dividing the Bata'ih region from the shore of the Persian Gulf. Kufa and Basra grew up on sites where there were already scattered villages, monasteries, or fire temples, but which had not yet played any political or economic role. These cities, founded immediately after Arab troops entered Mesopotamia, under the Caliphate of 'Umar, in 637–639, grew very fast thanks to a mixed population made up of Arabs, converts (*mawali*), and protected subjects (*dhimmi*). Some thirty years later, Kufa had more than 100,000 inhabitants, while Basra had more than 200,000. They were, in the truest sense, 'mushroom cities'.

Basra saw its greatest prosperity under the Abbasids. It was a major storage centre for Indian Ocean trade, the port for Baghdad, and was at that period served by numerous canals linking its various suburbs with the river. Near the West Gate was the Mirbad, a depot for caravans crossing the Arabian Steppe. The wharves along the riverside were the centre of business life, because of the market, but also of intellectual life, with the great mosque and the libraries. Midway between Basra and Kufa – hence its name Wasit, 'in the middle' – a new town appeared about 695. It was founded by a governor anxious to exert firmer control over Basra and Kufa, and with them it completed the trio of major urban foundations of the second half of the seventh century.

The new Abbasid dynasty, which was the culmination of a movement originating in 750 or thereabouts in Khurasan, the centre of Iranian traditions, left Damascus which sympathized too much with the fallen Umayyad dynasty, and sought to fix its capital further east. In Iraq the Abbasids found a country rich in natural resources and urban traditions, a country midway between the Semitic World and the Iranian World. Mesopotamia now became once again the centre of politics and civilization.

The first Abbasid caliph, Abu' l'Abbas as-Saffah, established himself on the banks of the Euphrates, but not in Kufa or Basra, both noisy cities with 'Alid tendencies. He chose a point at Hashimiyya, near al-Anbar (from a Persian word meaning 'depot, granary', Greek *emporion*, and regarded by the Arabs as the plural of their word *nibr* with the same meaning), at the starting-point of the great navigable junction canal connecting the Euphrates and the Tigris — the Nahr 'Isa. The second Abbasid caliph, al-Mansur, established his residence at the other end of the Nahr 'Isa where it flowed into the Tigris. From these beginnings grew Baghdad. The importance of the Nahr 'Isa was the way it connected major currents of trade between the Upper Euphrates and the Lower Tigris. Beyond al-Anbar, in fact, the Euphrates was more and more swampy, and the Bata'ih, where it almost stagnated, impeded navigation. For this reason the Lower Tigris was preferable.

Baghdad was placed at the intersection of three river routes and two land routes. The Upper Tigris route led north to Mosul and Armenia, the Nahr 'Isa and Euphrates led north-west to Syria, the Lower Tigris led south-east towards the Persian Gulf and the Indian Ocean. The land routes ran south-west to Arabia and the holy cities of the Hijaz.

Like the site of Basra, the site of Baghdad was inhabited before Islam. There was a Sassanid castle with a pontoon-bridge over the Tigris, a village, and some Christian monasteries. The town's name recalls its origins; the name 'Baghdad' probably derives from an Iranian form 'Bag-dade', 'gift of God', and the name of its commercial quarter, al-Karkh, from the Armenian *kerka*, 'market'. Pre-Islamic Baghdad had merely a localized function, in common with many of these old inhabited centres. Al-Mansur was its real creator, and he called it 'Madinat as-Salam', the 'city of Peace'. Building was started in 762. Workmen were brought in from every quarter — more than 100,000 were employed at once — as well as specialists. These men were the city's earliest inhabitants, as well as its builders. And so in four years there arose a circular town arranged round the palace and the principal mosque, in the form of a series of concentric walls between which were the houses of private individuals and those belonging to the monarch's favourites. A rampart with 360 towers surrounded the whole thing. Four broad streets ran through the city in the form of a St. Andrew's Cross, and it was entered by four gates each set at an angle, with

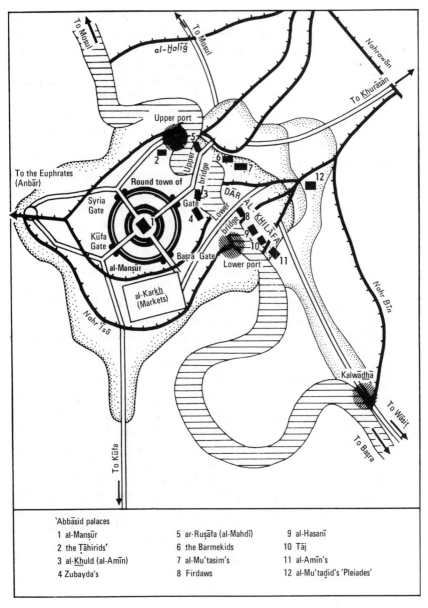

'Abbāsid palaces

1 al-Manṣūr	5 ar-Ruṣāfa (al-Mahdī)	9 al-Hasanī
2 the Ṭāhirids'	6 the Barmekids	10 Tāj
3 al-Khuld (al-Amīn)	7 al-Mu'taṣim's	11 al-Amīn's
4 Zubayda's	8 Firdaws	12 al-Mu'taḍid's 'Pleiades'

Fig. 12. Baghdad.

multiple defences, notably a ditch filled with water brought from the Nahr 'Isa and the Tigris. The circular ground-plan is Oriental in origin and reminiscent of the *Shahristan,* with its four gates, in contrast to the rectangular Hellenistic plan with a *cardo* and *decumanus.* One must also bear in mind the circular fortifications of the cities of central Asia and also the frequent occurrence of the circular plan with the Parthians. Opposite Seleucia, a Hellenistic city built on a rectangular plan, Ctesiphon had been built by the Parthians in the form of a circular camp.

This circular city of al-Mansur with its shops housed under arcades along the four converging streets, soon became too small, and lack of space obliged the town to spread in two directions, south towards the suburb of al-Karkh, a trading and craftsman area, and east beyond the river which could be crossed by a pontoon-bridge. It was here, far from the milling crowd, that the residential district grew up, with the caliph's palace, the dar al-Khilafa, as its most important feature. This move to extend the town on the east bank started in 768. Thirty or forty years later, under Harun ar-Rashid and al-Ma'mun, in the early ninth century, Baghdad was a densely populated urban area measuring about 10 kilometres by 9, roughly the same size as Paris within the outer boulevards. It then became the largest city in the world.

The caliph al-Mu'tasim (836–842) left Baghdad in 836 to found a new palatine centre on the site of Samarra, three days' march further north. This voluntary exile in a palace-city has parallels with Paris and Versailles. Here the explanation was the wish to escape the disturbances caused by the Turkish garrison when faced with the population of a large city which was always turbulent, particularly in the market-place. And so Samarra remained the centre of government for fifty-five years (836–892); the palace itself was surrounded by a very populous city. In 892, still in an attempt to escape the power of the Turkish guard, the caliph al-Mu'tamid returned to Baghdad, which necessitated an extension to the parts of the city which were on the east bank. The onset of the decline of Baghdad can be dated from the end of the tenth century; it continued in the eleventh century under the Seljuq Turks and was completed when the town was captured by Hulagu in 1258.

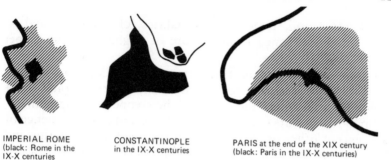

IMPERIAL ROME
(black: Rome in the
IX-X centuries

CONSTANTINOPLE
in the IX-X centuries

PARIS at the end of the XIX century
(black: Paris in the IX-X centuries)

BAGHDAD in the IX-X centuries

0   10 km

Fig. 13. Comparative sizes of some capital cities: Rome, Constantinople, Paris, and Baghdad.

However, the urban movement in Mesopotamia as a whole was not confined to Baghdad and Samarra, the two great Muslim foundations, but also affected towns already existing during the Sassanid era, which now experienced development in the topographic, economic, and human spheres. In Khuzistan, formerly Susiana, a country long accustomed to irrigation by means of huge dams, enabling sugar-cane and cotton to be grown, Tustar, Sus, and al-Ahwaz grew considerably. In Upper Mesopotamia, where cotton was grown in the Great Khabur Basin, the town which experienced growth was Mosul, famous for its fabrics (cf. 'muslin'), and its copper goods fashioned from the ore of Arghana on the Upper Tigris.

As well as Mesopotamia the former Sassanid kingdom also included Iran, a vast area in touch with many diverse cultures. First of all there was Turan, the home of the steppe-dwelling nomads, the Uralo-Altaic Turks. This was a race without any experience of towns except other people's, which it dreamed of plundering and living in as overlord. Indeed, the Turkish nomad's attitude towards the Iranian towns was identical with that of the Arab nomad towards the towns of Syria-Mesopotamia. Here, too, Turkish infiltrations were a prelude to the phase of conquest which began in the eleventh century. Still further east, Iran maintained contact, by a chain of oases, with Chinese civilization; along the so-called 'silk route' which led eventually to populations of agricultural settlers. Finally in the south-east, via the Pamir and Hindu Kush passes, it was possible to reach India, another civilization of agricultural settlers.

In Iran, unlike Mesopotamia, the geographical situation of the towns did not follow the river network but rather the caravan routes linking Mesopotamia with central Asia across Iran. The Arab conquest (642–652) assumed here a different guise from anything it may have known elsewhere. Whereas in Mesopotamia, whose Semitic or Semitized populations spoke Aramaic, the new arrivals were quickly absorbed, in Iran by contrast, resistance came from the old Persian element and from the national religion, which was fire-worship, Zoroastrianism, a cult also open to Buddhist and Manichaean influences. We have seen that the Barmekids, the Grand Viziers of the early Abbasids, were princes of Balkh (Bactra), servants of the great Buddhist monastery called 'Nawbahar' (i.e. 'New Monastery' from the Sanskrit *vihara* meaning 'monastery') of which they were the *paramaka* or abbots. This fact explains why Persia's conversion to Islam took a specific form, Shi'ism. The fact that some great authors writing in Arabic were of Persian origin did not prevent the survival and then the revival of the Persian language, particularly from the eleventh or twelfth centuries onwards.

The Arab conquerors began by settling in the modern parts of cities, side by side with the old town, which meant that the *medina* (Persian *shahristan*) was paralleled by the suburb, the *rabad* (Persian *birun*) which had a fortress, a great mosque, and a market. In this way a series of dual towns grew up and produced the phenomenon of twin cities, for example Merv, Balkh (which had a genuine second city, Baruqan, only a few miles from the first), Bukhara, and Samarkand. Later on these twin towns merged into one. In the Abbasid era, the *shahristan* became the civic centre once more, together with the great mosque and the market, which resulted in a return to the original urban nucleus.

The growth of a new urban population presupposed the development of irrigation, which involved a complex technique of undergound channels. The need to defend towns against the attacks of Turkish nomads made it imperative to build military outposts (*ribats*) and great circular walls round the larger cities with their suburbs under cultivation and their smallholders' villages. Thus at Samarkand and Bukhara there were ramparts 100 kilometres in circumference, walls which are reminiscent of that still more splendid wall built and rebuilt by the Chinese to keep these same Turanians at bay.

Major urban development was linked, in Iran as elsewhere, to the expansion of trade during the Muslim era, trade engaged in by a class of merchants whose wealth derived from the caravan traffic. Thus, prosperous cities were pre-eminently at key points, particularly Samarkand, which controlled the junction of the trade routes coming from India and Persia. Barthold estimates that under the Samanids, in the late ninth to tenth centuries, Samarkand had a population of about 500 000. The city was a most impressive sight, with four walls enclosing first the entire oasis region under cultivation (the 'long wall'), then the suburbs and the city (great wall with two gates), then the city proper (*shahristan*, with four gates), and finally in the centre the citadel. It was, like Baghdad, built on a radial plan. A great canal branching off in all directions provided the city with water; the streets were paved with stone and embellished with fountains and copper pools which showed how close the copper-mines were and emphasized the thriving copper-workers' craft. We are told by the geographer Ibn Hawqal that the public gardens contained cypresses trimmed to the most amazing shapes; horses, oxen, camels, and wild animals face to face, watching one another or locked in combat, in arrangements which recalled the art of the steppes.

The former Byzantine territories: Syria and Egypt

Let us consider Syria first. The towns fall into three categories. First there were the towns in the interior which had begun to decline during the Byzantine era but then experienced a revival based on their role as a point of contact with Mesopotamia. Next were the ports, which had remained active throughout the Byzantine era and now received further stimulus. Finally there were the Cilician frontier towns which commanded the passes over the Taurus Mountains; they entered upon a period of peace when the frontiers became stabilized. The frontier towns which had been destroyed in Byzantine counter-attacks were rebuilt by the Abbasid caliphs, while new fortresses were also built.

Damascus was typical of the cities of the interior. It was an oasis set on the banks of the Nahr Barada, which flowed down from the eastern spurs of the Anti-Lebanon. It was a market-place set between the oasis-settlers and the nomads of the desert steppe (Badiyat ash-Sham), it was an old Aramaean city, paired with a Greek colony during the Hellenistic period, and it supplied corn to the armies guarding the Roman *limes*. Damascus then suffered a decline which was emphasized in the Byzantine period by the nomadization of the suburbs, but it revived when the Umayyad caliphs made it their capital. It was destined, like Kufa, to hold on to the settled areas without losing touch with the Arabian desert; its inhabitants kept the dual aim of enjoying the comforts of city life without totally forsaking the pleasures of the Bedouin existence with its unrestricted hunting.

The great mosque, with the caliph's palace beside it, the Green House (al-Khadra'), was set in the middle of the old city and became by degrees hemmed in by the growth of flourishing suburbs. The caliphs had to divert the course of the Barada and to redistribute water rights throughout the oasis, a policy resulting in an increase of the surface area under cultivation and the emergence of new market-gardening villages. In the early eighth century, under al-Walid, the original mosque acquired grandiose additions and became the Great Mosque of the Umayyads. Workmen for this building were requisitioned from all kinds of places, and mosaic-workers were called in locally and from Byzantium. And so Damascus enjoyed its highest prosperity at the time when it was the capital of the Umayyad Caliphate. In 750 the city was captured by the Abbasids, who destroyed the ancient ramparts and profaned the tomb of the Umayyads, and it sank to the level of a provincial town. Even so, it always remained a populous place, the centre of considerable agricultural and craft production. Damascus remained famous for its plums, grapes, and apricots which were preserved and exported all over the world, as were steel goods, 'damascened' coppers, and 'damasks' such as silk and cotton.

As well as Damascus, mention must be made of Jerusalem which was an important religious centre living mainly on the income to be had from from the religious pilgrimages which Jews, Muslims, and Christians made there. Homs and Hama, towns in the Orontes Valley, and more importantly Antioch and Aleppo, must also be noted. The most important ports were those of as-Suwaydiyya, of Antioch, of Lattakiya (Laodicea, al-Ladhiqiyya), and all the former Phoenician ports — Tripoli, Jbayl (Byblos), Sayda (Sidon), Sur (Tyre), and 'Akka (Acre). They all experienced a revival during the Muslim era; fresh quays were built, new jetties put in place, thanks to the application of advanced techniques of submarine construction, as described by the geographer Muqaddasi in connection with the port of Acre in the early ninth century.

The Cilician frontier towns were known by the collective term 'ath-Thughur', 'frontier places' or 'marches'. The need to mount guard over the passes across the Taurus Mountains, which required annual expeditions and constant construction works, is the key to the history of these fortresses during the Muslim era; they were repeatedly destroyed and rebuilt, depopulated and repopulated. They were important centres of consumption because the military required a great number of men, horses, provisions, clothes, wea-

pons, and building materials. Another feature of these towns was
their ethnic variety. They contained Negroes, Slavs, Iranians, and
Armenians, and many other ethnic types. Urban life along the
frontiers, at Tarsus, Adana, and Massisa, had an atmosphere all its
own, and here too one may note an appreciable tendency to expansion, at least up to the second half of the tenth century, when
Nicephorus Phocas waged his campaigns.

In Egypt, the second part of the Byzantine Empire which fell to
Islam, it is possible to trace in detail, thanks to surviving papyri,
the way the process of ruralization in full swing at the end of the
Byzantine era slowed down and finally stopped. The Muslim conquest meant that a vast economy based on exchange superseded an
economy which, though not entirely rural, was in many respects
tending to become so. This change-over, which we know about
from information supplied by geographers and travellers, was also
accompanied by urban growth, the course of which can be followed in the archaeology and topography of the great continuous
creation of the Muslim era, namely Fustat-Cairo.

Before the Muslim era this site was occupied by the little
Graeco-Roman city of Babylon, the situation of which corres-
ponds, in Old Cairo today, to the Qasr ash-Sham' quarter. The
name 'Babylon', derived from an old local Egyptian name, fell into
disuse with the Arabs, but continued to be used by the Copts. The
word reappears, spelt in various ways ('Babalyun', 'Babiloine',
'Babillonia') in Western documents and in European literature to
indicate Cairo. This Egyptian Babylon was a fortress, a strategic
point on the apex of the Nile Delta. It dominated the land route
which led from Syria to the West, to Ifriqiya and the Maghreb and
avoided the Delta itself, which was a major obstacle because of the
way the Nile breaks up into innumerable rivulets and channels.
But here on the Island of Roda, the island of the Nilometer, the
Nile could be crossed easily by two pontoon-bridges. Moreover,
the site was the starting-point of the canal affording access to the
waters of the Red Sea. This canal belonged to the Pharaohs, then
to the Romans ('Trajan's river', *Trajani amnis*), and then to the
caliph, the Commander of the Faithful (Khalij amir al-Mu'minin).
In addition to these routes there was also the great river route of

the Nile running from south to north and linking Upper Egypt with the Delta.

It would be more accurate to describe the site of Cairo as a low-lying bank consisting of a plain and a series of alluvial terraces stretching as far as the advanced spurs of the Jabal Muqattam, known as the 'Jabal Yashkur'. Later on, some marshes (*birka*) were reclaimed and yielded good land for vegetable-growing.

Historically speaking, Cairo was a succession of cities. Babylon was followed by Fustat, founded after the conquest in 641 by 'Amr, the leader of the Arab invaders, in the form of a camp, to the north of the ancient city. The name 'Fustat' means either a 'military tent' or, more probably, a 'defensive moat' (Byzantine *fossaton*, Latin *fossatum*). The history of Fustat is a clear record of the transition from a camp to a town. Until the early eighth century the public services, staffed by Coptic civil servants writing in Greek, remained in Babylon, then came a decisive change under 'Abd al-Malik, with the adoption of Arabic by the civil service and the introduction of a Muslim-style currency. A new urban centre grew up; public buildings were put up at Fustat, depots, an arsenal, a port, a whole complex of installations which showed that river life was attracted to the new centre and which enlarged the original Fustat with its Great Mosque of 'Amr, the Governmental Palace (Dar al-imara), and market-places.

In 749–750 a new town was founded north of Fustat by the Abbasid generals bent on pursuing the last Umayyad caliph. This second town, al-'Askar, 'the camp', also included a governmental palace and market-place alongside a great mosque.

In 872, Ibn Tulun, the governor of Egypt in the name of the Abbasid caliph but in fact the founder of an independent local dynasty, built a huge palace at the foot of Muqattam, then in 875 a great mosque on the Jabal Yashkur. This mosque revealed influences from Samarra, where the minaret with a spiral staircase marked the transposition, on a round plan, of the architecture of the former Mesopotamian ziggurats. Ibn Tulun also built a hippodrome (*maydan*) for polo, and the new town received its finishing touch when land was shared out between officers and servants, hence the name 'al-Qata'i'', 'the Concessions', by which it was known.

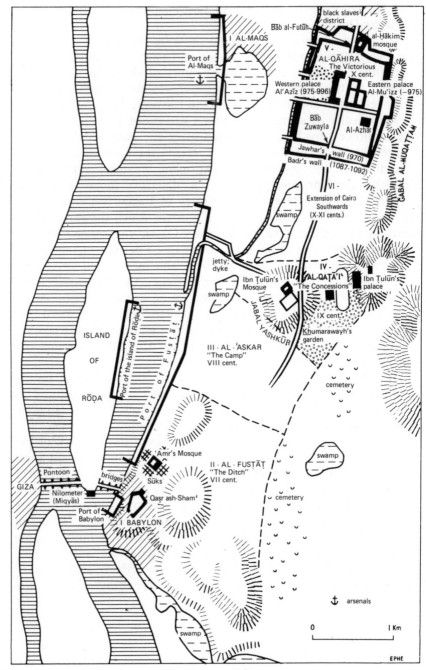

Fig. 14. Fustat-Cairo.

Finally, under the Fatimids, Cairo was founded. The Fatimids left North Africa in 969 via the oasis route and reached the Nile Valley. To the north of the existing installations they founded a new town with palaces and a mosque (al-Azhar, founded in 972); the new town was called 'al-Qahira', which means 'the town founded when the planet Mars was rising' and it grew very rapidly round the official buildings. The peak of Cairo's development came during the tenth and eleventh centuries, a period when an uninterrupted series of buildings joined it, in the south, to al-Qata'i'. At that time the urban area had about 500,000 inhabitants.

The second half of the eleventh century, however, saw the beginning of its decline, with the disturbances of al-Mustansir's reign (1035–1094): the famine of 1054 and the sacking of the Fatimid palaces by the soldiery in 1060. At this period was formed the Kharab, 'the desert region', a ditch growing wider and wider between al-Qahira and al-Fustat, until a fire severely damaged Fustat in 1168 and finally decided that the future of the city lay in Cairo.

Territories formerly within the barbarian West: North Africa, Spain, and Sicily

North Africa, the most important unit in this region, experienced between the eighth and eleventh centuries a set of general conditions which favoured unusually intense urban growth. It was a transit area between the most westerly points of Islam and the Muslim East, between Spain and Sicily, between the Muslim possessions and the world of the Sudan and the Sahara. It experienced considerable growth, based on the trans-Sahara trade which, in turn, ensured that urban modes of life travelled from Sijilmasa, Wargla, and Mzab in the northern Sahara to the banks of the Niger. The foundation and development of towns such as Fez or Kairouan were connected with this southern aspect of Maghrebi trade, with the rise of the great caravan towns which sprang up at the termini of the gold and slave routes.

The first Arab attack on Ifriqiya and the successes of the conquest despite the resistance of the Berbers of the interior, were followed in 670 by the foundation of Kairouan by 'Uqba. The town was planned as a defensive redoubt, a parade-ground, a jumping-off ground, all of which functions are expressed in its name 'al-Qayrawan', 'garrison town'. Indeed Kairouan was situated in a key position on the edge of the Sahara, the steppe-like plains and the *chotts* of southern Tunisia. It commanded, as did Kufa, Damascus, and Fustat further east, a major oasis route which it could jeopardize or protect at will; in this case it was the oasis route from Egypt.

At the time of the great Kharijite uprisings of the mid eighth century Kairouan was captured on several occasions by the rebel Berbers and its walls were destroyed. In 772 the walls and the great mosque were rebuilt. The chroniclers tell us that this was the town's second foundation; the prelude to the considerable extension of Kairouan under the Aghlabids (800–909). This period saw the construction of enormous reservoirs and tanks which were supplied by an aqueduct 25 kilometres long; in addition the great mosque was rebuilt because it was now too small, a fact which reflected urban expansion, as in the case of Damascus and Cordoba. At the same time there sprang up round the city a great number of new centres, a series of residential towns consisting of palaces rapidly surrounded by markets and forming the centre of new and populous cities.

In 800–801, towards the south-east, was built al-Qasr al-qadim, the 'Old Palace', or al-'Abbasiyya (in honour of the master, the 'Abbasid' caliph), where Charlemagne's envoys were entertained. This was yet another new city with a five-gate rampart, numerous baths, caravanserais and markets, a mosque like the one at Samarra, and a hippodrome (*maydan*). Though the court left the city in 877, it remained inhabited.

Another town was built in 876–877, ar-Raqqada, south-west of Kairouan, with a circumference of 24,000 cubits (more than 10 kilometres), but containing vast open spaces in the form of parks, public squares, and gardens. After the fall of the Aghlabids and after the conquest of Kairouan by the Fatimids, ar-Raqqada was pillaged by the inhabitants of Kairouan close by, who were jealous of the new city.

Finally in 948–949, under the Fatimids, a third subsidiary town sprang up to the east of Kairouan, namely Sabra Mansuriyya, founded by the Fatimid caliph al-Mansur after a revolt at Kairouan. The town had five gates, each of which brought in 26,000 dirhems a day in toll charges. As in the case of Samarra, the ruling power was obliged to yield to the population of the capital. Sabra, a palace-city and also a commercial centre, was soon absorbed into the larger area of Kairouan and became a suburb inside the ramparts, thus affording yet another instance of proliferation by urban explosion, followed by reabsorption, as in the case of Fustat-Cairo or Cordoba.

Along with the other urban foundations in Ifriqiya mention must be made of Tunis, founded soon after Kairouan. The ancient city of Carthage was now no more than a heap of ruins, so it was abandoned and the new city was built on one of its former suburbs Tynes. The building of the arsenal and the fleet was undertaken by an Egyptian labour force. Politically, Tunis belonged to the territory of the Fatimids or their vassals, Zirids or Hammadids. In addition to Tunis one must mention Mahdiyya, founded in 915, east of Kairouan, on the coast; Ashir, founded in 935, north of Hodna; Algiers, Miliana, and Medea, founded in 946; and the Qal'a of the Banu Hammad, founded in 1007.

In the central Maghreb, Tahert, founded in 761, 10 kilometres west of the modern Tiaret, was the capital of the Kharijite Rustamids. It was captured by the Fatimids in 908 and the Kharijites, driven out of Tahert, pushed southwards and took refuge in the desert. In the tenth century they founded Sedrata, near Wargla. During the persecutions which took place in the late tenth and the early eleventh centuries, they fell back once more into desert regions, the solitary wastes of the salt-marshes of the Mzab, where they drilled wells to a depth of hundreds of metres. The year 1077 saw the beginnings of the pentapolis of Mzab, which was yet another example of urban civilization. Other foundations were Tenes (875–876) and Oran (902–903). The latter was founded by Andalusian adventurers who organized a market with the local Berbers the results of which were so profitable that it warranted, after the first phase in tents, the building of a small fortress and then a town.

In the further Maghreb, in Morocco, the same process took place as in central Maghreb, namely, the almost total disappearance of the older Roman centres: Volubilis, Septem (Ceuta), and Tingis (Tanga, Tangier). In 788, upon the arrival of Idris the Younger, who, it should be noted, was an Oriental as were the Aghlabids, the Fatimids, and the Rustamids, also great city-builders, Tangier was the biggest centre dominating what is now called the Strait of Gibraltar. In 808 Fez was founded (see above, p. 71).

Fez is the perfect example of the reintroduction of an Oriental-type urban civilization into a Berber rural society. It was a city by virtue of its walls, its suburbs, its markets, its industries, its middle class (*fasi*). Its population was drawn from two sources: Cordobans who had been expelled from their city after one of its suburbs had revolted, and Kairouanians who used to constitute the unruly militia of the governors of Ifriqiya until their dismissal. And so the two halves of the city grew up on either side of the river, the Oued Fez, namely 'Adwat al-Andalus and 'Adwat al-Qarawiyyin, each with its great mosque, its *suqs*, its mint. One of the town's many charms was the water flowing everywhere. Water was diverted from the Oued Fez along channels and runnels into the houses, which were built round a grassy patio. The streets of the town were paved and, according to the tenth-century geographer Ibn Hawqal, every summer evening water from the river was flushed into the market-places to cleanse the ground and wash the paving-stones. In addition the river supplied water for twenty public baths and 300 mills. Fez grew rapidly, so that by the late tenth and early eleventh century it had about 100,000 inhabitants.

Basra in northern Morocco dates from the same period. Only a few traces of its outer wall have been preserved. It was very thick, built of roughstone, and flanked by semicircular towers of Oriental design; in fact this kind of tower is characteristic of Abbasid art, and reached Morocco via Egypt and Ifriqiya. Other foundations were Oudjda, in 994, Igli, built in the ninth century in the Sus al-Aqsa and connected with the termini of the trans-Sahara caravan trail and, lastly, a town founded by the Almoravids who arrived from the south via the Sudan caravan trail, namely Marrakesh.

This somewhat rapid survey of the urban history of North Africa suffices to convey some idea of the enormous revival of city life and the urban explosion in the area. This development is connected with the intensification of links between the Maghreb and the East, Spain, and Sicily, and above all with the opening of a new commercial horizon, the Sudan, the world of gold and slaves which was now accessible via the tracks crossing the Sahara. In addition, this urban development was connected with a very powerful demographic upsurge. During the early Middle Ages Barbary was a reservoir of manpower, as is evident from the colonizing of the Sahara by Berber camel-drivers, the conquest of Spain by more Berber contingents, the conquest of Sicily under the Aghlabids, and of Syria and Egypt under the Fatimids.

The same general considerations apply to Spain, with one reservation, the list of Muslim foundations is much shorter, and urban expansion depended to a greater extent on the development of ancient cities, which thus enjoyed a revival after the decline they had suffered during the barbarian era. These included the cities of Baetica, the area of the Baetis (Guadalquivir); Cordoba (Corduba, Qurtuba), and Seville (Hispalis, Ishbiliya); Cadiz (Gades, Qadis), Malaga (Malacca, Malaqa); cities of the Tagus: Toledo (Toletum, Tulaytula), Lisbon (Olisipo, Ushbuna); lastly, cities of the Ebro: Saragossa (Caesarea Augusta, Saraqusta). The only two genuinely new major foundations (and they were very important ones) were, as we have seen, the two great ports and arsenals of the Emirate of Cordoba, namely Almeria (al-Mariyya, 'the watchtower'), on the Mediterranean, and al-Qasr (or Qasr Abi Danis, Alcacer do Sal), on the Setubal Lagoon, facing the sea. These two cities which were founded at more or less the same period, by the earliest Umayyad princes in Spain after their accession to power, indicate that Muslim Spain was opening up trade on to the Mediterranean and the Atlantic. However, Almeria, founded in 756, seemed the more important of the two, for not only was it a large port but also an active commercial city with diversified industries, as is evident from the 'Aumaric fairs' referred to in the French *chansons de geste*. Silk cloth was manufactured there from silk produced in the Alpujarras, mountains which rose behind the city, and there were also great naval dockyards which provoked a development of the wood, iron, and sailcloth industries.

Nevertheless, the major urban phenomenon of the Iberian Peninsula under the Muslims was the development and flowering of Cordoba. The former capital of Roman Baetica, Corduba, was an insignificant affair when the Muslims arrived on the scene at the beginning of the eighth century. The major town, if such an expression is appropriate to the period, was Toledo, the capital of the Visigothic kings. Cordoba enjoyed a favourable position, with a Roman bridge marking the limit to which the Guadalquivir was navigable upstream. In 719 the sixth governor, representing the Umayyad caliphs of Damascus, moved from Seville to Cordoba and initiated the first building work of his governorship; he built walls, restored the old Roman bridge, and built water-mills on a jetty, using the current of the river. This was the period when the southern suburb came into being, with the Muslim cemetery as an important feature. From that point the city grew very fast, spilling over its walls to the north, east, and west while the suburb continued to expand southwards.

The major period of Cordoba's development occurred in the tenth century and particularly in the reigns of al-Hakam II and Hisham II. The city itself, *al-Madina*, in the centre, had seven gates. Beyond them, twenty-one districts made up the suburbs, which now extended in every direction: nine districts in the west, seven in the east, three in the north, and two in the south, on the other side of the river, in the area known as 'Calahorra'. The increase in population which this indicates was also reflected in the successive additions made to the famous mosque of Cordoba. In 785, 'Abd ar-Rahman I renovated the old mosque; in 833, 'Abd ar-Rahman II added nine new triforia at the south end; in 961, al-Hakan II built eleven more triforia, also on the south side; finally in 977, al-Mansur increased the building by a third, this time on the east side, with eight new naves. And so the dimensions of the building correspond to a city containing some 300,000 inhabitants.

Another phenomenon which was typical of the growth of Cordoba is the expansion best described as 'overspill'. Here, too,

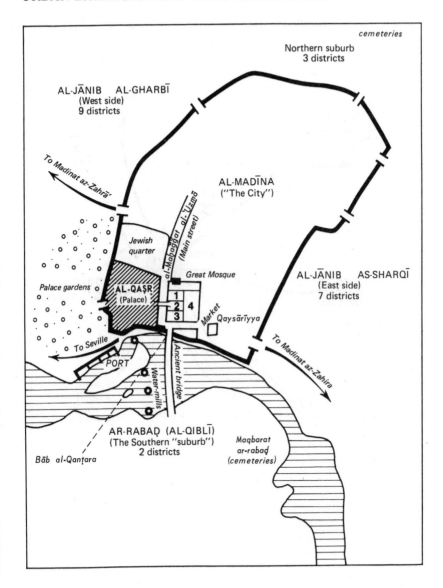

Fig. 15. Cordoba.

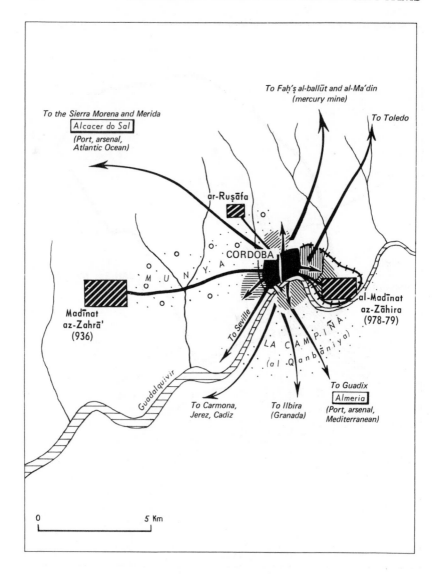

Fig. 16. The surroundings and offshoots of Cordoba.

caliphs' residences outside the populous city formed the nucleus of new towns, centres of growth by stages in the style of the Aghlabid and Fatimid palaces of Kairouan. First of all, about 3 kilometres to the north-west, as early as the reign of 'Abd ar-Rahman I, ar-Rusafa grew up, rather like the Rusafa in Syria which was for a time the residence of the Umayyad caliphs of Damascus. But ar-Rusafa was not the caliphs' only creation; other ones sprang up in the gardens surrounding the city, involving the development and populating of the Cordoban Plain (*fahs*) which became invaded by suburbs, cemeteries, and gardens.

However, the most famous of all was Madinat az-Zahra', founded in 936 for one of 'Abd ar-Rahman III's favourites whose name it bears. Situated 5 kilometres north-west of Cordoba, it was a princely and administrative residence, the centre of the civil service (*dawawin*) and was protected by Slav guards. Here too can be seen the same desire to keep a capital under permanent control, while remaining far enough away from it to avoid the risk, inherent in an ever-denser population, of riots such as the 'suburb' suffered in the ninth century. The building of Madinat az-Zahra' was a major operation which took decades to complete and employed 10,000 workmen. Slabs of marble were imported from Carthage and Sfax, where they were removed from ancient sites. The city had such flourishing markets that any merchant wishing to set up trade there had to pay a tax of 400 dirhems.

In 978—979, the *hajib* al-Mansur, a chamberlain who seized power to found a dynasty of Mayors of the palace, the 'Amirids, decided to build a new capital to symbolize his newly gained power. He left his residence at al-'Amiriyya, 'the Amirid', and established himself to the east of Cordoba, in Madinat az-Zahira, the 'City in Bloom' (from an adjective of which az-Zahra', the name of the favourite cited above, is as it were a superlative form). The new residence rapidly grew into a settlement which merged with Cordoba, and the name Madinat az-Zahira came to designate all the eastern suburbs of the capital.

As may be seen, the urban rhythm of Cordoba's growth was intense — a ring of suburbs, urban explosion followed by reabsorption. The city, the suburbs, and the adventitious towns of Madinat az-Zahra' and Madinat az-Zahira constituted a veritable urban region, a 'Greater Cordoba' containing about 500,000 souls, which would be a considerable figure in the East at that period. Paris, by far the largest city in Western Christendom, still had no more than 200,000 to 300,000 inhabitants even in the fourteenth century.

Finally we must look at Sicily, where Palermo, as Muslim travellers quite rightly observe, presents the same type of evolution as Cordoba. In the centre was the old part, the 'old palace' (al-Qasr al-qadim, *Cassaro vecchio*), ringed by modern suburbs. According to Ibn Hawqal, writing in the tenth century, the Qasr al-qadim, surrounded by a stone wall with nine gates, contained the great mosque, the main market-place, and the residences of the wealthy merchants. Round this were four districts. Khalisa, 'the White One' or 'the Pure One', was the princely and administrative city, protected by a wall with four gates and containing the palace, the administrative buildings, the arsenal, and the gardens, in later times the residence of the Norman kings. Next was the Saqaliba district, which was the biggest, and was populated, as is clear from its name, by Slav slaves. It contained the commercial port and its quays, without a protective wall but with a broad sea-front. Then came the district known as the 'Ibn Siqlab Mosque area', also of considerable extent and stretching out into the countryside with its gardens and mills turning beside streams: a garden suburb (*fahs*) which supplied the city with food. Finally there was the 'New district', al-Jadid, whose very name points to the size of this urban area.

Some interesting details about Palermo are related by the monk Theodosius who was taken prisoner at the fall of Syracuse in 878 and was held in captivity in Palermo. He gives us a good idea of the teeming masses in a Muslim city: "[It is] a very famous, very populous city, which has an enormous population of natives and foreigners. It seems as though the entire Saracen race has poured into it. From east to west, from the north to the sea, the city could not cope any more with the number of its new inhabitants. So they started to build houses outside its walls, and there sprang up close by the city several others just as prosperous, and also surrounded by walls."

We have seen the Muslim city in the process of expansion, from one end of Islam to the other. We must now examine the kind of work done there, the kind of activities engaged in, and the social upheavals which resulted.

CHAPTER 7

Social movements and the organization of labour

Social life and social evolution in cities are governed by two major factors; on the one hand the influx of gold and the increase in money circulation, on the other hand the acceleration of urban rhythm and the resultant production of consumer goods. The diversification of methods of payment, the intensive minting of currencies and their more rapid circulation, the extension of credit and of banking operations, the consumer demand resulting from the development of the great metropolises, all led to a speeding up of commercial activity, a revival of agricultural and craft production, a drop in the value of precious metals and a long-term rise in prices, maintained by a constant influx of money metals greater than the increase in volume of production, despite the progress achieved in this latter area.

This rise in prices benefited almost exclusively the merchant class and court circles. The concentration of wealth in the hands of the merchants encouraged them to reinvest it, to conclude more and more profitable business deals, while court circles, by means of taxation and their banker agents, drained away a considerable part of the new wealth and lived in unbelievable luxury. The prosperity of the merchant class as exemplified in the urban villa, and the luxury of the court milieu symbolized by the royal residence, were the mainstay of the material civilization of the cities and, by means of patronage, the mainstay of civilization itself.

At the same time the great mass of the people grew poorer, because their wages failed to keep up with rising prices, there being a constantly available labour force. And so the over-all problem of rising prices and prosperity was accompanied by subsidiary problems resulting from the unequal distribution of profit and interest among the different classes.

The urban invasion of the countryside resulted in the break-up of the close domanial structure. Wealth began to be expressed in chattels instead of real estate. Financial distress and a loss of power hit the local aristocracy, who were landed proprietors. This disintegration of the domanial structure brought with it social upheaval: the uprisings of the humbler country-folk matched the slave and plebeian uprisings in the cities. All these social movements were sporadic at first and then fused into one enormous collective movement uniting all rebels, whether slave or freedman, town-dweller or peasant; this 'Qarmat movement' rocked the entire Muslim World in the tenth century and led to a new way of organizing labour — the guilds.

The merchant class and the court

The only people to derive any benefit from the discrepancy in the distribution of wealth were the merchants, as we learn from the Pseudo-Denys of Tell Mahre, writing in the second half of the eighth century. Indeed, the activities of these merchants formed the spearhead of the economic expansion. The Levantine World has a long tradition of showing initiative in commerce. Now it pooled capital resources and founded trading and banking companies. The merchant-cum-contractor founded industries, provided work, supplied the raw materials, advanced the money, and undertook to find an outlet for the products. He was adventurous, he struck out into foreign lands and reached the Sudan, where he traded gold for salt and trinkets, loading his camels to capacity. He reached the Indian Ocean too, where, like Sindbad the Sailor, he bartered his wares over and over again. Rich cargoes putting in at Basra meant fat profits; for example the cargo of a ship coming from China was reckoned at 500,000 dinars. In the area of the Russian rivers, slaves constituted the merchandise which sold at the highest profit in the market-places of the Muslim East. This was the era when fortunes were quickly made, and trading subsidiaries sprang up in vast numbers along the routes of the known world. Hence the rise of the merchant class, embodied in the typical prosperous Muslim merchant, who might equally well be a Jew or a Christian.

Such a merchant could call on great capital reserves, either his own or his family's, and, in partnership with other merchants, he launched trading concerns based on the credit which all the participants guaranteed each other. Capital was constantly ploughed back into ever more ambitious undertakings, in the hectic world of business as reflected in the Hebrew documents of the Geniza of Old Cairo. We have, for example, a letter from a Jewish merchant living in Syria, who seems from his appellation 'al-Maghribi' to have been born in North Africa. This letter, sent early in the eleventh century from Jerusalem to Cairo by Farama, refers to the arrival of ships in Sicily and asks for news of a Spanish ship and, indeed, of any other ships putting in at Alexandria. The writer hopes his correspondents in Kairouan and Tyre will reply promptly. Another document written in the mid tenth century shows the organization of a trading firm directed by a family group. The parent firm is at Fustat and is run by the head of the family and his eldest son; while the younger son is in charge of the Aden branch, and has already made two journeys to India which included trips to Colombo in Ceylon. The maternal uncle of these young men was sent to represent the firm in India and he died there.

The great merchant was an educated man, and we may well imagine him surrounded by his ledgers, his correspondence, and his letters of credit. There are, moreover, technical treatises still in existence which were explicitly intended for civil servants, but the contents of which reveal a practical general culture suitable for businessmen and designed for them. Abu'l-Wafa' (940–997), Persian in origin but living in Khurasan and Baghdad, wrote a book of popular arithmetic "on what is necessary for scribes and prefects to know about arithmetical science". These merchants also knew the art of cipher and secret messages. They familiarized themselves with Indian numerals, which we call 'Arabic', based on nine signs and a nought. From the mid ninth century onwards this system appears in scientific treatises, then it moved from scholarly circles to commerical ones. The rich merchant often possessed real culture along with this practical knowledge, and indeed liked to air his religious erudition and to write poetry. In Spain in the early eleventh century the brother of the poet Ibn al-Labbana also wrote poetry, but he did not earn his living at it because he was a merchant. On the other hand the poet Abu Bakr Ibn 'Abd al-'Aziz, when he made a considerable sum of money by one of his writings, settled in Almeria and embarked on a prosperous business career.

The great merchant played the part of patron and benefactor by giving alms and affording help to the poorer people in the community. He contributed towards the embellishment of places of worship – mosques, synagogues, or churches – and pious foundations, a term which in Islam included any structure erected for the good of the people, such as schools or fountains. The merchant offered food and shelter to students and teachers, and he entertained people on pilgrimages. The wealthy merchants of the Jewish communities in Alexandria and Cairo bought back their co-religionists who had been captured by Muslim pirates, for a sum of thirty-three and one-third dinars per man, the price current throughout the Mediterranean, which constituted a kind of 'personal insurance' for all merchants when travelling.

The merchant lived on a grandiose scale in his stately townhouse, surrounded by a host of slaves and hangers-on, in the midst of his collections of books, travel souvenirs, and rare ornaments. His social rank, which was high, made him a person of considerable importance. For example, rich merchants suspected of being involved in a rebellion were arrested but entertained at the governor's table. Occasionally they had access to the councils of State. The typical *ghahbadh*, the powerful official banker in touch with the court, lending money to the caliph and to other key figures, was a privileged example of these relations. But there were others, for example suppliers to the palace, particularly of valuable merchandise, and tax-farmers. Jewish court bankers took charge of the money yielded by the al-Ahwaz tax, put it to work immediately in their vast sugar or fabric businesses, and gave the caliph promissory notes which could be drawn on their firms in Baghdad. In this way the *ghahbadhs* ensured the mobility of funds by a series of complex book-keeping entries between the provinces and the caliph's Treasury.

The highest rung on the merchant's ladder was the official rank of Vizier, which involved the control of the State finances. The Vizier enjoyed a most exalted position and wielded great influence, but some of them also suffered sudden disgrace, a resounding fall from power accompanied by the confiscation of their property, which put an end to their career. A famous example can be found in Cairo at the beginning of the reign of the Fatimid al-Mustansir (1036—1094). The Tustari brothers of Ahwaz, Jewish bankers and dealers in objects of value from the Indian Ocean and China, had obtained for the caliph az-Zahir (1021—1036) a beautiful Sudanese slave-girl. She gave birth to the future caliph al-Mustansir and after az-Zahir's death she ruled over Egypt during her son's minority with the help of her former masters. The 'reign' of the Tustari brothers lasted twelve years (1036—1048) and was finally ended by the Vizier, who was also Jewish in origin but had since become converted to Islam. Though he owed his position to the efforts of the Tustari brothers he had them assassinated by the Turkish guard. The Queen Mother (al-Walida) decided to avenge their death, and nine months later the Vizier was executed in his turn.

This is a particularly striking example, but by no means the only one. There are many more which would illustrate the wealth and power of this class of very powerful merchants, people of influence involved in court intrigue and forming a link between the palace milieu and the wealthy city circles. They were, together with the scribes of the civil service and the court, the main agents of economic activity in the Muslim World, the mainstay and the vehicle of its most brilliant civilization, from the eighth to the eleventh centuries.

The humbler folk in town and country

The economic centre of the city was the market, the *suq* with its own traditional population of craftsmen, labourers both free and slave, hawkers, and street-porters. As their means of subsistence grew more and more precarious this element of the population grew more and more unruly, and riots became frequent.

The country was the retreat of small landowners who had been ruined, and of poverty-stricken day-labourers. The rich usurers in the city turned them off their land by investing in real estate part of the fat profits they made in business. Year by year the town tightened its hold over the country. Moreover the rural populations were weighed down by the taxes which grew in proportion with the fall in the purchasing power of the currency, but were nevertheless rigidly insisted upon by the red-tape bureaucracy of this mighty centralized Empire. A detailed picture of the grinding poverty of the rural areas as regards Upper Mesopotamia and Syria is to be found in Christian sources (Nestorian and Jacobite), in Syriac chronicles of the ninth and tenth centuries, and in Egyptian papyri. The only recourse open was to run away from the villages. Everywhere there were refugees, displaced persons wandering aimlessly in an attempt to evade the taxes and their urban creditors, and gradually slipping into brigandage.

Disturbances became endemic in the rural areas. The government took steps to quell them in the hopes of restoring stability, collecting its taxes, and putting the land under cultivation. In Egypt, a special bureau was set up to trace fugitives and a compulsory identity card was introduced. People of substance were given a document bearing a stamp printed on it, but the lower orders had an identity mark on the skin of their arm or hand, or else a lead identity disc hung round their neck.

The extreme poverty of the humbler folk in town and country explains the sporadic existence of social movements imbued with magico-religious elements from the East and with messianism, fervent and constant expectation of the Mahdi (the word means 'he who is guided', or 'God's Inspired one'). These movements caused unrest in three different social classes: the slaves, the peasants, and the common folk in the towns.

In the case of the peasants there was a revival of older Iranian tendencies towards agrarian egalitarianism which had already under the Sassanids at the close of the fifth century inspired the Mazdakite movement which was linked socially with economic expansion and urban development. In the eighth and ninth centuries, Iran and Mesopotamia became the theatre of rebellions led by self-styled prophets continuing Mazdakite ideas, in particular Sunbadh the Magus (754—755) and Ustadhasis (766—769), both of whom inspired and led movements fed by the resentment provoked by the assassination of Abu Muslim, the apostle of the Abbasid-'Alid movement in its early stages. Later, in 774—775, there occurred a revolt in Armenia brought about by extortionate taxation and grinding poverty; then came the movement, led by the 'veiled Prophet' al-Muqanna' in Khurasan in 777—780. This was followed by a disturbance by the Batiniyya of Jurjan, the area at the southeastern end of the Caspian, where in 782—783 the 'Red standards' sect prevailed. About 800, in the reign of Harun ar-Rashid, the Khurramiya movement in Khurasan led to Babek's great revolt (816—838), which was the most serious of all.

Babek, invoking all previous social and religious claims, began stirring up the tribes in Azerbaijan. From his mountain fortress, where he wielded control and where he could regularly repair his shattered forces, he sent his men further and further afield, to Armenia in the west, Khurasan in the east, and Iraq in the south. In this way he disrupted the whole of Iran and part of Mesopotamia, pillaging caravans, hampering trade, and immobilizing several armies of Turkish mercenaries sent to fight him. In the end his fortress was captured and destroyed, and he was taken prisoner and handed over to the caliph al-Mu'tasim, who subjected him to a torture which matched in refinement the terrors he had caused. His hands and feet were cut off; he was paraded through Baghdad on an elephant bearing a placard with a list of his crimes; he was sewn into a fresh bullock skin with the horns on the level of his ears to ensure that his head was gradually compressed as the skin dried out; and he was strung up on the gibbet in this state until he died.

Another important peasant movement was the revolt of the

Zotts of Lower Mesopotamia in the reign of al-Ma'mun (813–833). These Zotts (Djatts or Tziganes) were Indians who came originally from the Lower Indus but had been deported to the swampy regions of Lower Mesopotamia, where in a wet reedy area they engaged in the breeding of buffalo. Here they endured grinding poverty until finally they revolted. Theirs was a protest of the outcasts of society, and they were soon joined by groups of runaway slaves. But they were defeated and then deported to the Byzantine frontiers, to northern Syria and the marshes of the Orontes, from where they moved on to Anatolia, then to the Balkans, and finally to Bohemia.

The first important slave uprising took place in 770, when the black labour force in the plantations and mines rebelled. But it was above all in 868 that these same black populations, this time in Lower Mesopotamia, began a revolt and fled into the swamps of the Lower Euphrates — the scene of the Zott uprising thirty years earlier — under the leadership of a Persian who assumed the title 'Sahib az-Zanj', 'Master of the Zanj'; he became known as 'the Rascal' ('al-Khabith'). He claimed descent from 'Ali and said he adhered to Mazdakite beliefs. Constantly at the head of his troops, he resisted the Caliphate for some fifteen years, until 883, causing appalling devastation. These rebellious slaves were joined by fresh fugitives. They succeeded in launching surprise attacks on the wealthy cities of the Persian Gulf and Lower Mesopotamia — Ubulla, Ahwaz, Basra, Wasit — plundering and laying them waste and slaughtering their inhabitants. They paralysed all trade between Baghdad and the Persian Gulf. The caliph's troops were held at bay not only by the fighting spirit of the rebels but also by the difficult terrain. In the end the caliph's brother, al-Muwaffaq, took over the operation and gradually drove the Zanj into a corner of the marshy region. After enduring a protracted siege in their last fortress, the leaders of the movement and their associates were taken prisoner and put to death.

Finally, the common people in the towns, whose poverty was, if possible, even worse than that of those in the country, were in a constant state of unrest. For instance, in Baghdad after the death of Harun ar-Rashid his succession was disputed by his two sons.

Disturbances resulted in the poverty-stricken people briefly gaining control of the city. This was known as 'the Revolt of the Naked'. In the reign of al-Ma'mun (813–833) the Coptic craftsmen of the Egyptian Delta revolted. This was a genuine social insurrection, in an area of luxury textile industries distributed among very many workshops in a series of small towns. Here too the movement spread and became concentrated in a marshy area, namely the marshes of the Delta, or more precisely Lake Bushtum. The situation was finally judged serious enough to warrant the dispatch of troops and the arrival of the caliph in person. The defeated rebels were deported in their thousands and sold as slaves in Syria and Mesopotamia. This shift of population also involved the transfer of certain Egyptian weaving techniques. The former rebels were also used later to fight the Zotts, because of their experience of warfare in swampy terrain.

And so, in the eighth and ninth centuries there occurred peasant uprisings inspired by the older Iranian egalitarianism, slave rebellions, and urban insurrections. In the tenth century these disorganized, aimless, heterogeneous movements fused into one great homogeneous uprising known as the Qarmat movement, which became in its early stages confused with the Fatimid movement and finally stretched from Iran and the Persian Gulf to Egypt and North Africa, with ramifications as far as Spain. The entire Muslim World was rocked by it.

Qarmatism was primarily the start of a new and different organization of labour by means of guilds. These were trade guilds with a social content and an initiatory character, differing profoundly from the *ministeria* of the Late Roman Empire and the Byzantine Empire. The *ministerium* (or *collegium*) of the Late Roman Empire was a State organization, an association of craftsmen controlled by State officials. This kind of institution had been adopted by the Byzantines in the form of *somata* or 'bodies', and also by the Sassanids. After the Muslim conquests the system had persisted and the governor and his agents undertook the control of the markets and the surveillance of the workshops. The picture changes in the tenth century. The new-style guild ceased to be an official organization, in fact it was sometimes in conflict with authority. From now on it was a close-knit association, a brotherhood in fact, with initiation rites, secret oaths, elected leaders known as 'masters', councils composed of these leaders, and a doctrine with both mystical and social elements.

From the outset, therefore, the Qarmat movement was social, mystical, and political in nature. Its doctrine, which was very syncretic and forged in the melting-pot of the Muslim World, contained elements from 'Alid (Shi'ite) Islam, heretical tendencies, Neoplatonism, Manichaeism, Mazdakism, and Babek-type egalitarianism. Qarmatism, with its artisan and commercial background, rested on a secret organization with various degrees of initiation and secret emissaries entrusted with the task of preparing for the coming of the 'hidden Imam', the Mahdi, and it also rested on an inter-confessional organization involving Christians, Jews, Mazdaans, and heretics. Uniting as it did the tendency to protest, so typical of the ninth and tenth centuries, which coincided with a point of extreme commercial, industrial, and urban development, and also grouping together in a single movement strikes, social crises, and revolts, Qarmatism developed a doctrine of its own insisting on individual liberty, the rejection of the strict law of Islam, and the affirmation of the relative nature of every system of human relationships.

In the political and temporal sphere, the movement resulted, in the tenth century, in the Fatimid Caliphate, whose power or doctrine travelled from Ifriqiya and Sicily to Egypt, Syria, and western Arabia, and on the other hand it led to the establishment of a Qarmat power in the countries near the Persian Gulf, namely eastern Arabia, Lower Mesopotamia, and the Iranian coast. In the social and spiritual realm, Qarmatism put forward a new model of Islamic brotherhood which emerged during the tenth century, first of all in regions controlled by the Fatimids and the Qarmats, and has kept some of its essential features in the Muslim World right to the present day.

It is, unfortunately, difficult to study in depth the history of such a secret movement which was so distrustful of written records and preferred oral information and initiation. A further difficulty is presented by the allusive and symbolic character of

Qarmat literature, so far as we can judge by what has come down to us. One fact at least is certain: the interest taken by the writers of this sect in the artisan classes and the world of work in general, its techniques and its organization — they extol the nobility of manual labour.

In the Sunni countries, non-Fatimid and non-Qarmat, the guilds were persecuted or at best kept under close scrutiny, subjected to innumerable restrictions which perpetuated a typical state of mistrust of authority, a state scarcely improved by the introduction of one or two modifications into attitude or ritual under the influence of new Qarmat guilds. In Fatimid countries, by contrast, the guilds enjoyed great prosperity and were in fact recognized by the State. Soon after the foundation of Cairo in 970 one of these guilds, the Guild of the Teachers and Students of the University of al-Azhar (inaugurated in 972) enjoyed great success. This demonstrates the importance accorded in Qarmat theory to knowledge and teaching, which is also confirmed by a famous encyclopedia, *The Epistles of the Brothers of Sincerity*, in which can be clearly seen the desire to honour every kind of work, whether intellectual or manual. And so the Qarmat movement flourished in Fatimid Egypt and contributed to the industrial and commercial development of the country, which, incidentally, served its purpose too, enabling it to spread to the Red Sea and the Indian Ocean. Later it was checked, at least in Egypt, by the Sunni Saladin who, in 1171, abruptly stripped the guilds of their privileges.

The inter-confessional nature of the guilds was completely different from attitudes in the West. It reminds us that the East stood for cosmopolitanism, openness, mingling, and syncretism, whereas the West was endogamous and hermetic. In Eastern guilds Jews, Christians, and Muslims were admitted on equal terms. Indeed, in some of them non-Muslims predominated, particularly goldsmiths, dealers in precious metals, and bankers, who tended to be mainly Jewish. Most of the doctors were Christians or Jews.

* * *

In conclusion I must, yet again, stress the link between the sudden economic development of the Muslim World, with its resultant social tensions, and the growth of this new guild movement. Of its many features including initiation rites, brotherly solidarity, oath, elected leaders, mystic and social doctrine, the last is understandably much the most important. It is what differentiates th : Muslim brotherhood from former organizations such as the *collegia* of the Late Roman Empire, the Byzantine *somata*, the trade associations of Sassanid Persia, which were all official and State-inspired, mere groups of workers kept under close scrutiny by the imperial civil servants, and subjected to a ruling dictated from above.

However, these new Muslim guilds were not completely free from traces of former models. On the contrary, it is precisely these Eastern survivals merged and recast so as to form a new synthesis which, as has been said, differentiated the tenth-century Muslim guild from the Western guilds of the eleventh and twelfth centuries. The latter did, admittedly, take up several features of the Eastern corporations but adapted them to a different setting which was endogamous and in some respects still rural. And finally we must observe the importance of the heterodox movements at the origin of the Muslim guilds, which may be compared with the Patarines in Italy in the eleventh century or the Albigenses in the Aquitaine Basin, who were, like the Qarmats, preoccupied with religious, economic, and mystico-social matters all at once. And it will come as no surprise to encounter in the Patarines and the Albigenses some Eastern, Manichaean elements, since both northern Italy and Aquitaine lay at the end of the great trade routes which linked the East and the West.

PART III

THE DYNAMICS OF TRADE

CHAPTER 8

Production and trading commodities

The main feature of the economic climate in which the Muslim World saw its production and output develop, was consumer demand. This was not only current consumption by the great urban areas, whose demands were ever more exacting both in quantity and quality because of the higher standard of living, but also the consumption of luxury goods arising from the demand of court circles and the wealthier sections of the population.

At this point we must draw up a production map which will give clearly a localized list of trading commodities. At the end of this inquiry, the map we have drawn will be no mere statement of these products, but will also highlight a set of problems. The study of each sector of production in relation to the centres of consumer demand will make it possible to differentiate products consumed on the spot from those which were exported some distance, i.e. trading commodities. In this way we can evaluate the evolution of needs, of the form and strength of the demand from major centres at various points in their history: creation, development, growth, and decline.

The ultimate aim is a geography of production which is dynamic both spatially (problems of supply) and temporally (problems of the variety of consumer demand). The study of productivity in major groupings of products will form the preliminary sketch for a drawing to show the lines of force of the commercial network, controlled by data on physical or human geography. In this way we shall study food crops, dairy produce, wood and the products of the forest, metals and weapons, textiles and cloths, the products of stone and soil, the products of the sea, the materials needed for writing such as papyrus, parchment, and paper, medicinal products, and finally slaves.

Food plants

The diet of sedentary populations in the East and the Mediterranean area was mainly vegetarian. It was based on cereals (flours, breads, porridge, and various pastas), on the olive tree, the oil from which made the perfect cooking fat, on vegetables and fruit, particularly grapes which also yielded wine, specific to the Ancient World in and around the Mediterranean, and on the date-palm, which was the staple diet of oasis-dwellers.

The diet of the nomad tribes of central Asia, Iran, Arabia, and the Sahara depended, on the other hand, on the produce of their flocks, i.e. meat, milk, cheese, etc. Their cooking fat was animal fat or butter.

The study of eating habits and diets, which is an important aspect, and indeed a motive force, of economic history, must go hand in hand with an examination of the movement of plants. The older crops of the Mediterranean Basin were predominantly those which grew in dry soil: cereals (corn, barley), olive trees, vines. The newer crops which were imported into the region all depended on irrigation: rice, sugar-cane, orange trees, date-palms, and likewise plants such as cotton or indigo needed for industry. The introduction of these new crops, whether tropical or subtropical, was of course connected with the extension of irrigated zones and the progress of technology. This transference of crops was made possible, or at least intensified, by the creation of the Muslim World. By uniting the area round the Indian Ocean with the Mediterranean area it brought into contact with each other two zones producing complementary crops. Henceforward the major trade routes which were used to exchange one kind of produce for another were also used to transfer crops. The study of the points in time at which this happened, the routes taken, the progressive area they covered, the resulting enrichment of the vegetation landscape, is an essential chapter of economic history.

Consumer demand was dominated by the need of major centres for food crops. This fact is of fundamental importance, both in cause and effect. One notable consequence was the growing of market-garden produce round cities in the form of a garden suburb (*fahs*). It is also worth noting that certain crops occurred in areas where the physical conditions did not favour their growth, and where people were satisfied with slightly inferior produce so long as it was easily available. This happened in the West, where the vine was grown in the north of France and in northern Europe even beyond its 'natural' limit. Examples of this abound in the Muslim World: sugar-cane in northern Spain, cotton in some areas of North Africa, vines in the monasteries of Upper Egypt, transplanted there for religious reasons. But alongside these commodities there were others, world-famous specialities, which, thanks to the development of large-scale trade, were exported to areas where they arrived in perfect condition. Travellers and geographers, for instance, refer to 'well-known products exported to every country'. We may mention dates from the Jerid, nuts from Tebessa, figs and currants from Malaga, plums and conserves from Damascus.

Cereals, particularly corn and barley, had been grown in the Mediterranean for a very long time. Their production was based on three extensive areas, the traditional 'granaries' of the Ancient World. Egypt was densely populated and therefore a heavy consumer country, but she still had enormous exportable surpluses. These took the form of the *annona* dispatched successively to Rome, Constantinople, Mecca, Medina, and Damascus. The corn trade was one of the most important items in Egypt's exports. It went by caravan to the oases in Libya and the eastern Sahara and to Nubia, or by boat to Cyrenaica, the Arabian ports of the Red Sea, Aden and the Persian Gulf, Oman, Bahrain, and Basra, whence it reached Baghdad. Syria exported grain by means of caravans to the Arabian interior and, via the bend in the

Euphrates, to Mesopotamia, in the form of sacks of flour loaded on to boats which sailed down the river to Baghdad and the other cities of Iraq. And so, what with the grain arriving from Egypt after sailing round Arabia, and the flour from Syria coming down the Euphrates and the Nahr 'Isa, we find yet again, Baghdad at the centre of a vast trade in solid foods. The other granary was North Africa, mainly Ifriqiya, particularly the Medjerda Plain; Béja sent a daily consignment to Kairouan and Tunis of 1,000 camel-loads of cereals. But corn and barley were also found in the central and western Maghreb, in the Constantine and Setif areas, on the Atlantic coast, and on the high Moroccan plains. This North African corn was exported by boat to Spain and Sicily and by caravan to Sijilmasa, the western Sahara, and the Sudan. The Berber caravaneers later introduced into the Sudanese Sahel between the tenth and eleventh centuries the method of growing corn by irrigation during the dry season.

Meanwhile sorghum, a cereal grown originally in black Africa, travelled in the opposite direction, northwards into Nubia and Upper Egypt, the Libyan oases and Cyrenaica, parts of the Algerian Tell, and southern Morocco.

Rice, the major Asiatic cereal, spread to the Mediterranean Basin at this period, from India and Lower Mesopotamia, where it was already known before the Christian era. From Lower Mesopotamia it spread to all the places in the Muslim Mediterranean where conditions favoured its growth, namely hot areas with low swampy or irrigated soil. For instance, it grew in the Ghor (Ghawr) Depression, i.e. on the banks of the Dead Sea and the Jordan, in Fayyum and the Egyptian oases, in southern Morocco (as-Sus al-Aqsa), by means of irrigation, and especially in southern Spain, where the Guadalqivir and the *huertas* in the Valencia region ensured a generous crop. Thus, to the cereals grown for so long in the Roman Mediterranean, the Muslim World added sorghum from the South and rice from the East.

Another basic source of food was the olive tree, the specifically Mediterranean tree in that it covers an area corresponding to that of the Mediterranean climate itself. There were many great centres of production and export of oil. Ifriqiya and the Tunisian Sahel formed 'the forest of olive trees', a magnificent adornment inherited from the Roman era and persisting until it was laid waste in the eleventh century. Sfax was the major exporting port — 'the oil port', as Ibn Hawqal calls it — and it sent oil to Egypt where no olive trees grew, to Sicily, Italy, Byzantium, and the central Maghreb. Syria could boast olive trees from southern Palestine to the Antioch region. She was a major exporting country and delivered oil by caravan to Egypt and Arabia, and, via the bend in the Euphrates, to Mesopotamia. Spain exported to the western Maghreb oil from the Guadalqivir area, particularly from Aljarafe (ash-Sharaf) to the north-east of Seville. The western Maghreb, incidentally, witnessed the spread of the olive tree in the regions of Fez and Meknes, known as 'Meknes of the olive trees', where it tended to supersede the argan tree. In the central Maghreb, the Kabylia Mountains reached the stage of massive output, but only for local consumption. Egypt, which does not enjoy a Mediterranean climate, and did not grow olive trees, bought oil from Syria and Ifriqiya, or else consumed oil produced locally from horse-radish, sesame, rape, colza, lettuce seed, colocasia, linseed, and the castor-oil plant. Before we leave the olive tree we must remember that it supplied industries depending on oil, namely soaps and bath oils, on which perfumes are based. Here too the major centres of manufacture and export were Syria and Ifriqiya.

Like the olive tree, the vine was a very old Mediterranean crop which had spread originally from Syria, where it was widely used in religious ritual. Islam forbade the drinking of wine, and one or two particularly pious caliphs such as al-Hakam II of Cordoba and the Fatimid al-Hakim, threatened to uproot all the vines. But practice proved more tolerant than theory, so that the drinking of wine remained a widespread habit throughout the Muslim World, and the courts of the caliphs often rang to the sound of Bacchic verse. The vine grew all over the lands of the Mediterranean but the important areas producing and also exporting famous vintages were Palestine with its famous Ascalon wine, northern Syria, where Bayt-Ras (Chalybonis) had been known since ancient times, the Nile Delta with its Damietta and Maryut wines, the Ifriqiyan Sahel and finally southern Spain: Malaga, Priego, and the wine of

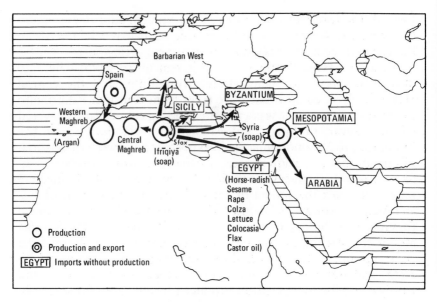

Fig. 17. The trade in olive oil in the Muslim Mediterranean.

Jerez (sherry), which was obtained from stock brought in from Shiraz in Persia. The prize wine-list, so obligingly given us by Muslim writers, proves that wine-growing was still appreciated despite its condemnation by the Koran, and this situation did not change until, in the eleventh century, Islam changed its image. The countries listed above also produced quantities of currants: Damascus and Hebron in Syria-Palestine, Esne in Upper Egypt, and Malaga in Spain.

The date-palm belonged originally to the part of Mesopotamia near the Persian Gulf where conditions were most favourable to it. Before the Muslim conquests it had already reached southern Syria, Egypt, and southern Tunisia. With the conquests it spread still further into northern Syria, Cilicia in particular (with the palm groves of Malatya and 'Ayn Zarba), to Spain (Elche, Jaen), and above all into the western Sahara, where the increase in camel-rearing, well-boring, and palm-growing were interconnected and were the essential factors in the colonization of the desert. The most important areas where dates were grown and exported were the shores of the Persian Gulf, southern Tunisia, and southern Algeria: al-Jerid, 'the date country', and the Biskra region, the Zab.

Sugar-cane was introduced from India into Sassanid Meso-potamia under Chosroes I Anushirwan (531–579). Susiana, or Khuzistan, became a major plantation centre, the main supplier for the entire Muslim East. There was already, at this early date, a link between sugar-cane plantations and a black-slave labour force provided by Negroes imported from the east coast of Africa. The growing of sugar-cane then spread from Susiana to the Mediterra-nean Basin during the Muslim era. In Egypt, from the close of the eighth century, all the most fertile soil was planted with sugar-cane. From there sugar-cane spread to Syria, southern Morocco (the Oued Sus region), the south coast of Spain, the Ebro Valley, and Sicily. But Egypt remained the major Mediterranean centre in the production and export of sugar and she herself consumed enormous quantities of it, at least at the court of the Fatimids: on festal occasions the trees were covered with tiny sugar figures, which shows what progress had been made in its manufacture. The area was famous for sweetmeats, confectionery, pastries, and pre-serves; the last were one of the key exports from Damascus, and it must be remembered that 'desserts' are Oriental in origin. Part of this manufactured sugar reached Byzantium and the West; the earliest mention of a consignment of *sukkar* (*zucchero*) reaching Venice is dated 996.

To sum up, vegetables and fruit were grown more and more in the garden suburbs which had developed round cities, by methods of irrigation which were constantly being improved, and a model of which might be seen in Spain in the *huertas* of the Levante. At this period artichokes, spinach, shalotts, bananas, citrons, lemons, and oranges, became widely known in the Mediterranean. The orange tree was introduced into Syria from Mesopotamia in 943; then it is mentioned about 970 in Sicily and in southern Morocco; at the end of the tenth century it had also reached Malaga and the Vega de Granada; by 1047 it was found in Egypt on the terraces of houses, set in boxes so as to form orangeries; by 1068 it was growing in Cyrenaica. And so we have the Mediterranean garden, a garden-oasis, with its irrigation channels, its vegetables, and its typical fruit trees. It is utterly different from the garden of antiquity which had already acquired the carrot, the cherry, the peach, and the apricot during the Hellenistic period. Later on this Mediterranean garden was to be further diversified by new plants from America: beans, tomatoes, potatoes, maize, and prickly pear

It is clear that the eighth and ninth centuries taken as a whole constituted an important stage in the history of food crops, both by virtue of the introduction of new species and by virtue of the development of growing techniques.

Stock-rearing

A distinction must, of course, be made between sedentary stock-rearing which used animals for domestic purposes, and nomad stock-rearing, which was far more important because of the various uses to which the animals were put. They were used for food in the shape of meat, fat, butter, milk, and cream; they also provided industrial raw materials such as wool and leather; and they were used as transport. The beast of burden, whether horse, camel, mule, or donkey, was the basis of the caravan (Persian *karvan*; Arabic *qafila*), a long string of transport animals weaving a network of overland trade routes. Finally, they were used as a source of energy when they operated hydraulic machines used in irrigation (*norias*).

The Muslim World saw the development of techniques in animal management, particularly equestrian techniques, under the influence of the civilizations of central Asia: stirrups, trappings, harnessing collar, polo (*cawgan*), and tattoos. The economic, social, and cultural implications of techniques in rearing and managing animals were enormous, hence the necessity of studying the zones of stock-breeding, their extent, their proliferation, and the transfer of animal species.

The camel came originally from two major centres; firstly, central Asia, the home of the camel with two humps known as the

'Bactrian', the region of the two great rivers, Oxus and Amu Darya; secondly, Arabia, more specifically central Arabia, the high grazing lands of the Nejd, 'the mother of camels', the home of the one-humped dromedary. Between the eighth and eleventh centuries the main areas of camel-rearing were central Asia, Iran, and Mesopotamia on the one hand, and Arabia (Nejd, Oman, Hadramawt, Hijaz) and Ethiopia and Nubia on the other, which had, particularly in Bedja territory, desert landscapes similar to those in Arabia, and finally the oases of the western Sahara. The camel-rearing area also extended to northern Syria, Asia Minor, the Ponto-Caspian Steppes of southern Russia, Spain, and the Sudan. Techniques of selection and cross-breeding became more varied, as in the great herds of Sequiet al-Hamra, yielding the powerful, slow pack-animal as well as the swift mount used to carry news.

There were four main breeds of horse. The Turco-Mongol horse of central Asia was small, thickset and stocky, sturdy, strong, and reliable, and was used as the cavalry in the great Asiatic invasions. This breed was found as far east as northern China and as far west as the steppes of eastern and central Europe. The Iranian horse was large and powerful, and could carry a warrior clad in heavy

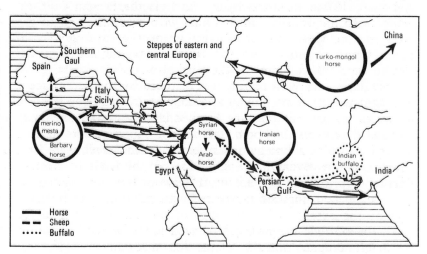

Fig. 18. Transfers and introductions of animals in the Muslim World.

armour, the *iswar* (plural *asawira*; Persian *asvar*, 'cataphract'). This breed was exported in quantities; it reached India via the Persian Gulf, and the dealers in Iranian horses were the beginnings of Mahratta cavalry. The barb, i.e. Barbary (Berber) horse, came from Numidia, more precisely from the high plateaux and the edge of the Sahara. It was quite small but very strong and vigorous. Since ancient times the horses of every country in the western Mediterranean had acquired more and more Barbary blood, particularly in Italy, Spain, and southern Gaul. The conquest of Spain and Sicily by troops of predominantly Berber stock strengthened this tendency, which culminated in the Andalusian horse or Spanish jennet, whose name (Spanish *jinete*) goes back to the Zanata, a large confederation of nomad Berber horsemen living on the high plateaux of the Maghreb. Finally, there was the Syrian breed of horse which resulted, as far back as Roman times, from the crossing of Barbary stallions, imported from northern Syria, with Iranian horses. These animals grazed on the winter pastures of the desert steppes (Badiyat ash-Sham), and in Muslim times they spread to the Nejd, a region of high pastures in central Arabia. The Arab thoroughbred was a perfect saddle-horse, delicately made, spirited, and swift. It was exported to the East via the Persian Gulf, together with the Iranian horses which went to India, and to the West, via the Mediterranean. Egypt became the meeting-point of the Syrian-Arab horse and the North African horse: later its cavalry was as much feared by the Mongols as the Crusaders.

This development in rearing was matched by the development of techniques, as is attested by a voluminous literature on the care of horses, and on farriery. The detailed classification of the qualities and defects of the horse — its illnesses, its paces, its coats — yielded a vast terminology and several methods which were later adopted in the Byzantine Empire and in the lands of Western Christendom, as may be seen by various words in our vocabulary.

An important question connected with the rearing of horses is that of the extent and availability of the plants they need for food, for example barley and lucerne. The steppes and fringes of the deserts provided natural grazing, but in regions under cultivation bearing heavy crops and laid out in gardens, artificial grazing had to be created by means of irrigated grassland. Lucerne, which came originally from Persia, spread to Mesopotamia, Egypt, and Spain, and in the other direction from central Asia into China.

Sheep were used by the nomads as food, and especially for wool, and so it is natural that the extent and progress of their rearing were bound up with the fortunes of the wool industry. England in the twelfth and thirteenth centuries offered the same phenomenon in that the large flocks attached to the English monasteries provided the raw materials for the Flemish cloth industry.

The Muslim World, during the period which concerns us, was the sole wool-producing area, if we take into account only a large output of superior quality. First and foremost was the 'sheep country', that is the high plateaux of North Africa, which produced a sheep with outstanding fleece, dense but fine and curly. This sheep, which became acclimatized in Spain when the Berbers entered the country, was known there, as we have seen, under the name of *merino*, either from the name of the Banu Marin, a Berber nomad tribe from the western Maghreb, or from the Arabic *marin*, 'gentle, soft, supple'. Not only did this breed of sheep reach Spain, but so also did the rearing methods peculiar to the Berbers of North Africa, which were communal practices used in mass rearing, in which the flock owned by the community was entrusted, when the time came to change pastures, to a head shepherd surrounded by helpers, all of whom were specialists and knew the good summer grazing land in the mountain regions. In this respect Spain had an outstanding organization which developed into the *mesta*, a pastoral institution which persisted in the country up to the twentieth century, with its privileges, and with its own routes, grazing lands, and jurisdiction. The terms of pastoral technique, in Castilian, Valencian, or Portuguese, are often Arabic in origin: *mesta* comes from *mashta; mostrenco*, 'with no known master', comes from *mushtarak*; and *alganame*, 'chief shepherd', comes from *al-Ghannam*. From the Muslim period onwards (eighth to eleventh centuries) there sprang up in certain places associations of shepherds and flock-owners — local *mestas*, in fact. It was, therefore, at this period that the general organization of the *mesta* began, which took definitive shape in the twelfth century with the

Reconquista. Clearly, when Spain embraced Christianity once more she merely developed, in this instance as in so many others, an earlier Muslim institution. The *merino* sheep and the *mesta* were the two basic Berber contributions to Spain.

The rearing of horned cattle was less important in the Muslim World because it requires a more humid climate and a richer vegetation. And so this kind of stock-rearing was only practised on the coastal plains of Morocco, in a few favourable spots in the Algerian Tell, and in Spain. It is interesting to note the arrival of the buffalo from India along with the gipsy Tzigane migrations. They came from the marshy regions of the Indus Delta, which is the type of ground the buffalo seeks out and finds most suited to his needs. When the Zotts, as we have seen, were deported in the eighth century to the swamps of Lower Mesopotamia they took their beasts with them. From there they moved into northern Syria, where their buffaloes became acclimatized to the swamps of the Orontes.

The over-all picture, then, is of the extension and improvement of stock-rearing. This brought many disadvantages: the destruction of crops and forests, particularly by shepherds who burnt them down so as to create new grazing ground, the impoverishment of the soil, and the devastation of young shoots. In Spain the abuses of the *mesta* were to ruin a considerable part of the country. The forests of the Muslim World were precarious, exposed as they were to such treatment, to say nothing of climatic conditions. In the Mediterranean and throughout the Muslim East they had reached the end of their natural life, having been reduced virtually to steppe tending more and more to desert. The problem of the abuse of stock-rearing obviously creates another problem of considerable importance, namely the abuse of the forest.

Timber and the products of the forest

The areas of genuine forest were very limited in the Muslim World. The forests on the southern shores of the Caspian Sea were the continuation eastward of the Pontic forest which ran from the northern coast of Asia Minor to the south coast of the Caspian and the Elburz Mountains. The forests of northern Syria, similarly, were a continuation of the forests on the edge of the Anatolian Plateau, which thus extended from the southern coast of Asia Minor to the Anti-Taurus and the Lebanon. There were one or two forests in Sicily, in the Maghreb, and in Spain, and that was all; apart from these wooded patches there was absolutely no woodland throughout Mesopotamia, Arabia, Palestine, Egypt, Cyrenaica, Tripolitania, Ifriqiya, and the Sahara.

Outside the Muslim World the nearest forests were to be found mainly on the northern coasts of the Mediterranean, in the barbarian West in the Apennines, Alps, Istria, and Dalmatia, and in the Byzantine Empire in the Balkans and Asia Minor. Far to the east, beyond an immense zone of steppes and deserts and the vast extent of the Indian Ocean, lay the forests of the west coast of India, with, most particularly, the teak of Malabar.

The original woodland areas of the Orient and the southern Mediterranean had long since been exhausted, having been intensively

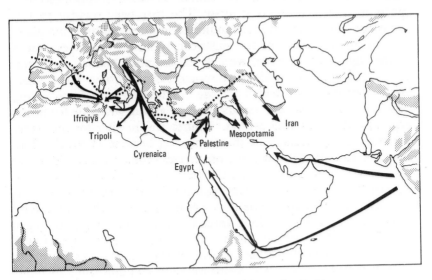

Fig. 19. Imports of timber into the Muslim World.

exploited by the older civilizations of Mesopotamia, Phoenicia, and Egypt. They had provided the materials for centres of industry, town-building and, above all, shipbuilding, particularly for the Phoenician navy. Irreparable damage was caused at this time, rendered still worse by the reckless depredations made by the Romans. The Lebanon, a famous example, was a major supplier of cedar to all the navies in the eastern Mediterranean. Already, by the early Middle Ages, it had ceased exporting wood, and everyone knows what state it is in today: what was once one of the finest tracts of woodland in the world can now boast only one or two rare specimens.

However, in the eighth to the eleventh centuries, the woodland cover was less damaged than it is today. An example of this relatively good growth is the Jabal Ansariyya, 'Mountain of the Alaouites', which, in the tenth and eleventh centuries, produced a large amount of wood for export, whereas today it is almost completely bare.

The question of forest areas was the more urgent for the Muslim Empire in that the demand for timber increased in enormous proportions as new uses for it arose. The first need was for fuel in industry: the old Mediterranean industries of metallurgy and glassmaking or new ones like the sugar-cane industry. The West Indies in the eighteenth century, were to experience a similar deforestation because of the needs of the sugar-cane industry. Then building timber was also needed for the building-yards of fast-growing cities and for irrigation, because wood was indispensable for hoisting apparatus and well-casings. Timber was needed for the navy, for the trading fleets, now increasing fast because of the development of commercial relations, on the sea, and on waterways (Nile river-craft), and also for battle fleets which were waging war against Byzantium in a long struggle for the domination of the sea. Because of the improvement in naval technique the ships, now much bigger, with their long yards for lateen sails, required longer pieces of wood, which meant larger trees. Lastly, wood was needed for cabinet-making, which received a stimulus from the ever-increasing luxury. The Cairo Museum contains some splendid examples of these carved, chiselled, and inlaid woods. It should be noted in this connection that the wood was assembled in small pieces. It constituted a precious material which had to be used up, right down to the tiniest fragment. This had a paradoxical result: the techniques were more developed here than in the wood-producing countries which supplied the vast logs of timber; indeed in the fourteenth century Moorish workers were called in from Spain to make the *artesonados* ceilings in the Palace of the Popes at Avignon.

There was, then, a great demand for timber, especially in Meso-potamia, Egypt, and Ifriqiya, which were important consumer countries but also areas without any woodland resources of their own. Egypt was particularly remarkable in this respect. She was a country with no forests but she made up for this by having highly developed industries requiring a good deal of fuel (the sugar indus-try, for example), irrigation systems with hydraulic machines, large cities, especially the new Fatimid Cairo, which made heavy demands on timber for building and for cabinet-making, and lastly a very sizeable fleet, on river and on the sea, with two fronts to defend, namely the Mediterranean and the Red Sea.

Three ways were used to solve the timber shortage. First, the meagre local resources were carefully organized. In Fatimid Egypt every scrap of wood capable of being used in shipbuilding was set aside for the State arsenals. State forests were also maintained, with an entire organization created to oversee and control the felling of trees. Another method was for Syrian and Egyptian ships to launch attacks against the Byzantine coasts of Anatolia and Dalmatia, with the object of timber-cutting: cypress, pines, and firs. Lastly, and most important of all, trade was brought into play, and wood was imported from more or less distant countries pos-sessing forests. Timber from Armenia, for example, was floated down the Tigris to Baghdad. India supplied teak (*saj*), which reached Mesopotamia via the Persian Gulf and Egypt via the Red Sea and the Canal of the Caliph, Commander of the Faithful, a route en-abling it to reach the timber depot (Sahil al-Khashabat) in whole lengths. The barbarian West sent its pines, firs, and larches from the Apennines, the Alps, and Istria, via Amalfi and Venice. Like the arms traffic, the traffic in naval timber, at least in the form of long pieces, was strictly forbidden at that time by the Byzantine emperors, who were fighting against Islam for naval hegemony in the eastern basin of the Mediterranean. In 971 the authorities at Constantinople set fire to three Venetian ships loaded with wood, two of which were about to leave for Mahdiyya, in Ifriqiya, and one for Tripoli. But these prohibitions were no more respected by the Venetian merchants than those concerning arms. Wood was far too profitable a business to be given up: contraband merchandise is always more lucrative than legal trade.

Thus the Muslim World was precariously placed as regards its supplies of timber; depending as it did on forests separated from it by routes subjected to all the vicissitudes inherent in doing business over long distances. This timber was, of course, very dear, and was paid for in gold. On this level the Muslim World was poor in contrast to the wealth of forests the West could boast, which seemed inexhaustible even up to the fourteenth century, by which date, however, difficulties began to be felt in the supply of wood to Western cities.

The same demand, along the same routes, governed the arrival of other products of the forest: pitch, food obtained by gathering such as honey, and above all products like furs obtained from hunting.

Metals

The short supply of timber directly restricted the metallurgic industries of the Muslim World. Wood or charcoal, which were fuels required in the processing of ore, were needed in large quantities because of antiquated methods which swallowed up entire forests. It took 150 cubic metres of charcoal to obtain only 10 kilogrammes of malleable iron. The metallurgy of the older Eastern civilizations simply devoured forests.

There was an even more basic limitation, namely the relative lack of metals in the Muslim World. The main reason for this was the poverty of mineral resources: there were few major metalliferous areas in the East. This poverty was aggravated by the reckless exploitation and consequent exhaustion of the few easily accessible veins of ore, a process which had been going on in some cases for thousands of years. Finally one must bear in mind the inadequate techniques available for processing ores, which allowed a considerable proportion of the metal to be wasted as slag.

Here too these inadequacies were palliated to some extent by trade with distant countries. Ships and caravans brought back from the remote — sometimes very remote — territories of the Muslim World either raw materials (gold, iron, tin), or manufactured goods (swords, copper utensils). The supplying countries, mining or metallurgical centres, were the Caucasus, the Urals, the Altai, India, black Africa, and the barbarian West. The supplies of metals on which Muslim economic life and civilization depended were precarious; once again they came from abroad and depended on long-distance trade.

To deal first with precious metals, gold and silver, which are the basis of the goldsmith's and silversmith's craft, we have already seen in connection with the mining areas supplying the mints, that the Muslim territories contained very few gold deposits. These were in Arabia and Armenia, to which must be added some washing of auriferous sand in Kirman and in Spain (Tagus). But, as we have seen, vast gold reserves were put back into circulation with the Muslim conquests, and, even more important, gold began to flow into the Muslim World from outside as a result of trade, with the North, the East, and the South. Asian gold came from the Caucasus, the Urals, the Altai, Tibet, and Turkestan, but African gold arrived in greater amounts. There were three major auriferous zones in the African continent: between the Nile and the Red Sea, the area of Nubia-Ethiopia; East Africa, where gold was brought by porters from the gold-fields in the interior worked by Negroes, to the counting-houses set up by the Muslims along the coast, which included Sufalat adh-dhahab (Sofala, perhaps the Ophir of ancient times), and then further north the counting-houses of the Zanj country; lastly, in West Africa, the Sudan (Senegal, Niger, and the 'Gold Coast'), from which the gold was carried by Berber caravans across the Sahara to the Maghreb.

All this gold was used to mint dinars and was the basis of a very considerable goldsmith industry. Workshops both in palace and town were everywhere very active, and gold was in constant circulation, being melted down over and over again, as is clear from the inventory of the Fatimid palaces, very little of whose contents has come down to us.

Silver was usually extracted from argentiferous lead-mines, and then subjected to a process which separated it from the lead. The two main areas used by the Muslim World to satisfy its needs for white metal were the wide argentiferous band in northern Iran from the Caucasus to Tien-chan together with the great Benjhir Mine north of Kabul, and Muslim Spain, which was so intensively exploited that all that remains nowadays is a few veins of lead. Silver, which supplied a considerable silversmith industry and was also used to mint dirhems, was imported in large quantities into Egypt, a country possessing no silver resources of its own, but holding it in almost as high regard as gold, as is evident from the bands of inscribed silver repoussé-work in the Cairo mosques.

The Muslim World was very poorly endowed with iron. It was obtained mainly from more or less oxidized surface deposits, which easily lent themselves to opencast working. These deposits, whose existence had been known for a long time, were found in the Lebanon, in North Africa, and in Spain, particularly at 'Iron Constantine' to the west of Cordoba, on the edge of the Sierra Morena. Here, too, the Muslim World was obliged to call upon neighbouring or distant lands. For example, it went to the Caucasus for ore and for specialists who were heirs to one of the most ancient traditions of metallurgy: the valleys of Dagestan specialized in the manufacture of cuirasses and coats of mail. But its main sources of supply were India and the barbarian West, which were familiar with specialized methods of producing steel and manufactured famous swords which were much sought after.

One of the most important steps forward in iron metallurgy was taken in India. This was the discovery, about the beginning of the Christian era, of molten steel. The process yields, by spheroidization of the molecules, a high-grade steel with a characteristic macrostructure and with designs impregnated in the mass of the steel and clearly visible on the sword-blades. Mediterranean coun-

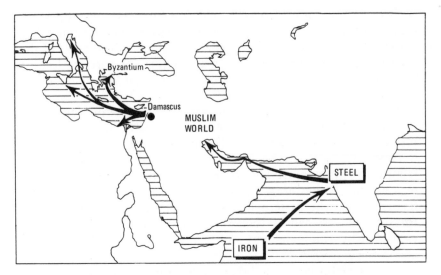

Fig. 20. The circulation of East African iron and Indian steel.

tries began importing this remarkable steel in Roman times: it was the *ferrum sericum*, from the 'Seres country', perhaps the Dravidian kingdom of the Cheras of the central and southern Dekkan. More and more of this steel was imported during the Muslim era, when Indian steel became known by the name of *hindawani* or *hindi* (which was, with the definite article, *al-hindi*, from which is derived the Spanish *alinde*, meaning a 'mirror of polished steel'). This steel, ready to be fashioned, reached Damascus and the other major centres where arms were manufactured, Toledo in particular. Steel was, however, imported direct from India in the form of swords, which were a legend throughout Arabic literature because of their strength, keen edge, and flexibility.

It should be observed that this steel manufactured in southern India was produced from an ore which came from the east coast of Africa, from the Zanj country, and which was judged superior to Indian ore for molten steel. This ore was crudely extracted by Negroes, then sent to India by Muslim merchants, where it was turned into Indian steel and sent on to the Muslim World as crude steel or in the form of swords. The itinerary taken by this steel, pieced together from various Oriental sources, demonstrates very clearly the importance of this trade in weighty objects and of the specialization of the centres of manufacture, on circuits leading from the raw material to the refined material and then to the finished product.

The barbarian West also possessed very many iron deposits in the form of surface deposits of pisolitic iron, 'iron-fields'. The eastern Alps of the Tyrol and Styria, Noricum of Roman times, were known at that time as a very active centre of arms manufacture. Mention must also be made of the Moselle and Meuse regions, the Rhine area, the Champagne area round Nogent-en-Bassigny, and the eastern Pyrenees. All these regions were richly forested and so had at their disposal reserves of fuel too. This explains why iron metallurgy was highly developed in Roman Gaul and in the eastern Alps.

It must be borne in mind that the barbarians kept on this industry, only too happy to be able to equip themselves fully with arms. They employed, moreover, new and remarkable techniques, producing blades superior to the Gallo-Roman hardened steel blades. Their specific innovation was the 'false Damascus' technique: very thin strips of metal of different types are made, some of soft iron, others of hard, steeled iron. These are sandwiched together in varying combinations, then soldered, flattened, forged and forged again, so that their final appearance bears a fairly close resemblance to genuine Damascus steel. But this appearance is obtained only after successive rollings, whereas genuine Damascus steel is obtained from the actual mass of steel by cooling after being molten in the melting-pot. In both cases the quality of the weapon is almost identical. That of the barbarian blades depends on a combination of extremely hard and less hard elements which imparts solidity, toughness, and sharpness as well as suppleness and flexibility. We have been able to study these weapons thanks to archaeological finds, particularly those made in the Merovingian cemeteries. Carolingian tombs are more disappointing, because the custom of burying the warrior with his weapons died out in the ninth century. But there are Carolingian swords in Scandinavia and in the area of the Russian rivers, where this funerary practice persisted up to the eleventh century.

We can in any case learn much about swords made in the West from a wealth of texts which have come down to us from the Carolingian and Ottonian empires and from the Muslim World. The *sayf al-Firanja* or 'Frankish swords', i.e. those made in the barbarian West, were famous. The Muslim World imported large numbers of them via the Bilad as-Saqaliba or Slav countries, and from Andalus, i.e. Muslim Spain. They were imported into the Muslim East along the Russian rivers and via the Caspian Sea, and into Mediterranean countries via the Rhône corridor or Venice, a city which specialized, as we have seen, in contraband trade and which, by selling arms and timber to the Muslim World, disobeyed the ban placed on such activities by the Byzantine emperors.

There remain copper and tin. The Muslim World was less favourably equipped for the production of copper than of iron. The main deposits were in central Asia, Upper Mesopotamia with the Arghana Mine, southern Morocco, and Spain. Tin was not produced locally but imported commercially from Britain and the Malay Peninsula, but zinc oxide or tutty (*tutiya*) was obtainable from Armenia and North Africa. The copper, bronze, and brass industries flourished: the artisan-cum-merchant was to be seen in all the *suqs* in Muslim cities.

To sum up, the Muslim World was obliged because of its lack of metals, with the exception of copper, to rely heavily on imports. Its expanding civilization cried out for useful metals for its daily needs and precious metals for its currency and its luxuries. It looked out on to the vast expanse of the barbarian West, richly endowed with ores and woodland which provided the fuel needed to process these ores. With this wealth of ore scarcely tapped, the West seemed a new country in comparison with older lands whose natural resources were almost exhausted.

Textiles

Muslim civilization was based to a considerable extent on textiles, which were, or course, used in clothing, but still more in furnishing. Eastern and Mediterranean furnishing was in fact dominated by the carpet, which was the most important, and sometimes the only, item of domestic furniture. Fabric was used for clothes and interior decoration, but also for tents and flags. Everywhere work-shops were busy producing high-quality fabrics: very delicate linens, wool or cotton muslin, silk figured with gold. These work-shops (*tiraz*) were commissioned to supply costly fabrics for use at court, luxury fabrics intended to increase the splendour of cere-monial occasions. They were also regarded as a kind of investment, and the term *Khizana* applied not only to the treasury but also to the wardrobe. Presents, wages, and rewards, were often given in the form of fabrics. The ceremonial robe embroidered with the sovereign's name was the origin of royal livery, and an entire hier-archy grew out of the varying degrees of sumptuousness of these official garments. Here we encounter an old custom of Oriental monarchies, both Sassanid and Byzantine, which was adopted by Muslim courts, especially the Abbasid court which was anxious to revive in its ceremony and etiquette the Iranian custom of the older monarchy. As in the case of food products, the older textiles in use for centuries were now challenged by more recent ones. The output of the former became stabilized or in some cases actually decreased in competition with the newer textiles.

These older textiles were two: wool, which we have already touched on when discussing sheep, and which came from central Asia, Armenia, North Africa, and Spain; and flax which came principally from Egypt, where it was grown throughout the Delta and at several points in the Nile Valley. The Egyptian soil — deep alluvial earth — suited it exactly, and the water so essential in the steeping of flax was provided in abundance by the canals and lagoons. The fibres yielded an excellent product which made pos-sible the manufacture of extremely fine fabrics — *qasab, Sharb, dabiqi*. The same conditions of production existed in Upper Meso-potamia and particularly in Susiana, to say nothing of other re-gions where production was limited by the shortage of water, in Syria, North Africa, and Spain. However, in Upper Mesopotamia flax later gave way to cotton and, in Susiana, to sugar-cane, plants which require the same physical and human conditions, namely a deep soil, water, and a plentiful labour force. Flax remained as a major textile plant only in Egypt where sugar-cane, but not cotton, became established.

Cotton, the new textile, came originally from India. It was introduced into Mesopotamia in the seventh century of the Christian era, and under the Muslims it grew in vast fields in Upper Mesopotamia, in the region of the Great Khabur, the Harran region, between the bed of the Euphrates and the Tigris. The earliest reference to cotton in Turkestan, on the Buddhist route linking India to China via the passes of the Hindu Kush and central Asia, occurs in the sixth century. In the following century, which saw the rise of the Muslim World, cotton-growing (*al-qutn*; Spanish *algodon*) spread to the Mediterranean. It was first seen in northern Syria, from the bend of the Euphrates as far as Aleppo, which was the natural continuation of the crops in the Great Khabur region; then cotton reached, on the one hand the Ghor (Ghawr), the tectonic rift-valley of the Dead Sea, where it encountered low, moist, warm earth, then the Damascus oasis, and on the other hand Cilicia, where it was found in the deltal alluvial plain, wedged between the Taurus and the Syrian reliefs. And so during the Middle Ages Syria was a major cotton-producer, but this textile did not really become established in Egypt, where flax, the traditional textile yielding the most outstanding products, was very strongly entrenched. Consequently, in the Middle Ages, Egypt had to apply to India and Syria for her cotton goods. Finally cotton reached North Africa, in particular the south of Tunisia (Jerid) and Morocco (Upper Valley of the Oumm er-Rebia, Plain of Tadla, and, by irrigation, as far as Sus al-Aqsa), Spain (Lower Valley of the Guadalquivir), Sicily (round Palermo), and later Cyprus, where cotton was developed under the Lusignans, and Crete during the Venetian era.

Another new textile was silk, which depended for its production on the mulberry tree and the raising of silkworms, which was in fact practised first in China, in central Asia, on the shores of the Caspian, and in Armenia. In the sixth century the silkworm was smuggled into the Byzantine Empire, in northern Syria. It is said

that a Nestorian monk from central Asia carried his precious burden inside a reed he used as a walking-stick, and the tale is a
pointer to the economic split between the Sassanid and Byzantine
worlds. Just as the cotton crops of Upper Mesopotamia were able
to spread only with the establishment of the Muslim World, so the
habit of raising silkworms did not spread until there existed a vast
territory which was economically unified. While on the subject of
the movement of products and techniques, it is interesting to note
that it was in the sixth century, when the silkworm reached the
Mediterranean from Turkestan, that cotton reached Turkestan
from India.

After the Muslim conquests the breeding of silkworms spread to
all the areas of the Mediterranean where it could possibly be carried out, because silk was in great demand in the expansion of the
luxury textile trade. Some of the producing areas were southern
Syria, Cyprus, southern Tunisia (Gabes region), and in particular
south-east Spain and Sicily. In the Alpujarras area and round Jaen
silk was introduced by the Syrians of Qinnasrin, a silkworm-
breeding centre of northern Syria, who came and settled in these
regions in the eighth century. Silk production became one of the
major innovations of Muslim Spain in western Europe. Sicilian silk
had to wait for the island to be incorporated in Western Christendom before it could reach southern and northern Italy.

In this way the production of silk developed widely throughout
the Muslim World. During the Sassanid era the imports of Chinese
silk went to the workshops in Iran and may have travelled further
to Byzantium. By contrast, in the Muslim era imports of raw silk
from China ceased abruptly, but imports of silk goods, a Chinese
speciality, were maintained at their usual level. The Muslim World,
moreover, did not process in its workshops all the silk it produced,
but exported vast amounts of it to Byzantium. The considerable
silk industry in Byzantium relied entirely on the supply of raw
materials from the Muslim World, despite the silk produced in the
Peloponnese, which may have begun as early as the tenth century,
though the earliest direct reference to it is in the twelfth century.

The dyeing materials most in use were indigo, kermes, and
saffron. Indigo, a blue dye, came from India and Mesopotamia and

was introduced into the hot, low, irrigated regions of the Syrian Ghor, the Libyan oases, the Chotts or salt flats of the Jerid, of Hodna, and of Sus al-Aqsa, and it ousted the growing of woad. Kermes or scarlet 'seed', an insect which is a parasite of the holm oak, used as a red dye (Arabic *qirmiz*, *qirmizi*, from which is derived the word 'crimson'), was processed in Armenia and Spain. It rivalled the *baqqam*, or Brazil-wood from India, but between them they ousted madder and purple (murex from Phoenicia). Saffron, used as a yellow dye, was the most prized and the most widely used of the Eastern dyes. It was the colour of the sun, the colour of the Sassanid rulers, and was used to dye clothing, but also to dye papers and official documents, under the influence of China where yellow was the imperial colour. Saffron, which was also used in cooking as a seasoning, was grown very widely indeed throughout the Muslim World.

The increasing variety of raw materials in textiles and dyes resulted in the progress and the spread of manufacturing techniques: looms with low-warp and high-warp, looms with pedals, Chinese in origin, a way of making carpets with knotted stitches (central Asia), the *susanjird* with its needle embroidery (Persia), the 'Gobelin' method of weaving (Egypt). The most famous products were imitated elsewhere: *irmini* carpets originally from Armenia were made in Spain, at Assyut in Upper Egypt, and at Tarsus in Syria; the *jurjani* material (from the name 'Jurjan') was made at Almeria in Spain; the *isfahani* at Antioch; the *dabiqi* (from Dabiq, a town in the Egyptian Delta) in Spain; the *'attabi* from Baghdad was made at Almeria; the *siqilli*, which means 'Sicilian', in Egypt, in Upper Mesopotamia, and in Spain. There was a general combination of techniques, and all the major centres were noted for the variety of their products and the world-wide renown of their fabrics.

Each city specialized in one particular cloth and each textile centre had its own fabric, which, independently of the other materials made there, assured the centre a specific outlet in world markets. Certain areas were genuine textile zones with whole towns and villages given over to the production of cloth. The sale of products on a commercial basis presupposed the existence of merchants to procure the raw materials and to be responsible for disposing of the finished product. These fabrics bore on the edge the names of the towns where they were made. The town of Fasa in Fars, for example, was known for its brocades, its *washy*, a material made of thick, watered silk made fashionable at court by the caliph al-Muʿtasim, its precious wool carpets, its blankets made of *Khazz* (floss silk) with a spotted design reserved for the caliph, and its *susanjird* (raised needle embroidery). This was better than the kind produced at Qurqub because it had more body: the embroidery in Fars was done on wool whereas at Qurqub it was done on silk. Fasa produced materials which were a blend of wool and silk and also pure silks (*harir*) which were everywhere in great demand. The area of Fars-Khuzistan also possessed, at Qurqub itself, an official workshop supplying exclusively the needs of the caliph and his court. The region was a great cloth-making unit, a major producer of precious or everyday fabrics, which were exported via the ports of Basra and Siraf.

Another major producing area was the Egyptian Delta, a centre where both luxury and everyday cloth was woven, beyond doubt the most important in the Mediterranean. The area exported goods to the Muslim East, the Indian Ocean, Syria, the Byzantine Empire, the Muslim West, and the Italian ports. Here the raw material for industry was flax processed locally but interwoven with silk imported from Syria, or with gold thread. Here too there was a great variety of products, ranging from an extremely sheer fabric, *sharb*, to heavy tapestries embroidered in gold. A series of little manufacturing towns — more than twenty — each with its *tiraz* and satellite villages working for it, directed Egypt's textile production. The more important towns were Damietta, Dabiq, Damira, and especially Tinnis, set in the lake which bore its name in those days (now Menzaleh). Tinnis, depending on boats for supplies, living on large-scale catches of fish, in a semi-aquatic setting, possessed in plenty the water needed for the steeping of flax, and the prevailing humidity made possible the twisting of fine cloth fibres. Five thousand looms produced annually the veil of the Kaʿba. These centres in the Delta all had their own speciality. Some wove white materials, others bleached fibres, engaged in the fulling of cloth, the glossing of linen, the glazing of silk goods (with gum from the Sudan); others specialized in dyeing or brocading with gold thread. All these products, together with the techniques used, were exported great distances, and imitations sprang up everywhere, for exarnle *qasal* and *dabiqi* were to be found in the workshops of Mesopotamia and Fars. And so, by the variety of its products, the Muslim World ranked, together with China and Byzantium, as one of the major producers and exporters of luxury fabrics.

Products of stone and soil

During the period we are considering the practice of stonemasonry had practically disappeared, except for smaller objects, such as capitals, plaques decorated in bas-relief, and ablution baths like the one at Madinat az-Zahra'. In fact most building was carried out in brick, both for walls and arched roofs, because timber was in such short supply. At Fustat, palm-trunks had to be specially requisitioned for the building of the ceiling in the Governmental Palace (Dar al-imara). Marble columns from ancient monuments were used to build mosques. Carthage, for instance, was used as a quarry for the new towns of Kairouan and Tunis, and its columns, like those of Sfax, were also used to build Madinat az-Zahra'. Walls were usually made of brick and then covered on the inside with a thick veneer intended to conceal the poverty of the materials. This veneer was often plaster – carved, engraved, chiselled, painted, and gilded, as at Samarra, in the Tulunid houses in Egypt, and in North Africa at Sedrata; but even more common were decorated earthenware tiles, the product of Mesopotamian and Iranian techniques which were already used in the Achaemenid and Sassanid palaces and later spread throughout the Muslim Mediterranean; this was *zulayj* (Spanish *azulejo*). One reservation must be made; the Byzantine territories remained true to the sumptuous mosaic decoration made of gilded cubes of glass and coloured paste. The Umayyads of Damascus and later of Cordoba sent for Byzantine artists to decorate their great mosques; these artists trained pupils locally and they perpetuated the techniques of Byzantine mosaics in the Muslim World.

Another industry which derives ultimately from the earth is ceramics. Muslim civilization has left us a splendid series of dishes, vases, and ewers. Here, too, as in the wall-tiling, one discerns the techniques and decorative style of Sassanid Mesopotamia and Iran, but in the case of ceramics there were additional Chinese influences which travelled along the Rayy trail to Samarra where Chinese porcelain was found, or else along the Indian Ocean and Red Sea routes to Fustat-Cairo, where excavations have also brought some porcelain to light. The terms *sini* (porcelain) and *siniya* (porcelain dish) are derived from the actual name of China: as-Sin. The techniques used in ceramics are amazing, especially the technique of lustre ware which owes its sheen to gold reflections obtained by adding a metallic alloy to the paste before firing. The major centres were Rayy (Rhages) in Iran; Samarra in the ninth century; Egypt in the ninth and tenth centuries; North Africa; and tenth-century Spain, with Madinat az-Zahra', which was later taken over in the twelfth century by Catalayud. It was a persistent tradition – in the thirteenth and fourteenth centuries large 'Hispano-Moorish' gilded ceramic dishes were the inspiration for the majolicas of the Italian Renaissance.

Glass was another Mediterranean industry which had flourished since ancient times in the Phoenician towns of Tyre and Sidon and in Alexandria, which had excellent sand for glass-making. Syria and Egypt remained the major production centres during the Muslim era, both in respect of standard products and luxury goods. However, a new centre emerged in Iran, which exported in bulk the *'iraqi* glasses referred to in Spanish Christian documents of the tenth and eleventh centuries. These extremely high-quality glasses from Egypt, Syria or Iraq, coloured, gilded, enamelled, turned, and engraved, were exported to China, from which was imported porcelain in return. During the Crusades the warriors from the West pilfered Syrian coloured glasses in the belief that they were cut from precious stones, while the Venetians imported from Tyre all the pieces of broken glass, all the misshapen bits, so as to melt them down. This was the origin of the glass industry in Venice –

Murano glassware. Another glass-making centre grew up in Muslim Andalusia. In the ninth century 'Abbas b. Firnas is said to have discovered how to manufacture artificial crystal by blending the element going into the manufacture of glass and adding lead.

Finally, as far as precious stones are concerned, it may be said that the Muslims enjoyed at this period the monopoly of this particular trade. The emeralds (*smaragdos, zumrud*) of the Arabian Desert in Upper Egypt were, until the discovery of America, the only ones known in the world. The Pamirs, in the Badakhshan region, yielded a famous ruby, the *balakhsh* ruby, from which we have our 'balas ruby'. Diamonds came from India and Ceylon, and rock-crystal from the Maghreb and Spain. Everywhere treatises on precious stones were written, and from them derived the lapidaries of the medieval Western World, which dealt with stones and their magic properties. The techniques of cutting precious stones (hard stones) had reached a pitch of perfection; the facet-cutting and engraving were quite remarkable. We can judge this for ourselves if we inspect the intaglios, cameos, and superb pieces of rock-crystal fashioned into great ewers, basins, or globes, most of them from Fatimid Egypt and now exhibited at the Louvre in Paris, in the Treasury of St Mark's in Venice, and in other European museums. The techniques of glyptics, preserved and developed in the Muslim World, disappeared from the barbarian West, but were reintroduced at a later date.

Products of the sea

In the East, along vast stretches of coastline, such as the Red Sea, southern Arabia, and the Persian Gulf, fish was the basic food of the inhabitants. In the Mediterranean it was not so important because it was far less abundant; the continental shelf here is very narrow and gives way to very deep water without any transition. Fishing was possible only at one or two places, for instance the lagoons of the Nile Delta, the shallows of the Sicilian Strait and the east coast of Tunisia, the zone round the Strait of Gibraltar, and also the point at which the shelf juts out from the Atlantic coast

of Morocco. In all these places seafaring peoples lived and practised techniques of fishing which were centuries old. Lastly, the
tunny was caught at the time of its annual migration either by
harpoon, as is still done in the Sicilian Strait, or by means of a
madrague or tunny-net, which is a collection of nets into which
shoals of tunny are driven. These nets are still known as *tonnaria*
in Sicily. The word *madrague* comes from *madraba* (plural *mada-
rib*), 'net shaped like a narrow-necked bottle'.

Salt, another essential part of the diet, and also essential in
industry, whether for salting foodstuffs or processing fabrics and
leather, was collected in salt-pans along the coast or was extracted
as rock-salt inland. It supplied a flourishing trade with Negro territory, the Sudan. The caravans would load up with salt at Taghaza,
an oasis north of the Sahara (Taudeni), and then go on to the
banks of the Senegal and the Niger to barter it for gold and slaves.

Very costly materials also came out of the sea itself: coral,
pearls, tortoise-shell, and ambergris. Red coral is specific to the
Mediterranean, and was fished at Marsa' l'Kharaz, 'the trinket
port', La Calle, east of Bône. It was exported in vast quantities to
the Persian Gulf, which had no red coral, and to India, where it
was made into jewels, amulets, and lucky charms which were in
great demand. Red coral was a major item in the export trade to
the Indian Ocean carried on by Jewish firms in Fustat-Cairo.
Pearls, on the other hand, came from the Indian Ocean: the great
pearl fisheries of the Persian Gulf sent pearls to all the cities of the
Muslim World. Both coral and pearls required an over-all commercial organization of fisheries, considerable fishing fleets, control of
fishing by merchants and brokers, and State surveillance and taxation. Tortoise-shell came mainly from the east coast of Africa,
whence it was dispatched to Fustat-Cairo; here there were craftsmen who specialized in making tortoise-shell objects. Ambergris, a
concretion which forms in the digestive tract of the sperm whale,
was found on the coasts of the Indian Ocean and the Atlantic.
Pieces of this substance were washed up and collected on the
coasts of Arabia, East and West Africa, and on the Atlantic coast
of the Iberian Peninsula. It provided a perfume and a perfume base
used when several perfumes were blended.

The Muslims, therefore, dominated not only the trade in precious stones, but also that in the various priceless objects won from the sea.

Writing materials

In the Ancient World two materials were widely used for writing on, namely Egyptian papyrus and parchment. Papyrus was made from thin sheets of bark arranged in alternating horizontal and vertical layers, pressed down together into a single sheet, which was then stuck together with starch. Parchment was made from sheepskin which had been sliced very thin and polished. It was first made in Asia Minor ('parchment' comes from *pergamon*, or Pergamo), and was later made by the Seleucids, while the Lagids went on using papyrus. In the Roman and Byzantine empires Egyptian papyrus was customary for official documents; taking the form of a kind of stamped paper bearing a special protocol as a heading. Parchment, on the other hand, was used by the Parthian, Seleucid, and later the Sassanid monarchy.

The Umayyad Caliphate used papyrus in all its chanceries. In the eighth century it replaced the Greek protocol by an Arabic protocol, thereby pursuing a policy further exemplified in the creation of a Muslim-type currency and the introduction of Arabic into the civil service. The Abbasids, more sensitive to Persian customs, and their Iranian viziers, the Barmekids, replaced papyrus by parchment in the government offices of their new capital, Baghdad, where so many other Persian customs flourished in the mid eighth century.

But the close of the eighth century brought a most important development: Ja'far, Harun ar-Rashid's vizier and grandson of the promoter of the previous reform, Khalid b. Barmak, introduced the use of paper into government offices. The reasons for this reform advanced by Arabic writers were the lower cost of this material and above all the impossibility of scratching or washing paper without leaving traces, which was in fact possible in the case of papyrus and parchment. Paper could thus provide authentic documents.

Where did this paper come from? Both flax and hemp paper had been known in China since the first century. The oldest known documents made of paper are manuscripts of the second and third centuries which came from eastern Turkestan, an area exposed to Chinese influence until the eighth century, and which are now preserved in the British Museum. So the manufacture of paper had spread from China to central Asia. The Sassanid Empire did not manufacture paper but it did import it from China. In 751, by their victory over the Chinese on the banks of the River Talas, the armies of Islam opened up central Asia to the influence of the Muslim World, and this influence spread as far as Turkestan. The anecdote telling how Chinese prisoners introduced paper-manufacture into Samarkand, where flax and hemp were grown on a large scale, illustrates a historical fact, namely that Turkestan entered the politico-economic orbit of the Muslim World, and thereby facilitated the spread of Chinese techniques in the West. It is interesting to note that the vizier Ja'far, who founded the first paper-factory in Baghdad in 794 or 795, had a brother who was governor of Samarkand at exactly the same date.

And so the use of paper spread, in the ninth and tenth centuries, throughout the Muslim World. Factories were set up in Syria, which provided favourable conditions for the growing of hemp, in Sicily, in Andalusia, where in Jativa (Saetabis, Shatiba) they made *shatibi*, a name which is still given, in Morocco, to a kind of thick paper. Even in Egypt the production of papyrus was gradually abandoned, in fact a Koran on paper existed in Egypt as early as the tenth century. By the tenth and eleventh centuries documents were hardly, if at all, written on papyrus, which survived only in the use of its name, 'paper'. The Papal and Byzantine chanceries, which had traditionally used it hitherto, abandoned it at the close of the tenth century. The earliest paper documents in the West which have been preserved date back to the beginning of the twelfth century. This was an imported paper purchased from the factories in Spain and Sicily. Byzantium, on the other hand, bought paper from Syria or Egypt. Not until the thirteenth century did the actual techniques reach the West, with the installation of paper-factories in Italy and in south-west France.

Medicinal products

The development of what was called 'Judaeo-Arabic' medicine was really an extension of the older Greek corpus of medical knowledge translated into Syriac, Aramaic, or Arabic, in other words absorbed into the Semitic World. Jewish, Christian, and Muslim doctors all worked on the basis of this Greek knowledge even though they added to it medical knowledge from the ancient East — in particular the Iranian school of Junday-Shapur in Khuzistan — and India. The route taken by Greek medicine and indeed by Greek thought in general, is indistinguishable from the route travelled by Aristotle's ideas. These medical treatises went from Greece to Syria and were translated into Syriac, Aramaic, or Arabic; then they became known in major centres like Baghdad, Cairo, and Cordoba, where Spanish Jews translated them into Latin, in which form they reached the main centres of Western Christendom: Salerno in the ninth century, then Montpellier. In the eighth and eleventh centuries, Byzantium constituted an archaic and backward-looking unit, from a purely medical point of view. The East and the Latin countries of the West had come into closer and more lasting contact via the western Mediterranean under the Muslims than by direct exchanges with Byzantium. Simeon Seth in 1075 was the first person to discuss the virtues of sugar in Byzantium and to cite the remedies used by the Arabs, who themselves came to practise medicine only in the tenth century. It was the Nestorian Christians who went on running the medical school at Junday-Shapur for a considerable period. The influence of Indian science, already in favour at the Sassanid court, increased under the Abbasids from 750 onwards. New observations enriched the *materia medicinae*. This explains how sugar from the Khuzistan plantations was studied at Junday-Shapur and how it assumed paramount importance in the Eastern pharmacopoeia in the preparation of drugs and their easy absorption.

The spread of medical treatises and the greater number of medical centres, hospitals, and pharmacies in the Muslim World produced a corresponding increase in *materia medica*, drugs and medicines. These chemico-pharmaceutical studies made possible, in addition, the manufacture of luxury articles such as oils of roses, violets and wallflowers, ointments and pomades, rouge and scents, cooling drinks and syrups. The trade in drugs and toilet requisites was quite considerable, whether their origin was mineral, animal, or vegetable. For example, there was alum from Egypt, borax from Armenia and Egypt, sulphur from Sicily, and earth from Barca of Magham, near Toledo. There was castoreum from Bulghar, bezoar from Persia or the countries on the Chinese frontier, and theriac from Jerusalem, made from crushed serpents. Finally there were hemp and opium, both used a great deal in the Muslim World as inhalants and fumigations, and also in the practice of magic, since they are both narcotic plants. There was also a great demand for the gum-resin from the styrax or Syrian benjamin tree, balm from Judea, mint, rhubarb, and myrobalan from Transjordania, and cassia and castor-oil from Egypt.

Wine itself was regarded as a remedy, and drunk with spices added. Sugar took the place of honey in the composition of electuaries consisting of a blend of powders and medicinal extracts. There are many somewhat dubious stories about the origin of these drugs of long ago. 'Tabachir', for example, was supposedly made from the whitish gum exuded by a bamboo growing in China and on the Malabar coast, and then reduced to a fine ash. 'Tabachir' was regarded as a panacea until the seventeenth century, and was one of the most popular commodities in Alexandria, Pisa, and Venice, one of the most saleable goods of the Middle Ages. Very many other medicinal plants, 'simples', some of which are still in use, were actively sought after, picked, and exported, and many others were imported from India, China, the Indian Archipelago, or East Africa. The drug trade, therefore, was most important, and contributed to the development of long-distance barter and also to changes in men's way of life. This was the period when opium from Iran reached central Asia and the Far East.

Slaves

Following the example of the Ancient World and the Byzantine

Empire, the Muslim World was a civilization based on slavery. Motive power and energy were supplied to a large extent by the muscles of slaves, whether in the form of huge gangs working in the plantations and mines, where the labour force consisted entirely of slaves, or in the towns, where slaves and freemen laboured side by side. Domestic slavery should not be forgotten: women and eunuchs in the harem and servants, singers, and female musicians in the palaces of sovereigns and great nobles. The harem of 'Abd ar-Rahman III (912—961) at Cordoba had 6,300 women; the Fatimid Palace at Cairo had 12,000. The *sitara* or 'chamber orchestra' was an essential ingredient of luxury living, and there were special schools in Baghdad, Medina, and Cordoba, where musicians and dancers were trained, and were also taught literature, poetry, and grammar. Slaves who had been educated in this way would sometimes fetch astronomic prices, and some of them acquired great fame. A case in point was Ishraq as-Suwaida', the pretty little black girl who was famous in tenth-century Spain for her knowledge of grammar and prosody.

A final form of slavery, though by no means the least important, was military slavery. The bodyguards were almost all slaves, as is attested by the fact that the corps of *mamluks* in the ninth century at Fustat, under the Egyptian Tulunids, was composed of 24,000 Turks and 40,000 Negroes. The Umayyads in Spain, for their part, owned 10,000 slaves at Cordoba. This bodyguard of slaves, commanded by officers chosen from freeman, always played a vitally important role. Ibn Tulun was the son of an enfranchised Turkish slave, while Abu'l-Misk Kafur, ruler of Egypt (966—968), was a black eunuch.

Like the freemen of the Roman Empire and the eunuchs of Byzantium, these former slaves sometimes played key roles in the Muslim World. Their influence was mainly political and military, and was matched by the influence of that surging mass of human cattle, the slaves, who not only permeated political and military life but were also present on the economic and social scene. We have already noted the serious upheavals provoked by the Zanj Revolt in Lower Mesopotamia.

The slave-traffic was, then, of the utmost commercial importance.

But no slaves were to be had inside the Muslim World, because, once the phase of conquest was over, there was no room for anyone within the frontiers except Muslims or protected subjects (*dhimmi*) such as Jews, Christians, or Zoroastrians, none of whom could be reduced to slavery but for some rare exceptions, like the occasion when the Copts of the Delta revolted and were led away into slavery. Slaves had to be sought elsewhere in countries near and far, and obtained either by raids or by purchase from weaker, less tightly knit societies incapable of defending themselves.

There were three major areas where slaves might be found, three types of hunted humanity, three main reserves: first the Bilad as-Saqaliba, the 'slave country' *par excellence* (*saqlab*, 'slave'), the forest region of central and eastern Europe; then the Bilad al-Atrak, the Turks' country or Turkestan, that is to say the steppes of central Asia; finally the Bilad as-Sudan, the Negroes' country of the savannah and the fringes of the African jungle.

From the eighth to the eleventh centuries the Slavs occupied in the West those regions into which they had advanced as a result of Germanic migrations westwards (third to fourth centuries). They spread as far as the Elbe, the Saale, the eastern Alps, Istria, Dalmatia, the Balkans, or even the Peloponnese, where they were driven after the sixth century. In the East, the limit of their territory was more or less the edge of the great Nordic forest: Upper Dnieper, Upper Don, Upper Volga, with one or two outposts in the plain where the Polians faced the Drevlians. Behind Slav territory, towards the Baltic, dwelt the Finnish tribes whom Arab geographers also included in the general term 'Saqaliba'. In the steppes of southern Russia and the Danube lived Turco-Mongol tribes: the Khazars, Bulghars, and Magyars. The Slavs lived in the forests and by the rivers, fishing, hunting, and food-gathering. They were divided into loosely knit tribes, but they began, by about the tenth century, to crystallize into States in two regions, Bohemia and Poland. Moreover, from the eighth century onwards, the area of the rivers Volga, Don, and Dnieper was traversed by Scandinavians (Varegs, Rus) who founded in the ninth century the Russo-Scandinavian Principality of Kiev on the Dnieper, which became a third point of crystallization. Scandinavian trade exten-

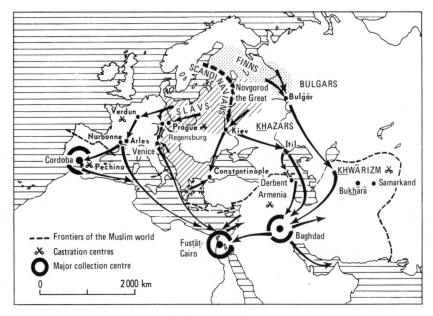

Fig. 21. The trade in Slav slaves.

ded down the North Sea and western Europe — stages along the route to Spain, the Muslim Maghreb, and the Mediterranean — towards the Caspian Sea and the Muslim East, and lastly to the Black Sea and Byzantium. It dealt mainly in Slav slaves, who were dispatched by the slave-exporting Principality of Kiev to the Muslim World and Byzantium.

Slaves also travelled eastward via the Khazars' territory on the Lower Volga, where Itil, a town on the Caspian Sea, levied taxes on the slaves, who were then dispatched either along the land route leading to Derbent and Armenia, a castration centre, or the Caspian route leading to Tabaristan, Rayy, and Baghdad. Another transit route ran through Greater Bulgaria via Bulghar at the confluence of the Volga and the Kama, and then led across the steppe to Khwarizm, where there was another great slave-market, serving central Asia, called Urgenc, which was in the Samanid Principality.

This Principality, which also took in Samarkand and Bukhara, both castration centres, was a slave-trading State, whose activity is attested by the great quantity of Samanid dirhems found along the Russian rivers, where they were used to pay for the convoys of slaves, and also the other products passing through Bulgaria, such as furs, honey, horses, and leathers. From Khwarizm the slaves finally reached Iran and then Mesopotamia, whence they made their way from market to market throughout the Muslim East.

The slave-trade with the West was in the hands of 'Frankish' and in particular Jewish merchants from the Upper Danube and the Rhine, and also merchants from the Meuse—Saône—Rhône corridor. From Bohemia, where Prague was a castration centre, the slaves went on to Regensburg. In the other direction they were sent from the Germanic markets on the Elbe and the Saale to Verdun, a great slave-trading centre and a castration centre, then via the Saône and the Rhône to Lyons. The existence of Radhanite Jewish merchants at Lyons is vouched for by Ibn Khurdadhbeh writing in 847, and by the pamphlets of the bishop of Lyons, Agobard, who died in 840. From Lyons the slaves moved on to Arles and Narbonne, whence they were taken to Spain or exported by sea direct to Egypt and Syria.

Lastly, in the south, Venice was the hub of the slave-trade. The Slav slaves from the Upper Danube and from the Rhineland via the Alpine passes, together with those captured nearer, in the eastern Alps, Istria, or Dalmatia, were all collected in Venice. Then they were exported by Venetian sailors to the ports of the Mediterranean Levant, and constituted a most profitable trade which increased the revenue Venice already drew from smuggling timber and arms.

It was an enormous trade and brought in fat profits. In the tenth century, Liutprand, referring to slave-traders and the 'manufacture' of eunuchs at Verdun, spoke of *immensum lucrum*. A further proof of the volume of the slave-trade may be seen in the figures of three successive censuses of Saqaliba carried out in Cordoba under 'Abd ar-Rahman III (912—961). These were 3,750, 6,087, and 13,750 men, which shows an increase of 10,000 slaves over a period of about fifty years, and at one single spot in the Muslim World. When the Caliphate of Cordoba was dismembered

at the beginning of the eleventh century, Slav officers, who had
once been slaves but had acquired their freedom, assumed the
leadership of several of the pocket kingdoms of the era of the
Reyes de Taifas (*Muluk at-Tawa'if*), notably those of Denia and
Valencia.

Whereas the Slavs were a forest race, the Turks inhabited the
steppes of central Asia as far as southern Russia. The most important points at which Turkish slaves entered the Muslim World
were, first, the region corresponding to Farghana, ash-Shash, and
Ma Wara' an-Nahr (i.e. Transoxiana), with the great markets of
Samarkand and Bukhara, and also Khwarizm which was, as we
have seen, the arrival-point of one of the major routes along which

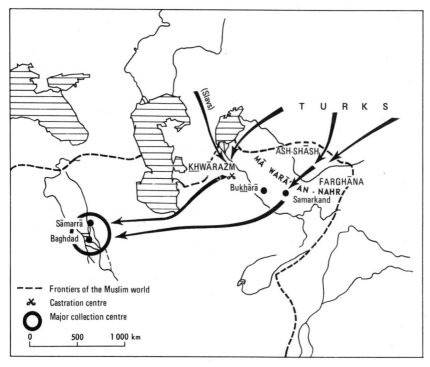

Fig. 22. The trade in Turkish slaves.

Slav slaves were imported, under the controlling influence of the
slave-exporting Principality of the Samanids (tenth century). From
these regions, the Turkish slaves were redistributed to all the slave-
markets in Iran, Mesopotamia, and the other regions of the Muslim World. Their primary function was to form the royal armed
guard (*mamluks*). The Abbasid Caliphate, an offshoot of a movement originating in Khurasan, organized bulk purchases in central
Asia. Al-Mu'tasim (833–842), in particular, formed a militia of
70,000 Turks which proved far too large and created such disturbances in Baghdad that he was obliged to leave and settle in
Samarra. From then on, Turkish infiltration was constant. Freed
slaves risen to officer rank grew extremely powerful, becoming
generals, captains of the guard, and even, as in the case of Ibn
Tulun in Egypt, genuine rulers. They made and unmade caliphs:
the return of the caliph to Baghdad in 892 was made in an attempt to rid himself of Turkish tutelage to which he was subjected
at Samarra. This infiltration into the army and the administration
facilitated the Islamization of the Turks still outside the borders of
the Caliphate and prepared the Muslim Empire for the Turkish
conquests of the eleventh century. The highest point of these
praetorian guards was reached in the mid thirteenth century, with
the *mamluks* in Egypt.

The Negro World was the third major source of slaves, and it
continued to provide slaves longer than any other, almost up to
modern times. There were several distinct groups: the Nubians of
the Upper Nile were imported via Aswan, the southern entrance
into Egypt and a centre where castration was carried out, particularly in its Christian monasteries; these were the Barabra, sometimes known even today as 'Barbarins' and reputed to be splendid
servants. The Ethiopians (Habash, Abyssinians) who were Semites,
were imported along the valleys of the Blue Nile and the Nile or
by the ports of the Red Sea, into Egypt or Arabia. The Somalis
from the Berbera area came via Zayla' to Aden and the great
redistribution market at Zabid, founded in the eighth century. The
Zanj on the east coast of Africa, i.e. the Bantus, supplied a rapidly
expanding market connected with the development of major Muslim trade in the Indian Ocean. These Negroes were seized in raids

or purchased, in exchange for shoddy goods, from the petty kings of the interior. They went from the counting-houses on the coast to Socotra and Aden, assembly-points from which they reached Egypt via the Red Sea or Mesopotamia via the Persian Gulf. We have seen that the enormous concentration of black slaves in Iraq led, in 868–883, to the terrible Zanj Revolt. The final source of supply was the western Sudan, where there were new areas in which slaves could be caught, areas which had been opened up by the organization of trans-Sahara trade in gold and slaves. The slaves were the Sarakole (Takrur) from Senegal, the Soninke from Ghana, the Songhai from Gao, and the Sao from Kanem, near Chad. They were exported to Nul Lamta and Sijilmasa, whence they travelled to Morocco and Spain, to Wargla and Jerid on their way to Ifriqiya, Fezzan, Tripolitania, and Cyrenaica *en route* for Egypt and the entire Muslim East.

Apart from the Slavs, the Turks, and the Negroes, various other peoples paid their tribute to slavery. Anglo-Saxon slaves were transported across Gaul to the Rhône corridor, northern Italy, and Venice, or else shipped direct via Ireland and the Atlantic to the ports of Muslim Spain, Lisbon and al-Qasr (Alcacer do Sal). Indian slaves travelled via the Hindu Kush, 'the slayer of Hindus', to Balkh and Samarkand. One must also take into account the prisoners captured by the Muslims in wars against the Byzantines or in raids against Christian kingdoms in northern Spain, the captives taken by the Vikings on their expeditions in western Europe and then sold to the Muslims by the Russian rivers route, and also the Lombards purchased by the merchants of Amalfi and other mercantile cities of southern Italy, which then resold them over the other side of the water, in Sicily, North Africa, and Egypt.

Slavery was one of the most important economic factors in the Muslim World. The steady supply of slaves enabled wars to be prosecuted and trade to be extended to central Asia, the great Nordic forest, the western Sudan, the East African coast, the British Isles, and India. But from the eleventh century onwards, the supply of slaves began to dry up. The major conquests were over; the Slavs embraced Christianity and were no longer sold to the Muslims, while the Turks embraced Islam and were thereby

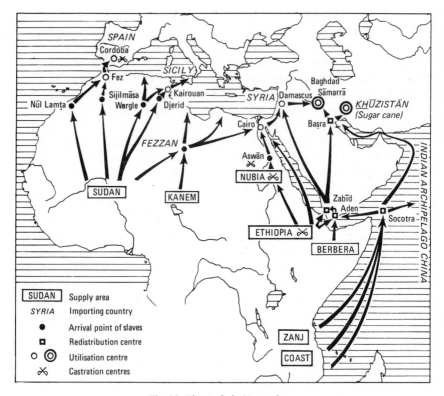

Fig. 23. The trade in Negro slaves.

exempted from slavery. There remained the Negroes, but here too
the advance of Islam pushed back even further the frontiers of
slave territory. The result was a crisis in slave labour which produced, as in the Late Roman Empire of the fourth century, new
forms of organization of labour. The barbarian invasions of the
eleventh century — by Turks, Hilalians, Almoravids — followed the
routes used by this vast slave-trade, and it was indeed the opening
up of these routes together with the creation of urban staging-
posts on the borders of the savage societies which supplied these
slaves, which paved the way for these hordes.

To sum up: the agricultural and industrial output of the Muslim World in the eighth to the eleventh centuries seems to display signs both of strength and of weakness. The strength is derived, in the first instance, from the nature of the period under review. The foundations of the economic hegemony of the Muslim World depended first and foremost on the positive heritage of very ancient civilizations whose techniques it took over and developed further. At the same time the Muslim World was able to palliate the negative after-effects of these ancient civilizations. For example, the existence of large-scale foreign trade to supply certain products, and the existence of an active urban network to process them, made possible the purchase of products which the Muslim World lacked or had lost because of the intensive exploitation indulged in by previous civilizations which were wasteful of their resources.

The precarious economy of the Muslim World resulted precisely from its lack of on the spot resources, particularly wood, metals, and water. The irrigation areas could not be extended indefinitely, and the limitation placed a check on the provision of vegetables as a basic food in the East. And so Islam's economic power was geared to the maintenance, at the very least, of the irrigation network and the road network, to the supply of gold, and to urban growth. This explains how a position of strength at a given period of history turns to weakness when the conditions of wider circulation are no longer fulfilled, i.e. the eleventh and twelfth centuries, under the effect of the following invasions: Turks all over the East, Hilalians in North Africa, Almoravids in Spain, Normans in Sicily, and Crusaders in Spain and Syria.

The crisis of the Muslim World, which is the perennial crisis of old, effete Oriental countries which fall to the invader, was aggravated by the successful rivalry of the newer countries in the West. These countries absorbed influences emanating precisely from the hub of the Muslim World, and were able to exploit their enormous resources of water, timber, and metals, which appeared even vaster when set against the resources of the older countries of the Muslim East which were by then all but exhausted.

CHAPTER 9

Commercial interchange in the Muslim World

The over-all direction of the monetary flow in the Muslim World and the general picture of new metal coming in to rejuvenate the money circuit has already been indicated. Thereafter we described the part played in the redistribution of specie by the cities of the Muslim World, which were centres of consumption and the driving forces of the economy as a whole. This study of the flow of money must be completed by a study of the main directions of the flow of merchandise. We must first turn our attention to the middlemen, whether Jews, Christians, or Muslims.

The middlemen of trade: the Jews

The substratum of Jewish commerce was a result of the diaspora, a dispersal caused by the first exile under Nebuchadnezzar; then by the second, after the destruction of the Temple in Jerusalem. The diaspora produced strings of Jewish communities established along all the major trade routes which were, therefore, identical with the path along which Judaization travelled. These routes, which were both religious and commercial, began in Sassanid Mesopotamia and ran as far as Armenia, the Caucasus and the Caspian, and the Khazar region (Lower Volga and Ponto-Caspian Steppes), and also reached Iran, Khurasan, Khwarizm, and Transoxiana and, lastly, the Persian Gulf and the Malabar coast of India.

From Byzantine Syria and Egypt the Jews moved first into northern Arabia and south-east Arabia (the Yemen), into Ethiopia and all the countries round the Red Sea, but also the oases along the 'Qsours' route (see above, p. 57) from Egypt as far as southern Morocco along the northern fringe of the Sahara. This second series of moves exerted a profound Jewish influence on the primitive Arab World, on the Eritrean World on the banks of the Red Sea, and on the world of the Sahara, where legends credit the Jews with the introduction of several techniques and the possession of vast territories south of the Jazirat al-Maghreb.

The third major migration of Jews was from Constantinople and Asia Minor to the Black Sea, the Tauric Chersonese, now the Crimea, and southern Russia, which was also the end of the route followed by Caspian Judaization, namely the Khazar region. Lastly the Jews moved from southern Italy and Spain, whose ancient mercantile cities had existed within a Semitic orbit ever since the Phoenicians colonized these areas, and which were also zones of transit through the straits, and they entered the barbarian West: Languedoc, the Loire Valley, the Rhône, Saône, Meuse, and Rhine valleys. In the Merovingian era Gregory of Tours refers to the 'Syri', by which he meant Christian Levantines and Jews.

These areas became the main centres of Jewish trade in the Middle Ages. Jewish communities were larger and more active in some places than in others. The most important was the Sassanid East, together with Mesopotamia, the land of exile in Babylon where the Jewish colony was headed by a political leader, the 'Exilarch', the Resh Galutha or 'leader of the Exile'; the land which radiated the influence of the religious leaders (*geonim*, singular *gaon*) of the two schools of theology at Sura, near Anbar and at Pumbedita, slightly further south; it was these two schools which produced what is known as the 'Babylon' (*babli*) Talmud. In Byzantine territory Palestine was the major Jewish centre with the school at Jerusalem, which, after the expulsion of the Jews, moved to Tiberias; here the so-called 'Jerusalem' (*yerushalmi*) Talmud was born. Egypt was another very lively centre, and it was the Jews in Alexandria who produced the Septuagint. Finally, in the barbarian West, we must mention the activity of the Jewish communities in southern Spain, which later provoked the Visigoth persecution, and also communities in Sicily and southern Italy, described in medieval Jewish chronicles written at Oria, Bari, and Rossano.

However, these centres were not in close touch with each other, and exemplify yet again the break between the barbarian West, the Byzantine area, and Sassanid territory, which thus constituted three distinct economic units. The Jewish communities, apart from being ill organized and rivalled by the 'Syri' were also the object of persecutions. The Sassanid persecutions provoked a Jewish migration into Armenia, the Caspian, and the Indian Ocean area. Byzantium, though it had welcomed the Persian invaders of the seventh century, turned the Jews out of Jerusalem and indulged in forced conversions; this too provoked further emigration towards the Black Sea and the Caspian. In Alexandria, anti-Semitism had raged since ancient times. In Byzantine Sicily the Jews also wished to escape from the domination of Constantinople which was concentrated in the maritime cities, so they went to Italy. The Visigoth kingdoms in the West proved no kinder. Violent persecutions afflicted the communities in the south (Malaga) and in Septimania (Narbonne) and initiated yet another emigration into Morocco, which further strengthened the various strands of Judaization. It is easy to see why these communities, on the whole, warmly welcomed the Muslim conquerors, in fact, in many places, especially Syria and Egypt, this went as far as open collusion, which made it easy for the conquerors to seize the country swiftly. Many of the Spanish Jews who had emigrated to Morocco returned to Spain in the wake of the Berber armies, and in fact they were later entrusted with the task of guarding the towns in the south of the peninsula while the Muslim troops continued their sweep northwards.

Within these Jewish communities, which were still only loosely connected with each other, a class of merchants and artisans was emerging who were loyal to the commercial spirit and the mercantile techniques of the Semitic East, and who had also retained the older manual skills: work in precious metals, dyeing, tanning, and glass-making. In the account of Jewish communities drawn up by the Rabbi Benjamin of Tudela in the twelfth century reference was made to merchants, bankers, doctors, dyers, goldsmiths, tanners, and glaziers. On the eve of the Muslim conquests the stage was set and ready for use.

This pre-Islamic Jewish substratum goes some way towards explaining the speed with which the Arab conquerors gained a hold, and the way Arabic spread to countries set outside the main bloc of Semitic dialects constituted by Arabia, Syria, and Mesopotamia. This meant in effect the spread of Arabic to Egypt and North Africa, at least in the cities and communication corridors situated outside the Berber-speaking mountain areas, as well as to Spain. It also explains the spread of Jewish trade which accompanied the rise of the Muslim Empire between the eighth and eleventh centuries. The establishment of an extended political organization with a unified economy was paralleled by the coherent and continuous network of Jewish mercantile communities. Older forms of Judaism, primitive, marginal, more or less isolated and placed as pioneers along the trade routes, now became firmly attached to the expanding centres of official Judaism. India, Khwarizm, the Caucasus, the Red Sea, the Sahara oases, and Spain now came into contact with orthodox rabbinism, with Mesopotamia and its *babli* Talmud, Palestine and its *yerushalmi* Talmud, Egypt and its centre in Alexandria. When, in the mid eighth century, the Abbasids founded Baghdad, which was to become the capital of the Caliphate and the hub of the economic activity of the Muslim World, the Jewish centres in Lower Mesopotamia established their religious pre-eminence and their intellectual supremacy.

The main Jewish community in Mesopotamia was the al-Karkh quarter, the merchant centre of Baghdad. The leader of the community (as was mentioned above) was the 'Exilarch', the Resh Galutha, the 'leader of the Exile', who was an important figure at the caliph's court and enjoyed a specific rank in official ceremonies. The two schools at Sura and Pumbedita, near Baghdad (the former was connected to the new capital by the Nahr Yahudiyya, 'the Jew's river'), were famous because of their leaders, who,

like the *gaon* Saadia in the ninth century, sent their *responsa* to all
the requests from the communities of the diaspora. Very few
gaonic 'replies' came from the schools in Babylonia. Similarly, it
was the *babli* Talmud which came to be adopted by the Western
forms of Judaism in Spain, Gaul, and the Rhineland. Finally, the
method of collecting money in the East — and also the West — was
often by money order from one community to another, on behalf
of the schools of Babylonia. For this reason Mesopotamia and
Khuzistan with its centre at Tustar, assumed the focal position of
world Judaism.

    Various currents of ideas — religious, philosophical, and mystical
— emerged and interacted with similar currents in Muslim circles.
Official rabbinism, conformist and accredited, was matched by
illuminism and mysticism (Kabbala). In particular the movement known as 'Qaraism' gained ground from 762 onwards; its
literal meaning is 'reading', and its aim is to go back to a Bible
stripped of all Talmudic commentaries. Old forms of Judaism and
small irregular groups joined this new movement, thereby creating
a second network of communities which paralleled the rabbinic
system. These communities were even more closely connected
with each other and therefore more efficient on the economic
level; their solidarity derived from the knowledge that they were
minority groups, rejected by official orthodoxy and subjected to
increasing persecution. This double network of Jewish communities based on the Mesopotamian centres was to prove vitally important for commercial relations.

    The fusion of small cells of Judaism from East to West was
achieved by official rabbinism within Muslim territory, just as
Christianity had spread within the framework of the Roman Empire. In the eighth to eleventh centuries many great Babylonian
gaons had been born in the countries round the Mediterranean, for
example Saadia, whose family came from North Africa.

    Any description of the network of intellectual and religious
exchanges between these communities is at the same time a de-
scription of the major Jewish trade routes; sometimes this plots
them very accurately, and it always sheds light on them. The
process of rabbinical centralization and the development of com-

mercial relations from the centres in Abbasid Mesopotamia kept pace with each other. These trade relations went beyond the limits of the Muslim World to form links with the distant rabbinical or Qaraite communities of the Negro country, the country of the Khazars and the Russian rivers, and the barbarian West.

Community organization provided the framework for commercial activity, the mould into which it fitted. This organization rested on a common responsibility, a solidarity which was essential to confidence wherever commercial transactions or credit operations were concerned. The Muslim authorities looked favourably on all this solid community organization — guarantors, correspondents, guilds, trading-houses with numerous branches — in that it helped them to keep order and levy taxes. The Eastern style of government rested, in the main, on a mosaic of communities for whom their religious leaders were responsible. Jews and Christians lived in a separate quarter which made it easy to check their movements. The community had a messenger who saw that news reached it quickly of the arrival, size, and load of incoming caravans; it had a relief fund, guarantors who entertained travellers, a judge for business matters, a supervisor of business deals and markets, and a superintendent in charge of slave ransoms, which, we are told, were fixed at a uniform rate throughout the Mediterranean.

Integrated land—sea trade was the speciality of the Radhanite Jews, known to us through a most important text of Ibn Khurdadhbeh (847). The term 'Radhanites' (*Radaniya*) seems to come from '(Nahr) Rudanu', 'the Rhône'; at least this is more plausible than the explanation put forward a hundred years ago by de Goeje, that the word came from the Persian *rahdhan*, 'one who knew the roads', 'a guide'. These merchants found many active communities scattered at intervals along the Meuse—Saône—Rhône corridor, from Verdun, Saint-Jean-de-Losne, and Lyons to Arles and Narbonne, the great port whose name persists in the surname 'Narboni', still very common among Mediterranean Jews. But Ibn Khurdadhbeh's text, important though it is, is not unique; it is confirmed by other passages in Arab and Persian writers, by the Geniza documents, and by Jewish and Latin chronicles of the Western World.

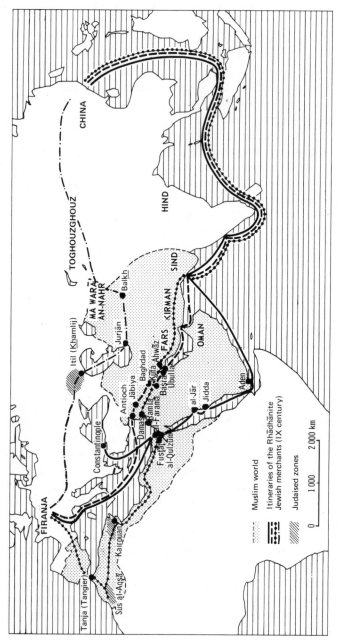

Fig. 24. Itineraries of Radhanite Jewish merchants.

CHINA

TOGHOUZGHOUZ

HIND

SIND

Itil (Khamlij)

MA WARA
AN-NAHR

Balkh

Jurjān

KIRMAN

FARS

OMAN

Antioch

Jābiya

Baghdad

al-Ahwāz

Kūfa

Baṣra

Ubulla

Constantinople

ar-Ramla

al-Farama

Damas

al-Jār

Jidda

Aden

Fustāṭ

al-Qulzūm

FIRANJA

Tanja (Tangier)

Sūs al-Aqṣā

Kairouan

Muslim world

Itineraries of the Rhādhānite
Jewish merchants (IX century)

Judaised zones

0   1 000   2 000 km

Thus a major part of all commercial interchange was in the hands of the Jews and their trading-houses, which did not specialize in this or that commodity, as was usual in the Middle Ages. The Jews bought and sold all the profitable commodities: cloth in the first instance, silks from the Muslim World, and brocades from the Byzantine Empire, which were sold in Christian Spain in the tenth century; wholesale trade in grain from Egypt to the Red Sea, the Persian Gulf, and Baghdad; the sugar trade, the great plantations of Susiana (Khuzistan, Ahwaz) supplying transfers of funds to Baghdad merely against a written statement and guaranteeing the farming of taxes throughout the province; trade in spices and drugs, in conjuction with Judaeo-Arab medicine; trade in gold, goldsmiths' wares, rarities from China, in a word everything costly and exotic; slave-trade, on all the frontiers of the Muslim World, with all that went with it, namely the 'manufacture' of eunuchs, the teaching and training of slaves; finally the dealings in currency and banking operations.

The importance of these Jewish merchants only increased at the court of the Abbasid caliphs, and perhaps still more under the Fatimids in Egypt, who held Jews in great esteem. This is shown in the careers of Jawhar (Paltiel), a southern Italian Jew who conquered Egypt and built Cairo for the Caliph al-Mu'izz (973—975), Jacob ibn Killis, vizier to al-'Aziz (975—986), and the Tustari brothers during the minority of al-Mustansir. Numerous pamphlets were directed against the Jews and the undue power they wielded at the Fatimid Court; the dynasty was actually accused of having Jewish origins, a fact which reveals the enormous jealousy people felt for the wealth and importance of the merchant-bankers and the rich communities of Alexandria and Cairo.

And so the commercial traditions established prior to the Muslim conquests enabled the Jews, when the vast Islamic Empire was built, to assume a role of primary importance. Gradually, through trade with the West, first under Charlemagne, then under Otto, the Jews ousted their Christian rivals, the 'Syri'. The latter were pre-eminently importers of Oriental luxury goods into the barbarian West; their centres were in the East and their outlets in the West. The Radhanite Jews, as is clear from Ibn Khurdadhbeh's text, were exporters of slaves, furs, and swords, with centres in the West (Rhine, Meuse, Saône, Rhône, Languedoc) and outlets in the Muslim East. The change of direction in the flow of trade was due partly to the way the huge Muslim Empire provided an ideal setting for the Jewish trade network already in existence.

In the eleventh century this flourishing Jewish trade took second place; it was supplanted in the West by Italian trading firms and banks, and in the East by Armenian merchants. The Jews were gradually driven out of the markets by various methods, such as mergers, marriages (in Italian cities), brutal treatment, bans, and massacres (in the Rhineland at the time of the First Crusade). They were excluded from major maritime trade by the Venetian prohibitions, and their activities were now confined to inland routes leading from the Upper Danube to the Slav countries. They became gradually relegated to a secondary role in commercial activities and were restricted to shopkeeping, lending, and usury. But between the eighth and eleventh centuries they were the undisputed masters of the routes and markets of the Old World. They were not, as we shall see, the only traders, but they were certainly the most important and most ubiquitous.

The middlemen of trade: Christians and Muslims

Up to the start of the Muslim era the Christian 'Syri' had dominated East—West trade, but then the Jews gradually took over from them the entire seaboard of the Mediterranean and the Indian Ocean, so that their only real importance was in more localized commerce in Egypt, Syria, Mesopotamia, Armenia, Iran, and central Asia. In these regions their trade depended on a chain of Jacobite and Nestorian communities. We have already seen the rank enjoyed by the Nestorian Catholicos at the Abbasid court; the Synods met at Baghdad. However, it is above all the economic role of the monasteries which must be stressed. They functioned as repositories for money and as banks, often used by important figures to conceal a fortune obtained by more or less fraudulent means, but they were also used as hotels for travellers, they retailed wine and other drinks, and lastly, they were used as centres where slaves were castrated, particularly in Armenia and Upper Egypt. It is possible, with the help of various details from Coptic, Syriac, and Arabic sources, to trace the network of commercial relations from one Christian centre to another, and to observe how it was linked with pious visits and pilgrimages. In this case, too, a climate favourable to commercial operations was created by the awareness of being a minority group and the feelings of mutual trust between several communities. The network thus established was, however, limited to routes in the interior.

The Armenians deserve a special mention. Their business deals took place in the zone where the Muslim World and the Byzantine Empire met, on the major route connecting Upper Mesopotamia with Trabzon. The subsequent Armenian expansion, with its wide extent and its commercial diaspora, is faintly reminiscent of the Jewish expansion. The Armenians moved into Upper Mesopotamia and from there to Baghdad, where they grew into a considerable colony. They also reached Asia Minor and Constantinople, where they became soldiers, architects, and traders. The Emperor Basil I, at the end of ninth century, was of Armenian origin. In northern Syria or Lesser Armenia they dominated trade at the time of the Crusades from the port of Ayas. Finally they reached Egypt, where the Fatimids' vizier at the end of the eleventh century, Badr al-Jamali, was an Armenian who formed a guard composed of Armenians and attracted to Cairo architects and businessmen of the same origins.

Muslim merchants used the following formula when writing business letters: "May God prosper your affairs and those of the Muslims." This underlines the fact that they were constantly doing business with merchants of different confessions, i.e. Jews or Christians.

We have seen the specifically Muslim trading which accompanied the great fairs at Mecca, held at the time of the Pilgrimage (Hajj). This trade was instituted for the pilgrims, great crowds of whom had to be fed, and also by the pilgrims, who brought merchandise into the country with them, and particularly precious stones for the jewellers' bazaars. The most famous was the tur-

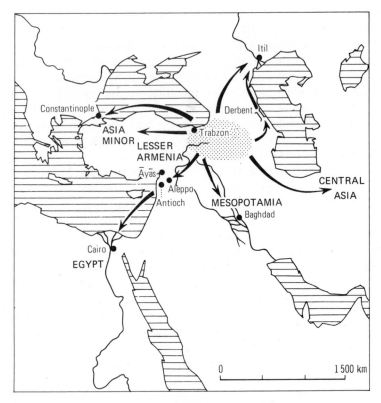

Fig. 25. Armenian trading connections.

quoise known as *makki* or 'Meccan', because it was sold in vast quantities at the time of Pilgrimage. Even so, these were closed communities, and thus, in the eyes of Islam which was the official, triumphant religion, they seemed heterodox communities, constituting therefore a network which could be the vehicle for commercial relations.

The model for this kind of community was provided by the Kharijites of North Africa, who split up into Sufrites and Ibadites and asserted their independence *vis-à-vis* the central government of the Caliphate. About 757 Sijilmasa, a great caravan city, was founded by the Kharijites when they sought refuge in the desert. It became the centre of a local dynasty, the Midrarids, and became by the close of the eighth century the major port of the desert and the largest market in gold and slaves. At the same period, in the central Maghreb, at Tiaret (Tahert), rose the star of the Rustamids who were of Persian origin and had fled to North Africa, where they inherited the aftermath of the great Kharijite movements which rocked the country for the whole of the first half of the eighth century. These Rustamids occupied all the central Maghreb and the entire desert façade. Towards the south-east, south of the Aghlabid States of Ifriqiya which were Sunni States recognizing the suzerainty of Baghdad, they stretched as far as Jabal Nefusa and the Ghadames oases. Towards the south-west, south of the Idrisid State of Fez, founded at the end of the eighth century, they went as far as Sijilmasa, where the Midrarids acknowledged their suzerainty, then, beyond, to Sus, Nul Lamta, and the Atlantic. In this way was formed a long strategic highway for Kharijite trade, from the Fezzan to southern Morocco; a route which commanded, in the south, because of the Hodna and Wargla oases, all trade with the Sudan by trans-Sahara caravan, and which enabled the Kharijites to extend their trade northwards right into the heart of the Maghreb. Tahert, nicknamed 'little Basra', the Rustamid capital, was at the head of a rigorist country, skilled and honest in business, running a whole State on the principle of the closed sect, with guarantors, brothers, and relationships from one community to another. No doubt there were also traces of influences persisting from the days of the older Berber and Saharan forms of Judaism.

In the early tenth century the Shi'ite Fatimids replaced the Aghlabids as the dominant force in Ifriqiya. In 909 the Fatimid army marched on Sijilmasa, laying waste the Kharijite city of Tahert on its way through. The last of the Tahert Rustamids withdrew southwards and founded Sedrata, near Wargla. Later, in the eleventh century, the persecuted Kharijites retreated into the salt-marshes of the Mzab, where they drilled wells and built cities, once again admirably situated at the end of the caravan routes from the land of gold and black slaves. Finally, at a more recent

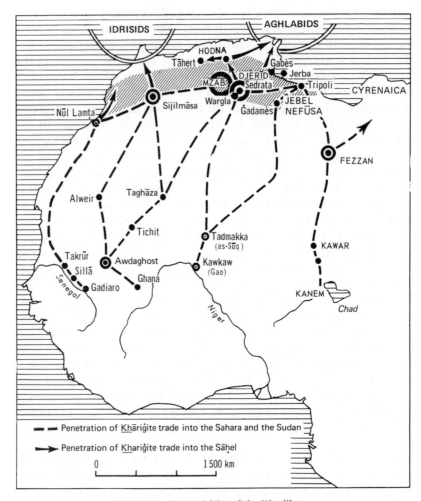

Fig. 26. Trading activities of the Kharijites.

date, Mzabite merchants made their way into the Sahel, where they were to be found as rich cloth-merchants, or else in every town in North Africa as modest grocers. They attracted gold coin into the Mzab and amassed it in small amounts which they buried later on when gold currency was in short supply. So the Mzab was another country which made heavy demands on gold.

Trade routes

The flow of commerce ran in various directions, along groups of roads all leading to the great urban centres of Bilad al-Islam. The north-east section was made up of the continental oasis routes which led from Mesopotamia to Iran and central Asia, then to the country of the Turks, to northern China or north-west India. The south-east part consisted of the sea routes of the Indian Ocean, leading from Mesopotamia and the Persian Gulf on the one hand, from Egypt and the Red Sea on the other, to the west coast of India, Malabar, then on to Ceylon, Indonesia, Indo-China, and southern China or to the Zanj country (east coast of Africa) and Madagascar. The south-west section consisted of the caravan routes from the Sahara, North Africa, to the country of the Negroes (Bilad as-Sudan). Lastly, the north-west section consisted of the sea, river, and continental routes leading either from Mesopotamia and Armenia to the countries round the Caspian and the Russian rivers and, beyond, to the Baltic countries and central Europe, or else from the Muslim ports on the Mediterranean to the Italian and Languedoc ports, either from Muslim Spain to the Iberian kingdoms in the north and, beyond, via the passes of the Pyrenees, to the Frankish West, or else, lastly, from Muslim Spain by the ocean route to Britain.

The north-east section

The route followed was more or less the old 'China route', but now it was developing fast and became crowded with caravans of horses and, above all, camels, the large two-humped Bactrian camels. These caravans climbed up from Mesopotamia to the Iranian Plateau, then passed north-eastwards through Khurasan, crossed the Oxus at Amu Darya or Jayhun and reached Transoxiana, the country 'on the other side of the river' (Ma wara'an-

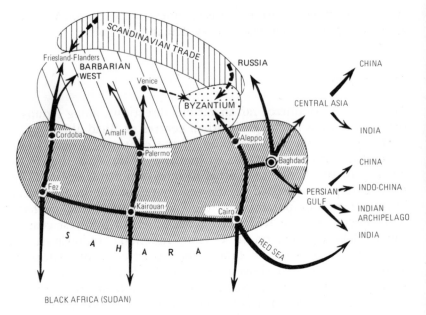

Fig. 27. Trading connections of the Muslim World.

Nahr), Shash, and Farghana. Then they had the choice of three possible routes: they went north-east into the steppes of the Turkish nomads; eastwards they followed the south side of Lake Balkash, then, going up the Ili or via Kashghar and the Tarim Basin they reached the elbow of the Yellow River, crossed the Ordos Steppes then the Great Wall of China, finally reaching the capital of northern China, Khumdan (Hsi-ngan); lastly there was the road running south-east via the passes of Hindu Kush – whose name recalls the hecatombs of Indian slaves who had travelled to the Muslim World, only to die of cold and fatigue when crossing these passes – along which the caravans went from Bamyan and Kabul to the Indus Valley which was under Muslim domination (Sind region) and, beyond, to the whole of northern India (Hind).

Three centres emerged as important. The first was Khurasan, round Merv, Herat, Balkh, and especially Nishapur, which rivalled Baghdad in the eleventh century. This area was situated at the fork in the major route from Baghdad to India, Khwarizm, and China. The second important centre, Khwarizm, was the region of the Oxus Delta, on the Aral Sea; together with cities like Urgenc, it was an extremely important trading centre, the pivot of trade with the Turks, India, and China, but also a key position on the routes from the Caspian, the country of the Bulghars, namely the Volga Valley, and from central Europe. Lastly, the third important centre was the group of oases of Ma wara' an-Nahr, which commanded the routes to the country of the Turks and to China.

The importance of the region thus defined was embodied in the dynasty of the Samanids (875—999), who in their heyday ruled over Khurasan, Khwarizm, and Ma wara' an-Nahr, in fact from the Turkish border in the east to the shores of the Caspian in the west. The Samanid capitals of Bukhara and Samarkand controlled the central Asian routes and indeed large quantities of Samanid currency have been discovered along the Russian rivers and also in the countries round the Baltic and the North Sea. These currencies were legal tender in the tenth century in the market at Mainz. The Arab traveller at-Tartushi, who came from Tortosa in Spain, saw, about 973, in the market at Mainz, dirhems minted at Samarkand in 913—915. We may note in passing the concentration of metal currency on the frontier regions of the Muslim World which imported a great deal — in this case the Khwarizm, Khurasan, and Ma wara'an-Nahr àrea. Imported merchandise travelled along the three main axes of circulation of this north-east section.

From the country of the Turks and the country of the Slavs, via Bulghar, products reached the Caspian, then the west and south of the Aral Sea round Urgenc. These imports were furs from the steppe and particularly from the Siberian forests, slaves — we have seen the enormous demand for *mamluks* from the Abbasid Caliphate — and finally metals, in the form of iron and weapons at which the Turks were acknowledged experts, copper and copper utensils, and felt which was a nomad speciality. In exchange, the Muslim World exported to the Turks silk cloth, mixed goods and, above all, coins.

Silk was imported from China (Chinese and Khotan silk) even though the development of silkworm-breeding in the Muslim

World had rapidly made it unnecessary to call on this source. However, embroidered Chinese silk and silk goods generally continued to be important as a luxury speciality, just as the Chinese, despite the technical perfection and artistic quality of their own product, went on ordering sumptuous cloth from the Muslim World. This is shown by indications in Chinese sources and by the influence of Irano-Muslim motifs on certain specimens of Chinese silk which have been preserved. But silk was not the only commodity involved in these transactions; China exported her porcelain, gold-tinted paper (above, pp. 187, 194), and jades. Taken as a whole, trade between the Muslim World and China via the central Asian route showed a more or less balanced flow of money in both directions.

From northern India, namely the Upper Indus, the valleys of the Himalayas and Tibet, the Muslims imported Hindu and Tibetan slaves, cloths from Kashmir made of goat's hair, perfumes, in particular musk from Tibet, which is a secretion of the musk deer. Trade with India, as with the Turks, resulted in a flight of money from Islam, both gold and silver. For India hoarded gold and turned to silver monometallism, the rupee (Sikh *rupya*, 'silver').

The south-east section

Here the commercial horizon is the Indian Ocean, a zone of west–east and east–west navigation, which alternated regularly with the rhythm of the monsoons (from the Arabic *mawsim*, plural *mawasim*, 'season', from which is derived the Portuguese *monção*). South of the Equator on the other hand is the area of the trade wind which blows from the south-east to the north-west. The dividing-line between the monsoon area and the trade-wind area was therefore the frontier between the zone covered by navigation and the unexplored empty zone.

The Indian Ocean was traditionally an area criss-crossed by Arab and Persian ships, by Alexandrian sailors from the first century of the Christian era, and by the Malaysian *prahu* in their outriggers; opinions concur in assigning a relatively early date to

Malaysian migrations to Madagascar. From the eighth to the eleventh centuries the Indian Ocean was dominated by Muslim sailors, with one highly important result, namely the transference of the triangular sail from this area to the Mediterranean, where it was called the 'lateen sail'. The Indian Ocean area facilitated essential trade exchanges, particularly the transfer of crops from India to the Persian Gulf and Syria on the one hand, and to the east coast of Africa, southern Arabia, the Red Sea, and Egypt, on the other. Betel, for example, was used in the Yemen as early as the ninth century. In this way the two routes, one via the Persian Gulf and the other via de Red Sea, joined together the Indian Ocean and the Mediterranean and united their techniques, their plants, and their customs.

However, there were various degrees of Muslim domination of the Indian Ocean. From the mid eighth century to the mid tenth, the Abbasid Caliphate, with its cities of Baghdad and Basra and their various needs, tended to dominate the Persian Gulf. At the close of the tenth century the Fatimid Caliphate created a rival kingdom which led to a struggle for supremacy between the Persian Gulf and the Red Sea. The ports of Qulzum (Clysma) and particularly 'Aydhab ensured a link between this sea on the one hand and the Mediterranean on the other.

However, the period from the eighth to the eleventh centuries was a time of expansion for Muslim trade along all the coasts of the Indian Ocean and along the roads of China. This expansion was based on settlements in very many places, on a Muslim-type ship built of teak, and on a strong dinar currency in use along these trade routes. On the east coast of Africa, the Zanj country, cities grew up, such as Mombasa and Barawa, where Kufic inscriptions dating from the eighth century have been found. The mosque at Zanzibar dates from the eleventh century. And behind the counting-houses, the process of Islamization continued deep into Africa, following the line linking the carrier depots used by the Negroes to bring their produce to the coastal depots. There was similar expansion on the Malabar coast, where mosques were built and where the Muslim colonies had their own judge, the *honarman*; in Ceylon (Sarandib in Arabic sources); in the Sunda

Islands, where Islamization occurred somewhat later, producing the millions of Muslims we have today, but where there is an Arabic inscription (in Java) dated as early as 1082; in Indo-China, where Arabic inscriptions, from the tenth to the twelfth centuries have been found; and finally in China, in the heyday of the T'ang dynasty and during the reigns of the first Sung emperors between the seventh and eleventh centuries. The Muslims were familiar with the great southern port of Canton, known as 'Khanfu' to Arab geographers.

Trade in the Indian Ocean followed a fixed pattern: before setting sail from Egypt the merchants took on board a cargo of wares which included coral, tortoise-shell combs, and iron bars or grain, which they exchanged in the islands or on the coasts of the Indian Ocean for the products of these countries, namely incense, ivory, rhinoceros horns, shells, camphor, Socotra aloes. These goods were then transported to China and exchanged yet again for the valuable products of that country — silk, porcelain, curios, etc. — which were brought back to Egypt and sold in the major Mediterranean markets.

But the merchants also supplied the Muslim World direct with tin from Malaya, timber, arms, indigo, and *baqqam* (Brazil-wood) from India and the Indian Archipelago, precious stones and pearls from Ceylon, the Persian Gulf, and the Red Sea , ambergris and tortoise-shell from the South Seas which supplied the makers of *objets d'art* sold in a special market in Fustat. Lastly the Indian Ocean was the main, if not the only, supplier of spice, perfumes, aromatics, and medicinal plants. The drug trade expanded from the eighth to the eleventh centuries, in conjunction with the advances made in Judaeo-Arab medicine. Alexandria was the main redistribution port of spices and drugs for the whole Mediterranean Basin, Cordoba, Western Christendom, and Byzantium. The Byzantine Emperor Leo the Armenian (813–820) attempted to put a stop to this trade, forbidding his subjects from travelling to Egypt and Syria and offering aromatic plants himself, 'like the ones we get from India'.

The south-west section

Here too trade continued and developed. The Muslim World took over and considerably extended an older network of trading connections, the one which had, from the fourth to the eighth centuries, impelled the Berber nomad camel-drivers to strike south across the Sahara and towards the Nigerian Sahel. Unfortunately little is known about this tremendously important development, one of the most significant in the early Middle Ages, either as regards its chronological details or its geographical progress, for lack of contemporary sources.

At all events, from the end of the eighth century (Sijilmasa was founded in 757) the trade of the Muslim World added this new caravan network to the older ones of the East and the Mediterranean, thus gaining access to the entire trading circuits of the Sudan, the Bilad as-Sudan, 'the Negro country'. As we have seen, this new commerce was in gold and slaves, but also in gum, used for glazing Spanish silk goods, and in ambergris from the Atlantic coast. The routes along which trade flowed were at the same time routes transmitting, from north to south, ancient Eastern and Mediterranean civilizations to the black tribes, new crops like corn and cotton, new livestock such as the camel and horse, and new techniques and social forms including the town and the State.

These routes fell into three major groups of caravan tracks, lined by wells and palm oases, from Jazirat al-Maghreb, 'the island or peninsula of the Maghreb', to the Sahel, the 'bank' of the Senegal and the Niger. The first group was in the west, beginning in southern Morocco (as-Sus al-Aqsa), and, beyond, at Fez; here the two major gateways of the desert were Nul Lamta, at the mouth of the Oued Nun, between the Oued Sus and the Oued Draa, and above all Sijilmasa, a large new caravan town which many rank in importance with the ancient caravan cities of Palmyra, Petra, and Mecca. Situated at the heart of the long palm grove of Tafilelt (Oued Ziz), Sijilmasa was always the stake in the struggles between the Rustamids and the Fatimids. It reached its peak of prosperity in the tenth century, at which period there was a colony of Sijilmasans at Awdaghost, the great southern Berber terminus. At that time the taxes on caravans returning from the Sudan brought the Fatimid ruler 400,000 dinars a year. However, in the eleventh century Sijilmasa was affected by the rivalry of Nul Lamta. Three routes started from these two major northern termini: one followed the Atlantic coast as far as Senegal (Takrur, Silla, Gadiaro), which was a two months' march away. The two others diverged on leaving Sijilmasa, one in the direction of Alweir, the other towards Taghaza, then they met again at the great southern terminus of Awdaghost. This town was in touch with the kingdom of Ghana and was split into a Muslim town of merchants and factors, and a town inhabited by Soninke Negroes. It was an imperial city with fabulous wealth and a strong force of warriors. These last two routes were shorter than the first for they took only a month and a half, but they were more costly.

The second group of caravan tracks consisted of those serving the central Maghreb, namely Tahert and southern Algeria. They started from the Kharijite refugee centres of Wargla, Sedrata, and Mzab, and went either to Taghaza and Awdaghost, or Tadmakka (now Essouk, as-Suq), in Adrar of the Ifoghas and beyond to Kawkaw (Gao) in Songhai country, another dual town of the same pattern as Awdaghost.

The third set of itineraries lay in the east and served Ifriqiya, Kairouan, and southern Tunisia. Their points of departure were the Jerid region (Tozeur, Nefta, Gabes), which is both Mediterranean and Saharan, and Tripolitania-Cyrenaica, a staging-post on the way to Egypt. From these centres the roads led either to the Niger via Ghadames and Tadmakka, or to Kanem (Lake Chad) via the Fezzan and the Kawar.

It was along these routes that gold flowed from the Sudan to the Maghreb, where it was sent on further throughout the Muslim World. The Maghrebi trading-houses maintained, at the southern end of these routes, a complex network of correspondents and factors trading for gold with the tribes of Negroes who specialized in gold-washing. This trade was on a colossal scale, in fact the tenth-century geographer Ibn Hawqal saw at Awdaghost a commercial document worth 40,000 dinars and several other sources mention excessively rich merchants involved in the Sudanese trade.

The commodity so much sought after was gold in plaited ropes, *tibr*. The most varied assortment of goods were bartered for gold; some agricultural and industrial products from the Maghreb and Egypt, and mixed cargoes too, consisting of trinkets made specially for trading with the Negroes, exactly the same kind of thing that was offered, from the seventeenth to the nineteenth centuries, by the European warehouses on the West African coast. During the Middle Ages there was in Ceuta a *suq* specializing in the manufacture of coral necklaces, glass beads, shells, and other trinkets. Even so, other products found their way south, such as corn, dates, short lengths of material for making loin-cloths, copper utensils (which reminds one of the way copper and brass objects were exported from Antwerp to Africa in the sixteenth century), leathers (from Zawila, Ghadames, Tafilelt, and Aghmat-Marrakesh), resinous woods and tar (to make leather bottles watertight and to treat mange in camels), takaout (tamarisk-gall, a tanning agent from southern Morocco), and salt, most of which was landed at Taghaza (Taudeni Salt-pan) and which the Negro World needed desperately and could not produce.

None of these commodities had great intrinsic value, but they acquired it by reason of the long and trying journey they made to the countries which lacked them. A geographer referred to the Berber traders as follows: "They take with them worthless merchandise and bring back great camel-loads of gold nuggets." And so this south-west sector was of vital importance in the monetary economy of the Muslim world. It was the gate through which gold flowed in, gold which made possible the large-scale minting and active circulation of dinars, and in fact mints (*dar as-sikka*, from which comes the Italian *zecca*) were set up at Sijilmasa and Wargla, at the northern end of the routes bringing gold from the Sudan.

The north-west section

Here, three areas must be distinguished from each other: Byzantium, the region of the Russian rivers, and the Christian West.

First, Byzantium. In this direction, too, the Muslim World showed a trading profit, the only difference being that the gold coming in was not in the form of nuggets but minted gold – the Byzantine *nomisma*. This trade derived its importance from the favourable geographical position of the Muslim World, which enclosed the Byzantine Empire on the east and south and was therefore the unavoidable through route for fine goods and expensive raw materials which were indispensable to the Byzantine luxury industries, and which all came from Asia and Africa.

The contacts between the Muslim World and Byzantium were of a similar nature to its contacts with China. They were relations between two advanced, well-governed, highly civilized polities. The trade linking the two States was governed by treaties, directed and controlled; it was an early form of mercantilism. It was carried on at Constantinople by colonies of Syrian merchants who possessed their own mosque in their quarter round the suburban Church of St Irene, an arrangement reminiscent of that obtaining in the Slav quarter of St Mammas, likewise in the suburbs. There were also colonies of Iraqi, Persian, Armenian (particularly at Trabzon), Bulgarian, and Italian merchants who acted as middlemen to this trade.

Business was constant and it benefited from the occasional privileged periods – the fairs at Trabzon for instance – and certain fixed meeting-places. As well as Constantinople, one must mention Lamos, on the river so named, which runs along the coasts of Anatolia and marked the frontier between the Muslim march of Tarsus and the Byzantine theme of Seleucia. The Lamos fairs were held when there was an exchange of prisoners between Muslims and Byzantines. On the Byzantine side we must note the presence of Greek specialist buyers, operating either at Constantinople or Trabzon, the *metaxopratai* (importers of new silk), the *prandiopratai* (importers of silk goods), and the *myrepsoi* (importers of perfumes).

One instance of the careful regulation of this commerce is the way the Muslim merchants were guaranteed the sale of all their products, of whatever quality or quantity. If the guilds of Byzantine purchasers left on the Muslim traders' hands part of the merchandise they were offering, the Prefect of the city was obliged to have them taken to the market-place and to see that they were

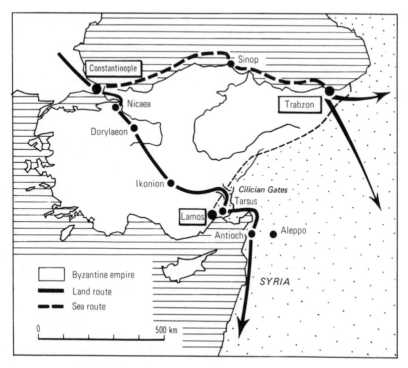

Fig. 28. Routes and centres of the trade with Byzantium.

suitably disposed of. Thus, Byzantine trade seems to have been essentially passive, a middleman's trade, which had to maintain a balance of payments between a mainly import trade (the Muslims) and a mainly export trade (the Venetians or the Amalfians). Constantinople functioned as a forwarding agent between East and West, a redistributor and also an exporter of manufactured goods made from products for which the raw materials had been imported from the Muslim World.

The commodities which the Byzantines dealt in were silk, silk goods, precious stones and pearls, ivory, spices, perfumes, aromatics, ebony, and mother of pearl from the Muslim World, and in the opposite direction one or two very high-quality materials, the

secret of whose manufacture was jealously guarded, for instance
brocades with a 'shot-silk' effect, the *hypocalamon* (Arabic *buqa-
lamun*). There was also linen imported from Thrace and Mace-
donia through the *othoniopratai* and livestock from Byzantine
Armenia, a major stock-breeding country specializing in cattle and
sheep and supplying Constantinople with wool and meat, while
exporting at the same time southwards to Muslim Syria in the
Muslim North. Taken as a whole, the trade of this region may be
expressed as a great flow of *nomismata* into the Muslim World,
which obviously meant a deficit for Byzantine trade, made still
worse by sums paid out as tribute by the emperors or *basileis* to
the caliphs. However, this cash loss was offset by purchases made
on the Byzantine market by Italians and Slavs.

   The second area of the north-west section was the region of the
Russian rivers on to which the Iranian countries looked, from the
Aral Sea to the Caspian, from Khwarizm, with Urgenc, to Arran
(Transcaucasia), with Bardha'a and Derbent (Bab al-abwab, 'the
gate of gates'). It was a region of steppes with the great Nordic
forest in the background, providing a striking backdrop for the
areas already prospected. It was a region of long, slow-moving,
very navigable rivers, the Volga, Don, and Dnieper, which rose in
the heart of the wooded zone and flowed into the Caspian and
Black Seas. Further north were other watercourses, like the Lovat,
and several lakes, affording access to the Baltic. It was an easy
matter to transfer from one river basin to another by *volok*, or
portage. The Caspian Sea, the Black Sea, and the Baltic Sea were
regarded as stages along a route which was a fusion of several, and
the Idrisi map shows them linked together by watercourses. On
these rivers there was considerable carriage of goods, either by
monoxyla, canoes made out of a single tree-trunk, or by large
boats like the ones used by Scandinavian merchants described in
Arabic sources. And so the Scandinavian-Slav trade was linked to
the trade of the Muslim World, which in these areas was confined
to the older trading populations, whether Iranian or Iranized, of
Khwarizm (Choresmia), Jurjan (Hyrcania), and Azerbaijan (Atropatene).

   Ibn Khurdadhbeh, in the mid ninth century, described the route

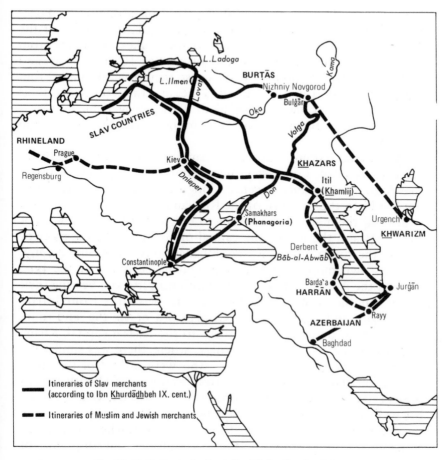

Fig. 29. Trade routes in the region of the Russian rivers.

taken by the Rus merchants: "The Rus, who belong to the Saqaliba tribes, travel from the most distant parts of Saqlaba [Esclavonia] to the Roman Sea [Mediterranean] and there they sell beaver skins and black fox skins, and swords too. The prince of the Romans claims one-tenth of their merchandise.... Then on their way back they go by sea to Samakhars, the city of the Jews [Phanagoria, on the Black Sea], and from there they return to the

Slav country. Or else they sail down the Tanais [Don], the Slavs'
river [Volga] and pass through Khamlij [Itil], the capital of the
Khazars, where the ruler of the country takes one-tenth from
them. There they embark on the Jurjan Sea [Caspian Sea] and
make for whatever point on the coast they have in mind. From
Jurjan or Rayy [on the site of Teheran] they transport their
merchandise by camel to Baghdad. There, Slav eunuchs act as
interpreters for them. They claim to be Christian and pay the
poll-tax as such."

Here we have proof that Russo-Scandinavian merchants actually
reached Baghdad. Conversely, many sources, duly collated, prove
that Muslim merchants travelled along the routes linking the Muslim World to the network of the Russian rivers. From Khwarizm a
road took them across the steppe to Bulghar, at the confluence of
the Volga and the Kama, the capital of Greater Bulgaria, more or
less on the future site of Kazan. Bulghar housed a Muslim colony,
with its own mosque and mint producing currency of the type
used by the Abbasid caliphs in the ninth century, and bearing their
name. Another route took the Muslim merchants from Jurjan,
Azerbaijan, and Arran via the Caspian Sea or via the land route
running from Bardha'a and Derbent to the Khazar capital, Khamlij (Itil) at the mouth of the Volga, where there was similarly a
district reserved for the Muslims, who were a third of the city's
population. The site of Itil has often been identified with that of
present-day Astrakhan, but no trace of the former Khazar capital
has ever been discovered, perhaps because of a subsequent rise in
the level of the Caspian Sea. From Itil, one reached Bulghar by
going up the Volga, then the Burtas country, at the confluence of
the Volga and the Oka, in the region of what was later Nijni-
Novgorod. But it was also possible, starting on the Lower Volga,
to travel towards the Don, then to Kuyafa (Kiev), where there was
a choice of routes, either the northern route to the Baltic, or the
one going south to the Black Sea and Byzantium, then west along
the Carpathians, through Prague and then via the Upper Danube
into the Rhineland countries were Samanid currency of the tenth
century was known. Let us remember in passing that this latter
route was the one taken by the Radhanite Jews who, as was indi-

cated above, came from the Rhine and the Danube to Prague, the Carpathians and Kiev, and finally to the country of the Khazars, who were converted to Judaism at the close of the eighth century.

All these itineraries are not only described in the sources and attested by actual geography and terrain, they are also traceable by very many finds of Muslim coins, from the seventh to the eleventh centuries, particularly Samanid coins of the tenth century. These were almost entirely silver currencies, dirhems, revealing a monometallic circulation of silver. The existence of gold is shown by one or two coins, but mainly in the written sources. Most of this gold was turned into jewellery, some of which may still be seen in Russian and Scandinavian museums, or it was re-exported to Constantinople to make possible the purchase of products of Byzantine industry.

Bilad as-Saqaliba sent to the Muslim World castrated slaves, furs, honey and wax from the bees in the great Nordic forest, swords which came from the Carolingian West to the Slav countries and were re-exported to the Muslim East, and horses and leathers from Bulghar. All these products passed through Khwarizm or Derbent on their way to the cities of Iran and Mesopotamia. In exchange, the Muslim World exported several products: gaudy cloths, various utensils, and in particular coins, silver coins and, to a far less extent, gold coins. The critical shortage of silver, which was the money metal throughout central Asia and Iran in the eleventh century, is explicable not only by the new conditions resulting from the expansion of the Seljuq Turks and Polovtses, but also by the drain incurred in trade with the Russian rivers area; in this sector the Muslim World showed a decidedly adverse balance of trade.

The third and last direction in which the north-west sector faced was the West. Here commercial exchanges went beyond the confines of Byzantium, whose own network of trading relations was as it were imprisoned within the larger movements of trade emanating from the Muslim World. Trade with the populations of Europe, at a time when it was still underdeveloped economically, depended on demand from the urban centres of Spain and the Maghreb. We have seen that the products of the forest, such as furs, timber for shipbuilding, slaves, metals, and arms, were all exported to the East along the routes of central Europe, from the Baltic and the Russian rivers, towards the metropolises in the East, especially Baghdad. These products also travelled westwards via Germany, the North Sea, and Carolingian Gaul, and reached the cities of the Western World, Cordoba in particular. In exchange for European products, the Muslim World provided its gold or silver currencies and one or two luxury products — mostly fabrics — which eluded the Byzantine middleman. This sector was another in which Muslim trade with the outside world ran at a deficit.

The middlemen of this trade were primarily Jews, particularly the Jews of Narbonne, a flourishing Jewish community which was one of a chain stretching from the Rhineland and Moselle to the Rhône corridor. These Narbonne Jews journeyed into Muslim Spain over the passes in the Pyrenees or by sea to Tortosa, then to North Africa, or else they went direct to the ports of the eastern Mediterranean.

As well as the Jews, the merchants of the Italian seaports played an increasingly important role. These were the Adriatic cities of Bari and especially Venice, Tyrrhenian cities like Salerno, Naples, Gaeta and especially Amalfi, whose citizens were, by the end of the tenth century, to be seen on the different markets of the Muslim Mediterranean — Almeria, Tunis, Alexandria, Fustat-Cairo, Antioch and, of course, Jerusalem, where their arrival was linked to the great pilgrimages with their annual fairs and important transactions. In Italy, the fairs at Pavia were famous and were frequented not only by the Venetians but also by people from the other side of the mountains, particularly the Anglo-Saxons who crossed the Alpine passes, and were required to pay taxes on slaves, swords, and tin.

Conversely the Orientals, Jews in particular, established themselves in Italian ports and in Lower Languedoc. We have noted that Jawhar, who subdued Egypt for the Fatimid caliph, was a Jew from southern Italy; we learn this fact from the Hebrew chronicle of Rabbi Ahima'as of Oria, a town situated between Brindisi and Taranto. There, Eastern communities transmitted commercial techniques and certain manufacturing processes like the embroidery of luxury fabrics, dyeing, and leather-working, which were to make possible the development of trade and production in the Italian cities from the close of the eleventh century. And so these Eastern Jews acted as initiators before being supplanted by their Christian rivals.

One more route must be mentioned, the Atlantic. It starts from what the Arabic texts call 'Baritaniya' or 'Birtaniya', meaning Anglo-Saxon England and the Celtic lands. From 'Britain' it went to Armorica, the Bay of Biscay, and the Muslim ports on the Atlantic, Lisbon and Alcacer do Sal, where the Anglo-Saxon slaves disembarked, and where cargoes of tin, furs, and swords were unloaded.

The study of the different trading sectors reveals the existence of groups of routes entering the Muslim World and going as far as the nerve centres of the economy, the major cities, which were interconnected by an active network of contacts.

The driving force behind all these commercial connections was the main caravan route, the trunk road from Samarkand, Bukhara, and Nishapur linking central Asia with Rayy, then Baghdad, then, via the Nahr'Isa and the Euphrates and the Upper Euphrates, with Aleppo, Antioch, and the commercial ports of Syria. In the southwest a route branched off and led to Damascus, Ascalon, Pelusa, and Alexandria and Fustat-Cairo in the Nile Delta; thence, via Cyrenaica, it continued to Kairouan, the high plateaux of the Maghreb and to Fez, the 'transit ports' of the Strait of Gibraltar, and to the towns of Andalusia, Seville, and Cordoba. Other important road networks joined the main one: the Russian rivers—Caspian—Rayy route, the Indian Ocean—Persian Gulf—Basra—Baghdad route, the Red Sea—'Aydhab or Qulzum—Nile Valley—Cairo route, trans-Sahara routes towards the Maghreb, routes from the Christian West to Spain and the ports of the Muslim Mediterranean.

Naturally enough, not all these routes were made by tne Muslims. In most cases, the Muslim conquests used networks or parts of routes laid down in former times but rendered indistinct or put out of action by the barbarian invasions. The formation of the Muslim World joined or rejoined together these trading areas which had hitherto remained more or less distinct from each other. In particular it gathered into the major economic orbit the territory of the Sahara-Sudan created by Berber expansion southwards from the fourth century onwards, and the territory of the Russian rivers which had been for some time in the process of organization by Slav, Finnish, and Scandinavian elements. On the other hand, demand from the major centres of consumption in the Muslim World stimulated the economic activity of the barbarian West, whose trade, money circulation, and urban development sprang into life at this instigation.

Conclusion

In the foregoing pages we have on several occasions regarded the Muslim World as split into three distinct parts: the Isthmus region, Iran and central Asia, and the Muslim West. Not only was such a division necessary for clarity of exposition, but it was reasonable in itself. Each of the three regions under examination corresponded to a set of geographical conditions whose effect was constant and inescapable, to an area which had reached a different stage of economic evolution from the others, and to a different part of the heritage of ancient civilization. If, by way of conclusion, we must seek the general picture, the over-all design, then it must be said that the Muslim World from the eighth to the eleventh centuries is not only the point of departure of the long history of the Muslim civilizations, but also the point of arrival — hitherto unsurpassed — of an even longer history, namely the history of the urban civilizations of the ancient East, the oldest human civilizations ever known, which had once been combined in the Empire of Alexander.

Not only was the Muslim World a focal point in time, but also in space. By virtue of its central position at the heart of the Ancient World, by its command of the Isthmus region between the two major sea areas, the Indian Ocean and the Mediterranean, by its possession of the major continental route, linking the steppes, the deserts, and the oases and running from central Asia to West Africa, the Muslim World was in direct contact with other major urban and civilized centres. It maintained fruitful exchanges, on an equal footing, with India, China, and Byzantium. But it also had contacts with more recent societies, whether nomad or forest-dwelling, which were still barbarian or had become so. These were the Turkish Steppes, the Russian rivers region, the Negro World, and the Christian West. To them it extended its influence and from them it drew energy. It formed a bridge between widely separated areas.

Hence the importance of routes which recorded the advance, the swift or slow, continuous or interrupted, progress of influences through this privileged transit area, the Muslim World up to the eleventh century. The result was the spread to the West − the Muslim West and beyond − of knowledge and skills acquired by the older countries of the East, modified and enriched by coming together in the same geographical area, and also the transmission of new influences which had come along the long-distance trade routes from India, central Asia, and China.

The urban network was also important. Towns were bound together by a network of economic and cultural relations; the road helped to transmit urban influences. The network of capital cities constituted the economic, social, and cultural framework of the Muslim World. From the eighth to the eleventh centuries the main points along this central axis, namely Baghdad, Damascus, Cairo, Kairouan, Fez, and Palermo, all of them important staging-posts on the route from Samarkand to Cordoba, bore witness to the amazing unity of a syncretic civilization with its vast movements of men, merchandise, and ideas, a civilization superimposed on the older regional, rural, or nomadic background.

Finally, monetary economy was important, and was expressed in an abundant minting of dinars made possible by the influx of new gold and the development of credit which doubled the circulation of currency. In the ninth century, Ibn Khurdadhbeh observed that the growth of wealth and commercial transactions was so great that actual cash could be seen changing hands in the smallest townships where, hitherto, simple barter had been the only method in use. And so the enlarged area of money circulation was matched by a greater power wielded by town over country.

But the dinar economy had both strengths and weaknesses. It depended on trade. It was geared to the upkeep of the roads, bound up with the domination of the network of trade relations abroad which enabled the Muslim World to obtain those goods it lacked and which were indispensable to its economy and its expanding civilization — timber, metals and arms, slaves, and especially gold. All this in an economy and a civilization accustomed to purchasing everything with gold and from a distance. But it only needed the links with the outside world to weaken, as a result of diversions or breaks in the roads, or gold to arrive less regularly, to induce a decline in the general economic situation, with one crisis after another, a slowing down of urban growth, and the consequent impossibility of resisting the greed of the barbarians. Accompanying all this was the use of mercenaries in the armies, a surge of invaders along the trade routes, and general collapse.

Indeed the second half of the eleventh century did bring crises, disturbances, invasions, and with them urban decline and the disruption of trade. Whole districts of Baghdad and Cairo stood in ruins; people left Kairouan and went to Mahdiyya; they left the Qual'a of the Banu Hammad for Bougie; Fez was taken by the Almoravids; the Caliphate of Cordoba was dismembered and succeeded by the Reyes de Taifas. The dislocation of the road system was matched by the break-up of the Muslim World into a Turkish Islam, an Egyptian Islam, a Maghrebi Islam, and a Spanish Islam. All the dormant particularisms emerged; the basic character of these areas which was there before the Muslim conquest but which it had modified, now came to life and produced, not one but *several* Muslim civilizations.

After the eleventh century the centre of gravity of the Ancient World swung from one place to another. From now on, the nerve centres and centres of influence of an expanding economy were no longer in the East, in the cities of the Muslim World. They moved westwards and became established in the mercantile cities of Italy and Flanders and, half-way along the great trade route linking them with each other, in the trade fairs of Champagne, where the

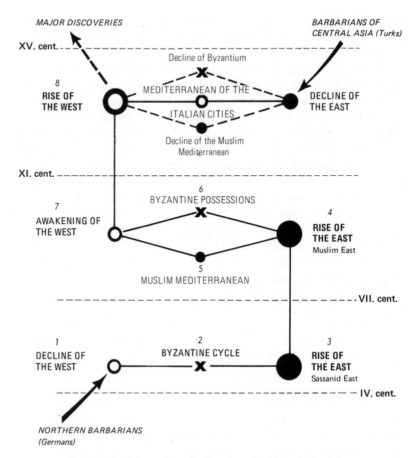

Fig. 30. World forces from the fourth to the fifteenth centuries.

products of Nordic lands and of Mediterranean countries were bought and sold. Despite violent alternations between buoyancy and depression it now became clear that economic power, the force of material expansion, and creative activity, were to be for centuries the privilege of western Europe.

However, even during its economic decline, the Muslim World long continued to influence the world in the realms of science, medicine, and philosophy. It played a conspicuous part in medicine especially, not only during the Renaissance but right up to the nineteenth century.

Set between China, India, Byzantium, and the medieval barbarian societies — Turkish, Negro, and Western — Muslim civilisation in its Golden Age, from the end of the ancient Empires to the emergence of the modern States, was a melting-pot in time and space, a great crossroads, a vast synthesis, an amazing meeting-place.

Index